PEARSON

my Student JOURNAL

This Student Journal belongs to

_____

PEARSON

Boston, Massachusetts
Chandler, Arizona
Glenview, Illinois
Upper Saddle River, New Jersey

Acknowledgments, which appear on page 400, constitute an extension
of this copyright page.

ISBN-13:   978-0-13-372701-2
ISBN-10:   0-13-372701-7
26   18

How to Use This Book vi

Core Concepts Handbook

Part 1 History and Geography 2
Part 2 Citizenship and Economics 8
Part 3 Culture 18

Chapter 1 **Early People**
Essential Question Preview 24
Connect to myStory 25
Section 1 26
Section 2 28
Section 3 30
Essential Question Writer's Workshop 32

Chapter 2 **Beginning of Civilization**
Essential Question Preview 34
Connect to myStory 35
Section 1 36
Section 2 38
Essential Question Writer's Workshop 40

Unit 1 Sum It Up 42

Chapter 3 **The Fertile Crescent**
Essential Question Preview 44
Connect to myStory 45
Section 1 46
Section 2 48
Section 3 50
Section 4 52
Essential Question Writer's Workshop 54

Chapter 4 **Ancient Egypt and Nubia**
Essential Question Preview 56
Connect to myStory 57
Section 1 58
Section 2 60
Section 3 62
Essential Question Writer's Workshop 64

Chapter 5 **Judaism and the Jewish People**
Essential Question Preview 66
Connect to myStory 67
Section 1 68
Section 2 70
Section 3 72
Essential Question Writer's Workshop 74

Unit 2 Sum It Up 76

Chapter 6 Civilizations of Early India
Essential Question Preview 78
Connect to myStory............................ 79
Section 1.. 80
Section 2.. 82
Section 3.. 84
Section 4.. 86
Essential Question Writer's Workshop 88

Chapter 7 India's Empires
Essential Question Preview 90
Connect to myStory............................ 91
Section 1.. 92
Section 2.. 94
Essential Question Writer's Workshop 96

Chapter 8 Ancient China
Essential Question Preview 98
Connect to myStory............................ 99
Section 1.. 100
Section 2.. 102
Section 3.. 104
Essential Question Writer's Workshop ... 106

Chapter 9 The Chinese Empire
Essential Question Preview 108
Connect to myStory.......................... 109
Section 1.. 110
Section 2.. 112
Section 3.. 114
Essential Question Writer's Workshop ... 116

Unit 3 Sum It Up 118

Chapter 10 The Ancient Greeks
Essential Question Preview 120
Connect to myStory.......................... 121
Section 1.. 122
Section 2.. 124
Section 3.. 126
Section 4.. 128
Essential Question Writer's Workshop ... 130

Chapter 11 Ancient Greek Civilization
Essential Question Preview 132
Connect to myStory.......................... 133
Section 1.. 134
Section 2.. 136
Section 3.. 138
Section 4.. 140
Essential Question Writer's Workshop ... 142

Unit 4 Sum It Up 144

Chapter 12 The Roman Republic
Essential Question Preview 146
Connect to myStory 147
Section 1 148
Section 2 150
Section 3 152
Section 4 154
Essential Question Writer's Workshop ... 156

Chapter 13 The Roman Empire and Christianity
Essential Question Preview 158
Connect to myStory 159
Section 1 160
Section 2 162
Section 3 164
Section 4 166
Section 5 168
Essential Question Writer's Workshop ... 170

Unit 5 Sum It Up 172

Chapter 14 The Byzantine Empire
Essential Question Preview 174
Connect to myStory 175
Section 1 176
Section 2 178
Section 3 180
Essential Question Writer's Workshop ... 182

Chapter 15 Islamic Civilization
Essential Question Preview 184
Connect to myStory 185
Section 1 186
Section 2 188
Section 3 190
Section 4 192
Essential Question Writer's Workshop ... 194

Unit 6 Sum It Up 196

Chapter 16 Early African Civilizations
Essential Question Preview 198
Connect to myStory 199
Section 1 200
Section 2 202
Section 3 204
Section 4 206
Essential Question Writer's Workshop ... 208

Chapter 17 China in the Middle Ages
Essential Question Preview 210
Connect to myStory 211
Section 1 212
Section 2 214
Section 3 216
Section 4 218
Essential Question Writer's Workshop ... 220

Chapter 18 Japan Before Modern Times
Essential Question Preview 222
Connect to myStory 223
Section 1 224
Section 2 226
Section 3 228
Essential Question Writer's Workshop ... 230

Unit 7 Sum It Up 232

Chapter 19 Mesoamerican Civilizations
Essential Question Preview 234
Connect to myStory 235
Section 1 236
Section 2 238
Essential Question Writer's Workshop ... 240

Chapter 20 Early North and South America
Essential Question Preview 242
Connect to myStory 243
Section 1 244
Section 2 246
Essential Question Writer's Workshop ... 248

Unit 8 Sum It Up 250

Chapter 21 A New Civilization in Europe
Essential Question Preview 252
Connect to myStory 253
Section 1 254
Section 2 256
Section 3 258
Essential Question Writer's Workshop ... 260

Chapter 22 Conflicts and Crusades
Essential Question Preview 262
Connect to myStory 263
Section 1 264
Section 2 266
Section 3 268
Section 4 270
Essential Question Writer's Workshop ... 272

Chapter 23 A Changing Medieval World
Essential Question Preview 274
Connect to myStory 275
Section 1 276
Section 2 278
Section 3 280
Essential Question Writer's Workshop ... 282

Unit 9 Sum It Up 284

Chapter 24 The Renaissance
Essential Question Preview 286
Connect to myStory 287
Section 1 288
Section 2 290
Section 3 292
Section 4 294
Essential Question Writer's Workshop ... 296

Chapter 25 The Reformation
Essential Question Preview 298
Connect to myStory 299
Section 1 300
Section 2 302
Section 3 304
Essential Question Writer's Workshop ... 306

Chapter 26 The Age of Exploration
Essential Question Preview 308
Connect to myStory 309
Section 1 310
Section 2 312
Section 3 314
Essential Question Writer's Workshop ... 316

Unit 10 Sum It Up 318

Chapter 27 European Colonization
Essential Question Preview 320
Connect to myStory.......................... 321
Section 1... 322
Section 2... 324
Section 3... 326
Section 4... 328
Essential Question Writer's Workshop ... 330

Chapter 28 The Rise of the Monarchy
Essential Question Preview 332
Connect to myStory.......................... 333
Section 1... 334
Section 2... 336
Section 3... 338
Section 4... 340
Essential Question Writer's Workshop ... 342

Chapter 29 An Age of Revolutions
Essential Question Preview 344
Connect to myStory.......................... 345
Section 1... 346
Section 2... 348
Section 3... 350
Section 4... 352
Essential Question Writer's Workshop ... 354

Unit 11 Sum It Up 356

Chapter 30 Nations, Industry, and Empires
Essential Question Preview 358
Connect to myStory.......................... 359
Section 1... 360
Section 2... 362
Section 3... 364
Section 4... 366
Essential Question Writer's Workshop ... 368

Chapter 31 Wars and Hardship
Essential Question Preview 370
Connect to myStory.......................... 371
Section 1... 372
Section 2... 374
Section 3... 376
Essential Question Writer's Workshop ... 378

Chapter 32 The Changing Postwar World
Essential Question Preview 380
Connect to myStory.......................... 381
Section 1... 382
Section 2... 384
Essential Question Writer's Workshop ... 386

Chapter 33 Today's World
Essential Question Preview 388
Connect to myStory.......................... 389
Section 1... 390
Section 2... 392
Section 3... 394
Essential Question Writer's Workshop ... 396

Unit 12 Sum It Up 398

How to Use This Book

The *myWorld History Student Journal* is a tool to help you process and record what you have learned from the Student Edition of *myWorld History*. As you complete the activities and essays in your Journal, you will be creating your own personal resource for reviewing the concepts, key terms, and maps from *myWorld History*. The Journal worksheets and writing exercises focus on the Essential Question, helping you uncover the relevance of each chapter to your life.

The **Essential Question Preview** will help you understand the chapter you are about to read. Begin with Connect to Your Life to find ways to relate the issues and principles of the Essential Questions to your life—your family, school, or community. Next, Connect to the Chapter invites you to flip through the chapter and chart your predictions on how the Essential Question relates to the countries in each chapter.

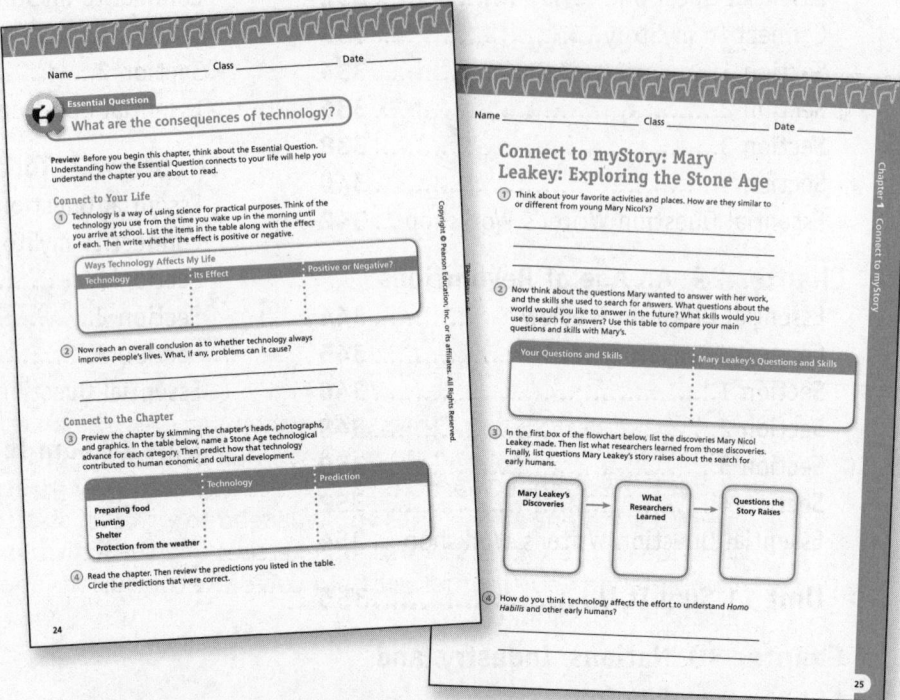

The **Word Wise** exercises give you the chance to really get to know and explore the key terms through word maps, crossword puzzles, and other game formats. You will synthesize concepts and create a detailed visual study guide by filling in the graphic organizers in **Take Notes**. Each Take Notes page ends with an exercise that helps you draw conclusions about the Essential Question.

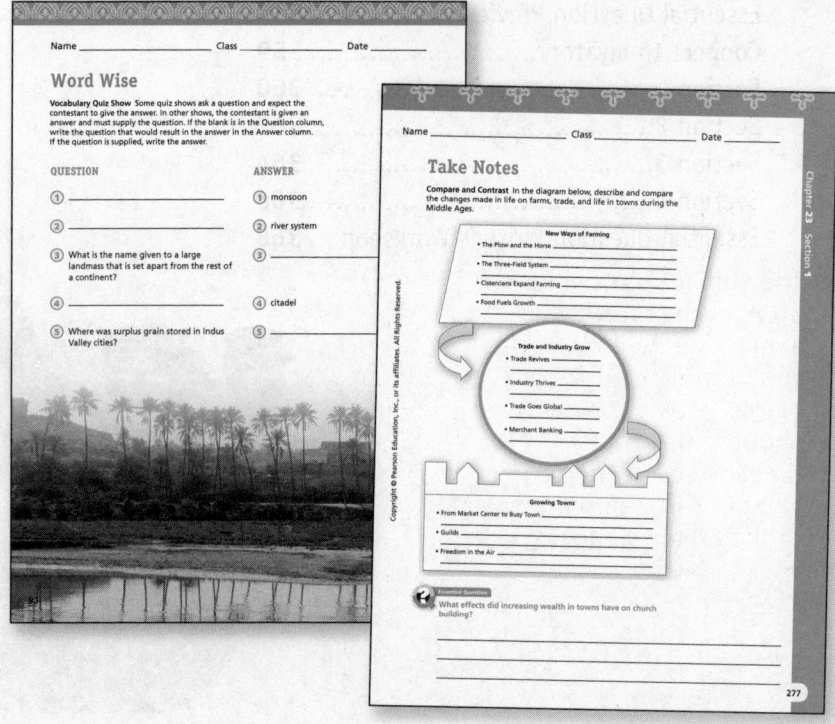

Name _____ Class _____ Date _____

Essential Question | Writer's Workshop

What are the consequences of technology?

Prepare to Write

Throughout this chapter, you have explored the Essential Question in your text, journal, and On Assignment at myworldhistory.com. Use your notes and what you've learned to write a five-paragraph essay describing how technology helped the development of civilizations in the Fertile Crescent.

Workshop Skill: Outline an Essay

Your essay will contain five paragraphs: an introduction, three body paragraphs, and a concluding paragraph. You will need to capture your reader's attention. Also, you will need to create a thesis statement.

The Hook Think about technology's role in the development of the Fertile Crescent. For example, the wheel and the discovery of how to make bronze were technologies that helped spread Sumerian culture. Then create a "hook" that will capture your reader's interest. For example, *How did the invention of the computer change our lives?* Notice how this makes the reader think about technology. On the lines below, write some hook ideas to generate interest in the technologies of the Fertile Crescent.

Hook idea 1: What would Sumer have done without the wheel?

Hook idea 2: _____

Hook idea 3: _____

The Thesis Statement Now state your thesis, which is the main idea of your essay. The thesis should state three ideas, in the form of topic sentences, that you will use to support your position. These ideas will be the focus of your body paragraphs.

In this case, the thesis statement is the last sentence in your introduction. Add your own ideas to the thesis statement given below.

Example *Technology was a key element in the development of ancient civilizations. The wheel and the invention of bronze helped Sumer become the first great civilization. Later empires like the _____ and the _____ built upon the Sumerian achievements. By the time of the Phoenicians, the development of _____, _____, and _____ had made technology necessary for economic survival in a changing world.*

54

The Introduction Your first paragraph is the introduction. This is how you will get your readers "hooked" on the topic and make them want to read more. The introduction includes your hook and thesis statement.

Body Paragraphs Your essay will include three body paragraphs, each with a topic sentence, main idea, supporting details, and conclusion. Use the chart below to piece together your three body paragraphs.

Body Paragraphs

Topic sentence:	Topic sentence:	Topic sentence:
Main idea:	Main idea:	Main idea:
Detail 1:	Detail 1:	Detail 1:
Detail 2:	Detail 2:	Detail 2:
Concluding sentence:	Concluding sentence:	Concluding sentence:

Conclusion Your last paragraph is your conclusion, in which you summarize the main ideas presented in your essay. This is your opportunity to get your point across to your readers. Review your big ideas and complete the conclusion below.

Example *The examples of Sumerian achievements in agriculture and metalwork and the use of Sumerian achievements by the _____, _____, and _____ show how technology spreads. The success of the Phoenicians demonstrated the importance of _____ in a growing*

Draft Your Essay

Review and revise your outline to be sure your thoughts are clearly presented. Then write your essay and proofread it with a writing partner.

55

The **Essential Question Writer's Workshop** provides you an end-of-chapter opportunity to show your understanding of chapter content by writing about the Essential Question. Each Workshop features instruction and practice with one of the skills you will need to write an essay and express your ideas. The Writer's Workshop exercises and the activities you have completed in your Journal will help you draw conclusions about the Chapter Essential Question.

The **Sum It Up** activities after each unit provide a map exercise that helps you locate the important places you have read about in the unit. A timeline activity helps you put the major events of the unit in sequence.

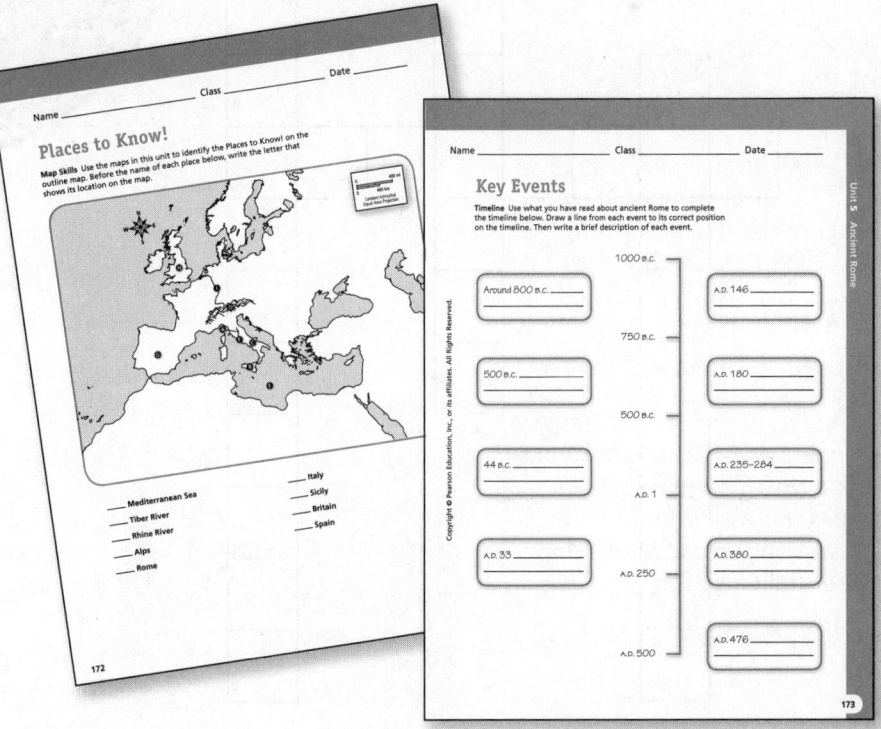

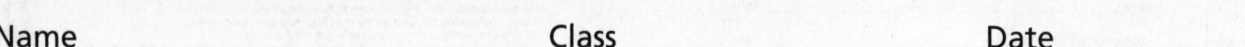

Core Concepts 1.1: Word Wise

Crossword Puzzle The *Across* and *Down* clues are definitions of key terms from this section. Fill in the numbered *Across* boxes with the correct key terms. Then, do the same with the *Down* clues.

Across	Down
1. a length of time that is important because of certain events or developments that occurred during that era	3. a person who studies, describes, and explains the past
2. a graphic organizer that shows events in the chronological order in which they happened	4. a list of events in the order in which they took place
	5. the time before humans invented writing

Core Concepts 1.2: Word Wise

Words In Context For each question below, write an answer that shows your understanding of the boldfaced key term.

(1) Why is an article written about a famous explorer considered a **secondary source**?

_____

_____

_____

(2) Why do museums collect and display **artifacts**?

_____

_____

_____

(3) When researching a topic, why must you be on guard against **bias**?

_____

_____

_____

(4) If you were doing a project about a famous battle, what **primary sources** might you use?

_____

_____

_____

Core Concepts 1.3: Word Wise

Word Bank Choose one word from the word bank to fill in each blank. When you have finished, you will have a short summary of important ideas from the section.

Word Bank
archaeology
anthropology
oral tradition

For centuries before people began to record information by writing,

history and culture was communicated to younger generations through

_____. By passing down information through songs and

storytelling, people were able to continue their traditions for hundreds

of years.

Today, people involved in the field of _____ study this

practice as well as other aspects of how different cultures developed. These

historians also depend on the findings of the people who work in

_____. Using evidence from artifacts, scientists in this field

determine how people behaved and what their culture was like.

Name _____ Class _____ Date _____

Core Concepts 1.4: Word Wise

Words In Context For each question below, write an answer that shows your understanding of the boldfaced key term.

(1) How does **absolute location** differ from **relative location**?

_____

_____

(2) What does the geographic theme of **place** describe about a location?

_____

_____

(3) The Midwest is one **region** of the United States. What characteristics make it a **region**?

_____

_____

(4) How can you see the theme of **movement** in a city like Washington, D.C.?

_____

_____

(5) How does **human-environment interaction** affect your life?

_____

_____

Core Concepts 1.5: Word Wise

Crossword Puzzle The *Across* and *Down* clues describe key terms from this section. Fill in the numbered *Across* boxes with the correct key terms. Then, do the same with the *Down* clues.

Across	Down
1. a map that shows a larger area than the main map	4. a standard map diagram that shows the cardinal directions
2. the map part that shows how much space on the map represents a given distance	
3. the map part that shows what the map symbols mean	

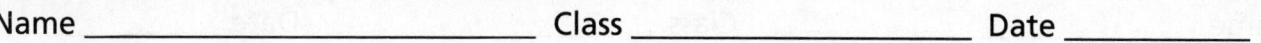

Name _____ Class _____ Date _____

Core Concepts 1.6: Word Wise

Word Map Follow the model below to make a word map. The key term *locate* is in the center oval. Write the definition in your own words at the upper left. In the upper right, list Characteristics, which means words or phrases that relate to the term. At the lower left, list Non-Characteristics, which means words and phrases that would not be associated with it. In the lower right, draw a picture of the key term or use it in a sentence.

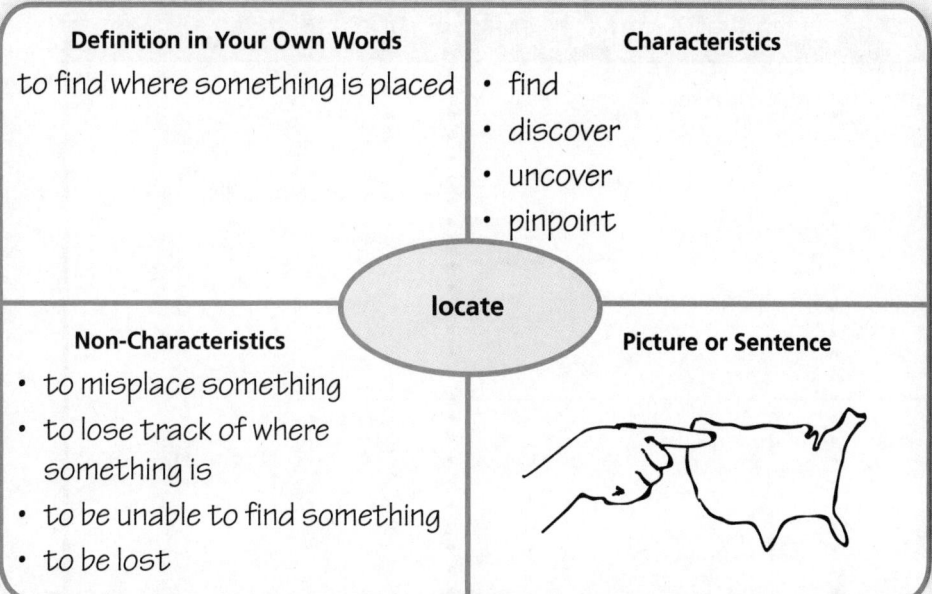

Definition in Your Own Words	**Characteristics**
to find where something is placed	• find • discover • uncover • pinpoint
Non-Characteristics	**Picture or Sentence**
• to misplace something • to lose track of where something is • to be unable to find something • to be lost	

*(center oval: **locate**)*

Now use the word map below to explore the meaning of the word *historical map*. You may use your student text, a dictionary, and/or a thesaurus to complete each of the four sections.

Definition in Your Own Words	**Characteristics**
Non-Characteristics	**Picture or Sentence**

*(center oval: **historical map**)*

Sum It Up

Be a History Detective Imagine that it has just been revealed that a famous American from a previous century was actually a spy for another country. You are a historian collecting information for a documentary about this American's secret life. Explain how you would use each type of resource listed in the table's column headings. Include a specific example of each kind of resource. (You will need to use your imagination for this part.)

Primary Sources	Secondary Sources	Artifacts

Core Concepts 2.1: Word Wise

Sentence Builder Complete the sentences using the information you learned in this section. Include terminal punctuation.

(1) Two goals of a **government** are _____

_____

(2) A **constitution** is a system _____

_____

(3) In a **limited government,** _____

_____

(4) In an **unlimited government,** _____

_____

(5) **Tyranny** can result in an abuse of power such as _____

_____

Core Concepts 2.2: Word Wise

Crossword Puzzle The *Across* and *Down* clues describe key terms from this section. Fill in the numbered *Across* boxes with the correct key terms. Then, do the same with the *Down* clues.

Across	Down
1. In the political system called _____, the government owns all the property. 2. One person or a small group holds all the power in a(n) _____ government. 3. In a(n) _____, the citizens have political power. 4. A city and surrounding area that form an independent state is a(n) _____.	5. another name for a nation or country 6. A(n) _____ consists of several nations or territories and may be quite large. 7. a country led by a king or a queen

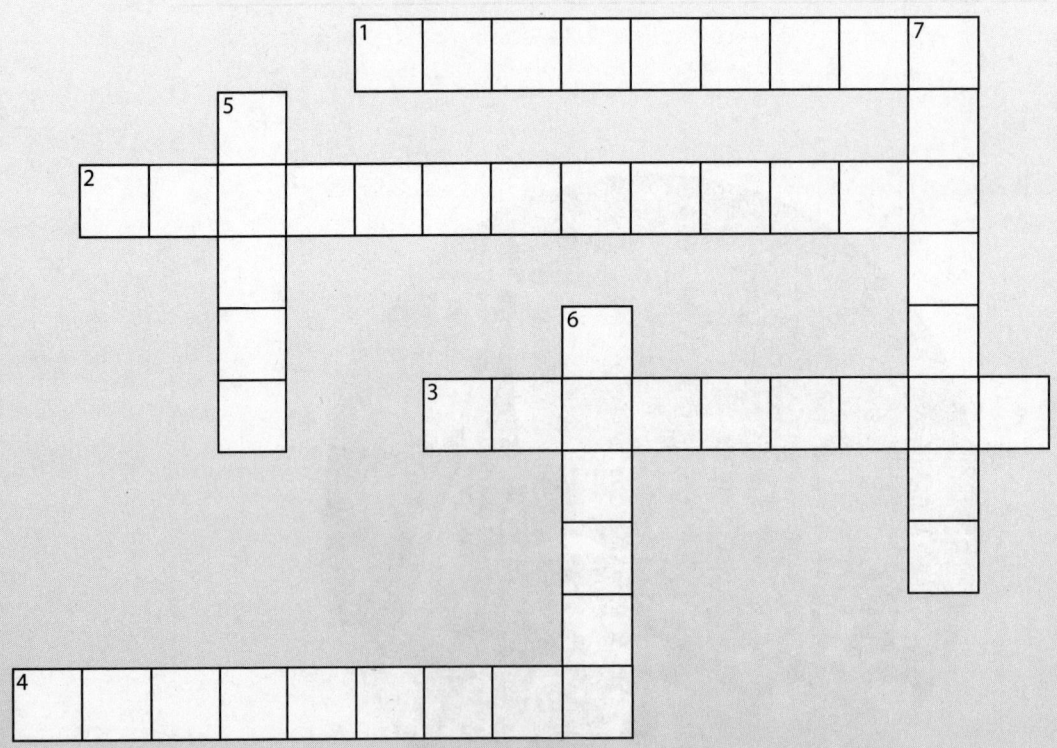

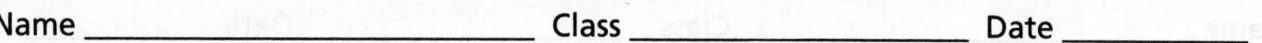

Core Concepts 2.3: Word Wise

Word Map Follow the model below to make a word map. The term *unitary system* is in the center oval. Write the definition in your own words at the upper left. In the upper right, list Characteristics, which means words or phrases that relate to the term. At the lower left, list Non-Characteristics, which means words and phrases that would not be associated with it. In the lower right, draw a picture of the key term or use it in a sentence.

Definition in Your Own Words	Characteristics
a central government that makes laws for the whole country	• single government • centralized government • most nations today
unitary system	
Non-Characteristics	Picture or Sentence
• federal system • divided government • confederal system • United States	A country with a unitary system has a very powerful central government.

Now use the word map below to explore the meaning of the term *federal system*. You may use your student text, a dictionary, and/or a thesaurus to complete each of the four sections.

Definition in Your Own Words	Characteristics
federal system	
Non-Characteristics	Picture or Sentence

Core Concepts 2.4: Word Wise

Word Bank Choose one word from the word bank to fill in each blank.
When you have finished, you will have a short summary of important ideas
from the section.

Word Bank

political party   civic life
citizens   civic participation
interest group

People born in the United States or who have completed the

naturalization process are U.S. _____. There are a number

of ways to take advantage of the privileges of citizenship. For example, you

may register to become a member of a _____ that reflects

your political views. Becoming involved with this group and other

organizations is a simple, effective way of participating in

_____. Voting, speaking out in meetings, signing petitions,

or simply staying informed are other kinds of _____.

If there is a certain issue about which you feel strongly, you may want to

join a related _____ dedicated to that particular cause.

Core Concepts 2.5: Word Wise

Vocabulary Quiz Show Some quiz shows ask a question and expect the contestant to give the answer. In other shows, the contestant is given an answer and must supply the question. If the blank is in the Question column, write the question that would result in the answer given. If the question is supplied, write the appropriate answer.

QUESTION	ANSWER
(1) _____	(1) incentive
(2) What describes the value of what you decide to give up when you make an economic choice?	(2) _____
(3) _____	(3) economics
(4) What do you call the amount of goods or services available for use?	(4) _____
(5) _____	(5) consumers
(6) What word describes the degree of desire for a good or a service?	(6) _____
(7) _____	(7) producers
(8) What is the term for having a limited quantity of resources to meet unlimited wants?	(8) _____

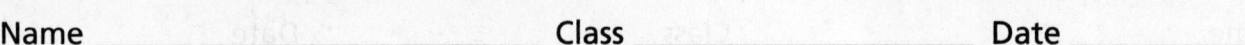

Name _____ Class _____ Date _____

Core Concepts 2.6: Word Wise

Crossword Puzzle The *Across* and *Down* clues describe key terms from this section. Fill in the numbered *Across* boxes with the correct key terms. Then, do the same with the *Down* clues.

Across	Down
1. an organized way for goods and services to be exchanged	2. a decline in economic growth for six or more months in a row.
5. the money earned by selling goods and services	3. The struggle among producers for consumers' money
6. the act of a company concentrating on just a few goods or services	4. A general increase in prices over time
7. the money left after subtracting the costs of doing business	

Name _____ Class _____ Date _____

Core Concepts 2.7: Word Wise

Words In Context For each question below, write an answer that shows your understanding of the boldfaced key term.

(1) What makes a person's way of life important in a **traditional economy**?

_____

_____

_____

(2) Who makes economic decisions in a **mixed economy** and why?

_____

_____

_____

(3) How do new businesses benefit from the freedom of a **market economy**?

_____

_____

_____

(4) How does a **command economy** differ from a market economy?

_____

_____

_____

15

Core Concepts 2.8: Word Wise

Sentence Builder Complete the sentences using the information you learned in this section. Include terminal punctuation.

(1) Grain is one example of an **export** from the United States because it is

_____

(2) You might **trade** your _____ for _____

_____

(3) Consumers benefit from **free trade** because _____

_____

(4) China **imports** _____ from _____

_____

(5) An example of a **tariff** is a _____

_____

(6) The purpose of a **trade barrier** is _____

_____

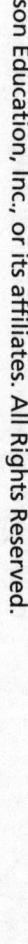

Name _____ Class _____ Date _____

Core Concepts 2.9: Word Wise

Word Bank Choose one word from the word bank to fill in each blank. When you have finished, you will have a short summary of important ideas from the section.

Word Bank

budget   credit
interest   invest
stocks   bonds
saving

You have options for using your money wisely. For example,

_____ funds in a bank, credit union, or other financial

institution ensures that you will have money for future use. You can take

some of that money and _____ it. Hopefully this will earn

you a profit. One way to do this is to buy _____, which are

certificates from a business or the government promising to pay back your

money plus additional money. Another way to do it is to purchase

_____, which give you shares of ownership in a company.

Of course, people also buy expensive things such as a car or a home

even though they do not have enough money to pay for it in full. To do this,

most people use _____. This means that they agree to pay

for their purchase over time. As they pay back the loan, they will also have

to pay _____. If this seems complex, don't worry. You can

create and stick to a money-management plan called a(n)

_____. It will help you save more and avoid borrowing too

much money.

Sum It Up

Think About It Use what you learned in this section to answer these questions about Myra and the way she uses her money.

(1) Your friend Myra is given $100. She wants to invest half of it so she can earn some more money. What do you think is the best way for her to do this? Why?

_____

_____

_____

(2) Myra plans to use the other $50 to buy a new pair of headphones. How might competition and specialization among headphone producers affect her choice?

_____

_____

_____

(3) Assume that Myra lives in a command economy. How do you think her headphone choices might be different from those in a market economy?

_____

_____

_____

(4) Name two disadvantages of a command economy.

_____

_____

_____

Name _____ Class _____ Date _____

Core Concepts 3.1: Word Wise

Sentence Builder Complete the sentences using the information you learned in this section. Include terminal punctuation.

① In modern American culture, one example of a **norm** is _____

_____

② Examples of **cultural traits** are language, _____

_____

③ Human activities define the **cultural landscape** by _____

_____

④ A nation's **culture** includes its _____

_____

⑤ A **culture region** can extend beyond a nation's borders because _____

_____

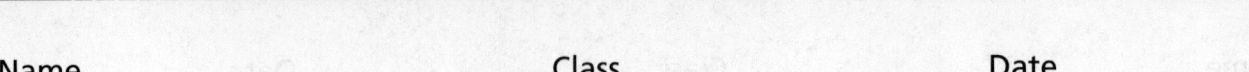

Name _____ Class _____ Date _____

Core Concepts 3.2: Word Wise

Words In Context For each question below, write an answer that shows your understanding of the boldfaced key term.

(1) Why do many people value **religion**, and what do they hope to gain from it?

_____

_____

_____

(2) Which situation would test your **ethics**: learning how to drive a car or deciding whether or not to copy someone else's homework? Explain.

_____

_____

_____

Core Concepts 3.3: Word Wise

Sentence Builder Complete the sentences using the information you learned in this section. Include terminal punctuation.

1 Ideas such as _____ and _____ spread

   outward from a **cultural hearth** when _____

   _____

2 One example of **diversity** is _____

   _____

3 Traders were partially responsible for **cultural diffusion** because _____

   _____

Core Concepts 3.4: Word Wise

Word Bank Choose one word from the word bank to fill in each blank.
When you have finished, you will have a short summary of important ideas
from the section.

Word Bank

irrigate   science   standard of living

Throughout history, cultural development has followed people's

discoveries about the natural world. New understandings in

_____ helped ancient groups change from a life of hunting

and gathering to farming. For example, technology like metalworking let

people create tools that helped them clear land and grow crops. When

people learned to _____ land, they increased their chances

for successful agriculture by making more land arable and providing some

protection against droughts.

As agriculture—and later industry—became central to world

economies, people were able to improve their _____ and

afford more goods and services.

Sum It Up

Draw and Label Imagine that you have been given the chance to create a new town with new cultural elements. Draw a scene of everyday life in your new town, representing and labeling all of the concepts listed in the key.

KEY

A = cultural trait   **B** = art   **C** = technology

Answer these questions about your town on a separate piece of paper:

1. Describe the technology you included. How does it affect daily life in the town?

2. Describe diversity in the town. How does this diversity influence the town's overall culture?

Name _____ Class _____ Date _____

What are the consequences of technology?

Preview Before you begin this chapter, think about the Essential Question. Understanding how the Essential Question connects to your life will help you understand the chapter you are about to read.

Connect to Your Life

1 Technology is a way of using science for practical purposes. Think of the technology you use from the time you wake up in the morning until you arrive at school. List the items in the table along with the effect of each. Then write whether the effect is positive or negative.

Ways Technology Affects My Life		
Technology	Its Effect	Positive or Negative?

2 Now reach an overall conclusion as to whether technology always improves people's lives. What, if any, problems can it cause?

_____

_____

Connect to the Chapter

3 Preview the chapter by skimming the chapter's heads, photographs, and graphics. In the table below, name a Stone Age technological advance for each category. Then predict how that technology contributed to human economic and cultural development.

	Technology	Prediction
Preparing food		
Hunting		
Shelter		
Protection from the weather		

4 Read the chapter. Then review the predictions you listed in the table. Circle the predictions that were correct.

Name _____ Class _____ Date _____

Connect to myStory: Mary Leakey: Exploring the Stone Age

1. Think about your favorite activities and places. How are they similar to or different from young Mary Nicol's?

_____

_____

_____

2. Now think about the questions Mary wanted to answer with her work, and the skills she used to search for answers. What questions about the world would you like to answer in the future? What skills would you use to search for answers? Use this table to compare your main questions and skills with Mary's.

Your Questions and Skills	Mary Leakey's Questions and Skills

3. In the first box of the flowchart below, list the discoveries Mary Nicol Leakey made. Then list what researchers learned from those discoveries. Finally, list questions Mary Leakey's story raises about the search for early humans.

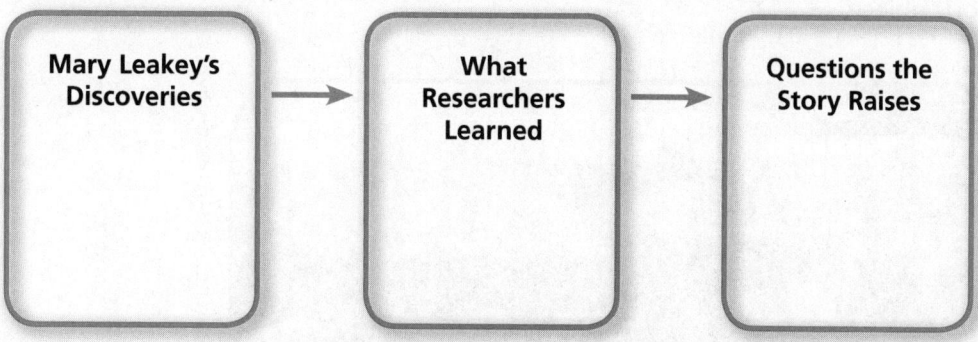

Mary Leakey's Discoveries	→	What Researchers Learned	→	Questions the Story Raises

4. How do you think technology affects the effort to understand *Homo Habilis* and other early humans?

_____

_____

Word Wise

Sentence Builder Complete the sentences using the information you learned in this section and the key terms below.

anthropology   archaeologist
prehistory   fossil
geologist   artifact

(1) Mary Leakey and other researchers studied people who lived long

ago in _____.

(2) Scientists in the field of _____

study how ancient human groups behaved.

(3) An _____ examines the things humans

from long ago left behind.

(4) A rocklike copy of a plant, a feather, or a bone is a _____.

(5) A tool, pot, or weapon from early human society is called an

_____.

(6) A _____ uses layering as a way to determine the age

of prehistoric objects.

Name _____ Class _____ Date _____

Take Notes

Identify Main Ideas and Details Scientists who study the earliest human history are on a journey of discovery. For each part of the journey listed below, give details that tell more about the main idea.

Studying the Distant Past		
Many kinds of scientists work together to study early humans.	Scientists have discovered several important clues to early human life.	Many questions still exist about the beginnings of human life.

Essential Question

Modern archaeologists make use of both hand tools and advanced scientific equipment. Why do you think both types of technology are necessary?

_____

_____

_____

Name _____ Class _____ Date _____

Word Wise

Word Map Follow the model below to make a word map. The key term *technology* is in the center oval. Write the definition in your own words at the upper left. In the upper right, list Characteristics, which means words or phrases that relate to the term. At the lower left, list Non-Characteristics, which means words and phrases that would *not* be associated with it. In the lower right, draw a picture of the key term *or* use it in a sentence.

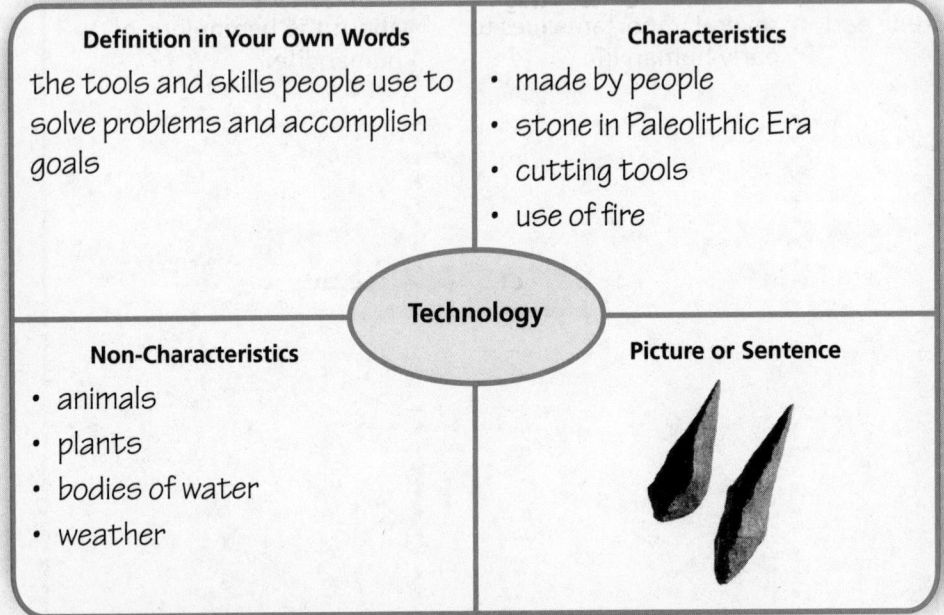

Definition in Your Own Words

the tools and skills people use to solve problems and accomplish goals

Characteristics

- made by people
- stone in Paleolithic Era
- cutting tools
- use of fire

Technology

Non-Characteristics

- animals
- plants
- bodies of water
- weather

Picture or Sentence

Now use the word map below to explore the meaning of the word *hunter-gatherers*. You may use your student text, a dictionary, and/or a thesaurus to complete each of the four sections.

Definition in Your Own Words

Characteristics

hunter-gatherers

Non-Characteristics

Picture or Sentence

Make word maps of your own on a separate piece of paper for these words: *culture* and *nomad*.

28

Name _____ Class _____ Date _____

Take Notes

Analyze Cause and Effect Use what you have read about hunter-gatherer societies to list ways that each change shown affected early human life.

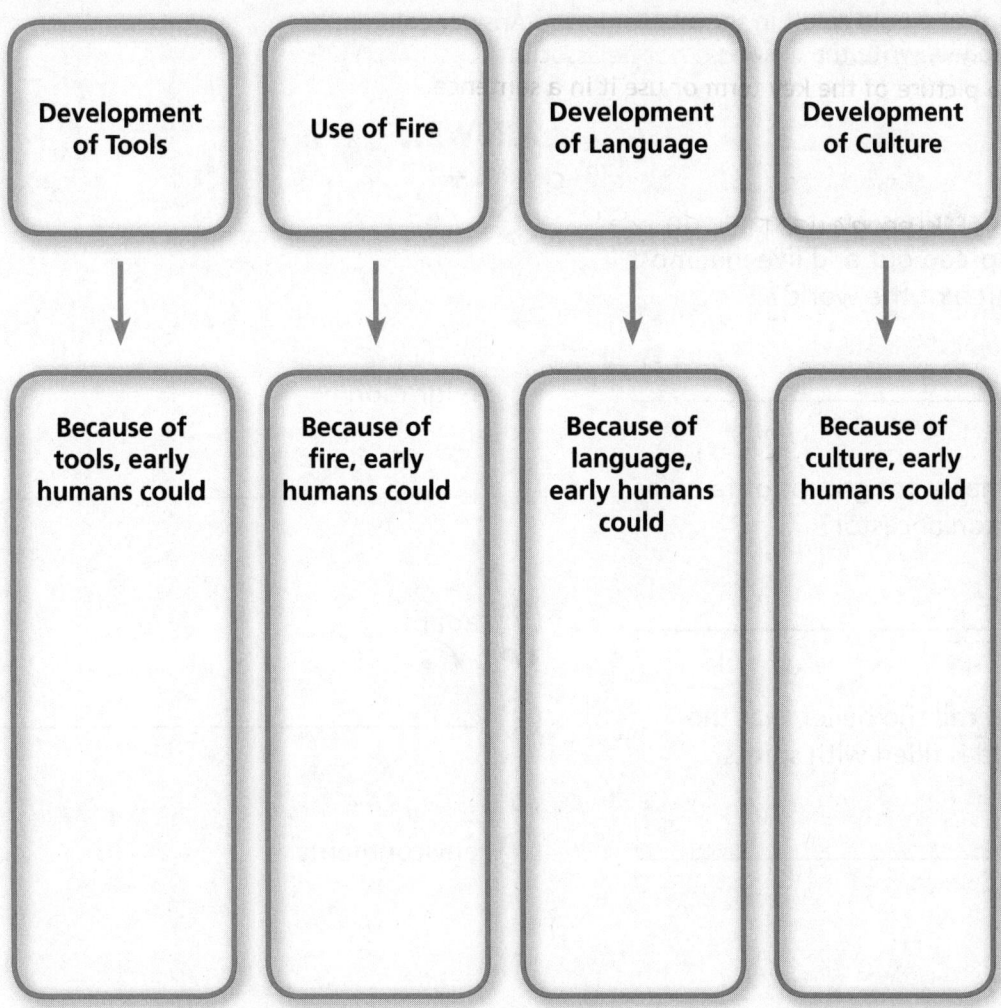

Development of Tools	Use of Fire	Development of Language	Development of Culture
Because of tools, early humans could	Because of fire, early humans could	Because of language, early humans could	Because of culture, early humans could

Essential Question

Choose one technological advance from this section. How did that technology benefit Stone Age people? How could that technology have unexpected results?

_____

_____

_____

Word Wise

Vocabulary Quiz Show Some quiz shows ask a question and expect the contestant to give the answer. In other shows, the contestant is given an answer and must supply the question. If the blank is in the Question column, write the question that would result in the answer in the Answer column. If the question is supplied, write the answer.

QUESTION	ANSWER
① What word describes what people do when they spread out and live in almost every land area of the world?	① _____
② _____	② migration
③ What is the name for groups of families with a common ancestor?	③ _____
④ _____	④ adapt
⑤ What do you call the belief that the natural world is filled with spirits?	⑤ _____
⑥ _____	⑥ environments

Name _____ Class _____ Date _____

Take Notes

Sequence As they populated Earth, early humans changed in many ways. Use information from *Populating the Earth* to complete the flowchart with some of these changes in the order in which they took place.

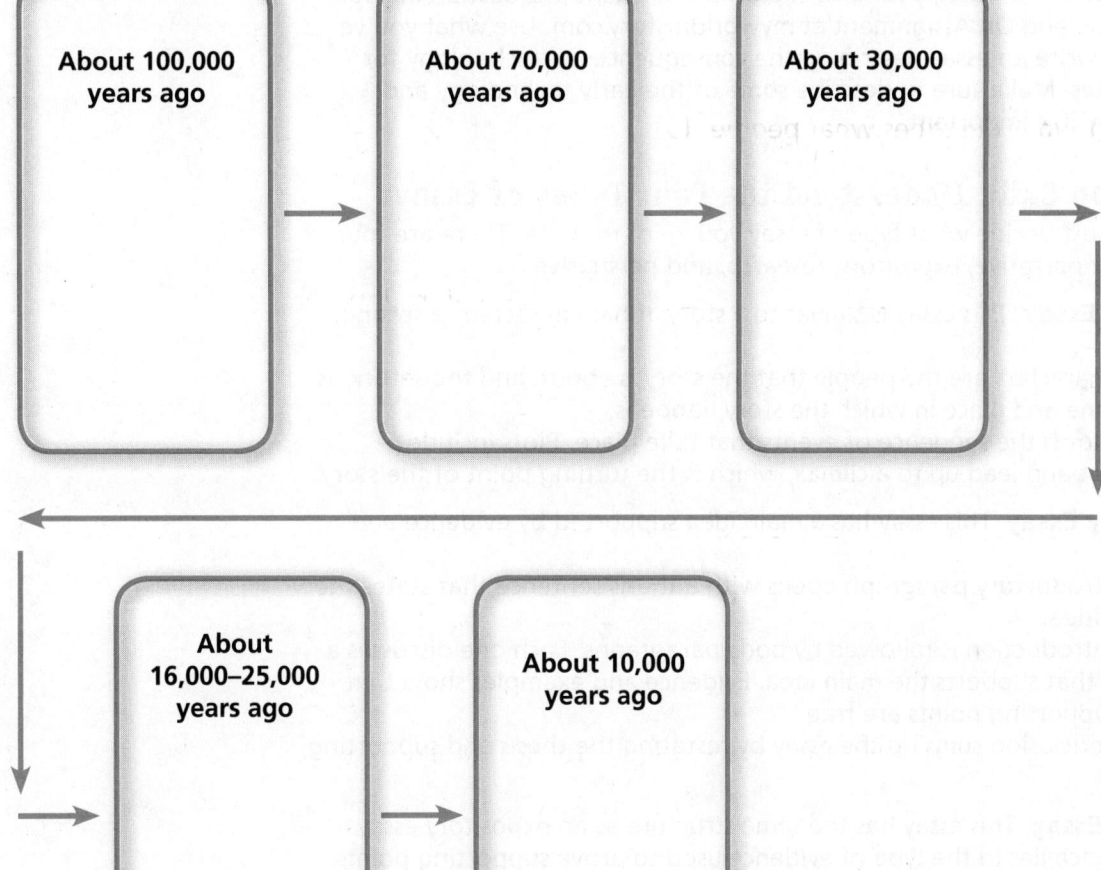

About 100,000 years ago

About 70,000 years ago

About 30,000 years ago

About 16,000–25,000 years ago

About 10,000 years ago

Essential Question

What technology helped people adapt to the last Ice Age? What other skills and tools would have helped Ice Age people survive?

_____

_____

_____

Name _____ Class _____ Date _____

Prepare to Write

Throughout this chapter, you have explored the Essential Question in your text, journal, and On Assignment at myworldhistory.com. Use what you've learned to write an essay describing the consequences of technology for early peoples. Make sure to describe some of the early technology and explain why it is important.

Workshop Skill: Understand the Four Types of Essays

First you must decide what type of essay you want to write. There are four essay types: narrative, expository, research, and persuasive.

Narrative Essay This essay is similar to a story. It has characters, a setting, and a plot.
- The characters are the people that the story is about, and the setting is the time and place in which the story happens.
- The plot is the sequence of events that take place. Plots include conflict and lead up to a climax, which is the turning point of the story.

Expository Essay This essay has a main idea supported by evidence and examples.
- An introductory paragraph opens with a thesis sentence that states the main idea.
- The introduction is followed by body paragraphs. Each one discusses a point that supports the main idea. Evidence and examples show that the supporting points are true.
- The conclusion sums up the essay by restating the thesis and supporting points.

Research Essay This essay has the same structure as an expository essay. The difference lies in the type of evidence used to prove supporting points.
- Evidence and examples should come from a broad range of reliable sources.
- Writers use quotations, footnotes, and a bibliography to show where they found the evidence used in the essay.

Persuasive Essay This essay is written when the author wants to persuade readers to adopt an opinion or to take action.
- The introduction tells why the topic is important. Then the thesis statement explains what the writer wants readers to think or do.
- In the body paragraphs, the writer uses both arguments and evidence to prove the supporting points.
- The conclusion reviews the main points and urges the reader to adopt the opinion or to take the action mentioned.

Identify Essay Types

Use what you have learned to identify the different essay types. Read the four descriptions in the table below. In the column on the right, write if the essay described is a narrative, expository, research, or persuasive one.

Essay Description	Type
1. The essay tries to convince readers that modern *Homo sapiens* developed separately in different parts of the world.	_____
2. The essay examines whether *Homo sapiens* first developed in Africa. It contains graphs, charts, statistics, and quotations from anthropologists. Sources are listed in footnotes.	_____
3. The essay states that the creation of technology helped humans to survive in hostile environments. It explains three major technologies in prehistory.	_____
4. The essay is a story that tells about the experiences of a young archeologist on her first expedition to Africa.	_____

Plan Your Essay

Use the following questions to help you make some decisions about your essay.

1. What do I want to say about the development of technology?

_____

2. Do I want to tell a story, explain an idea, present evidence, or persuade others about something?

_____

3. What type of essay will best help me accomplish my goal?

_____

Organize Your Essay

Now that you have decided on an essay type, outline your essay. Remember to have an introductory paragraph, three body paragraphs, and a conclusion. Then create your outline.

Draft Your Essay

Write your essay using the outline you created. When you have finished, proofread your essay.

Name _____ Class _____ Date _____

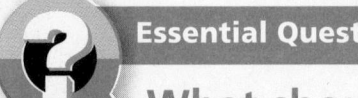

Essential Question

What should governments do?

Preview Before you begin this chapter, think about the Essential Question. Understanding how the Essential Question connects to your life will help you understand the chapter you are about to read.

Connect to Your Life

1. Think of ways that government affects your life every day. Then organize them by type of government. For example, your local government probably decides how much money your school can spend each year. The national government, however, makes some laws that affect schools. List your ideas in the table.

Government's Role in My Life			
School	Home	In My Community	Beyond My Community

2. Now think about whether you agree with the ways government affects your life. Why might some people support a particular government action and others oppose it?

_____

_____

Connect to the Chapter

3. Preview the chapter by skimming the chapter's heads, photographs, and graphics. Then make predictions about different parts of society where government might logically play a role. List your ideas in the table below.

Government's Role in Societies			
Safety and Defense	Laws	Economy	Social Services

4. After you have read the chapter, return to the table and circle your predictions that were correct.

Name _____ Class _____ Date _____

Connect to myStory: The Story of Gilgamesh

① Think about what you would have done if you had lived in the city of Uruk during the time of Gilgamesh. What are some ways you might have opposed Gilgamesh or persuaded him to reform?

_____

_____

② Now think about the experiences Gilgamesh had and how they changed him. In the table, list lessons he learned. Then list what you can learn from the story.

Lessons Gilgamesh Learns	Lessons I Can Learn From Gilgamesh

③ In the table below, list ways that Gilgamesh helped and hurt the people of Uruk. Write **B** next to actions that happened before Gilgamesh's travels and **A** next to those that happened after.

Harmful Actions	Helpful Actions

④ In what ways might leaders like Gilgamesh and their governments help early human communities form and develop? What values do leaders need in order to govern well?

_____

_____

Name _____ Class _____ Date _____

Word Wise

Words in Context For each question below, write an answer that shows your understanding of the boldfaced key term.

(1) Why is the birth of farming called a **revolution**?

Revolution=farmings modifies environment, causes people to remain in one place as a community →city

(2) What do people do when they **domesticate** plants and animals?

Herd them to fresh grass, so that they grow meat, milk

(3) How much food does a family have if there is a **surplus**?

Surplus more food than you need

(4) What are some examples of job **specialization**?

_____

_____

_____

Name _____ Class _____ Date _____

Take Notes

Analyze Cause and Effect Changes in agriculture had many effects on early
human populations. As you read, list some of these effects in the concept
web below.

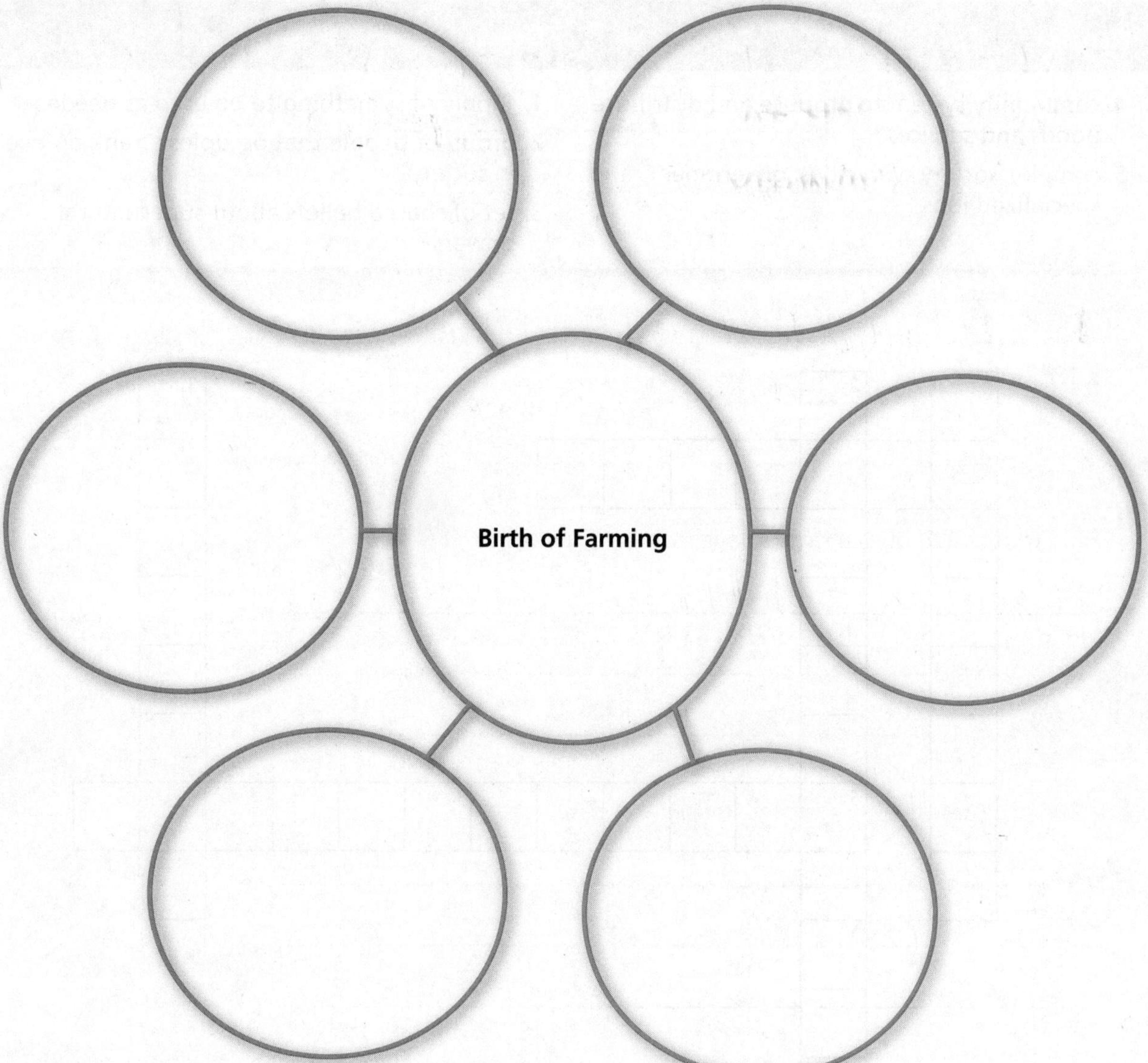

Birth of Farming

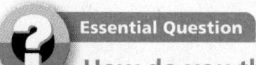 **Essential Question**

How do you think decision making would change as people moved
from hunter-gatherer bands to settled farming communities?

_____

_____

_____

Word Wise

Crossword Puzzle The *Across* and *Down* clues are definitions of key terms from this section. Fill in the numbered *Across* boxes with the correct key terms. Then do the same with the *Down* clues.

Across	Down
4. community system to produce and distribute goods and services	1. supply of something to be used as needed
5. complex society with cities, government, and specialized jobs	2. group of people that occupies a rank or level in society
	3. set of shared beliefs about supernatural powers

Name _____ Class _____ Date _____

Take Notes

Summarize As you read about cities and civilizations, briefly record the most important ideas about each feature of civilization.

Cities	Organized Government	Established Religion	Job Specialization

Social Classes	Public Works	Arts and Architecture	Writing

Essential Question

How was a strong government linked to public works? Do you think organizing such projects was a necessary job for early governments to do?

_____

_____

_____

Essential Question   Writer's Workshop

What should governments do?

Prepare to Write

Throughout this chapter, you have explored the Essential Question in your text, journal, and On Assignment at myworldhistory.com. Use what you've learned to write an essay describing the role of government in three features of civilization. Focus your essay on the city of Uruk. Make sure to identify and describe the three features of civilization you will discuss. Then explain what you think governments did to help those features develop in Uruk.

Workshop Skill: Use the Writing Process

Writing is a bit like learning a sport. Sometimes you work on one skill and discover you have to return and brush up on another skill first. In the writing process, you complete four basic steps but you sometimes have to repeat some of them along the way.

In this lesson, you will learn about the four basic steps in writing an essay. The steps are prewriting, drafting, revising, and presenting. Each step has several parts that help you communicate your ideas effectively.

Prewrite This step includes everything you do before you start writing. First, choose three features of civilization. Then brainstorm about the jobs government can do. You could use the chapter images or subheadings to get ideas. Collect ideas in note form or use a graphic organizer such as a flowchart. Then make an outline. It should list a main idea or thesis about the role of government in developing civilizations. Briefly mention the three features you will use to support your thesis. Then return to the chapter and look for evidence (such as quotes and examples) that tells about government's role in developing each feature. Add these to your outline.

Draft Start putting your ideas into sentences and paragraphs. Follow your outline, but don't worry too much about spelling, grammar, or even complete sentences. Just get your ideas onto paper. Mark places where you may need to get more information. Think about how you can explain your ideas to readers. Try to start each paragraph by identifying the feature of civilization in a topic sentence that communicates its main point. This will help you know what else has to go in the paragraph.

Revise Read over your draft. Ask yourself if your ideas and explanations make sense. Think about whether idea A belongs before or after idea B. Move text around until the arguments flow clearly. Then read your draft out loud, listening for sentences that ramble on. Shorten them or create two sentences. On the other hand, if you have too many short sentences, use sentence combining to create interest. Read a third time to find and fix spelling and grammar errors. As with drafting, you may find that you need to get more information or write more text.

Present Create a clean, double-spaced copy of your essay. Add your name, date, and a title according to the format your teacher has requested.

Here is a sample table to help you brainstorm. Think about the ideas you identified when you reviewed the chapter:

What Governments Did		
Feature 1: Public Works	Feature 2: Social Classes	Feature 3: Cities
• organized workers	• gave power to groups such as priests and rulers	• built roads to help people get in and out of the city

Use a Graphic Organizer

Now create and complete your own graphic organizer to brainstorm ideas for your essay. Use the style shown above or try a concept web.

Draft Your Essay

Use the graphic organizer you created to collect ideas for your essay. Then follow the steps in this workshop to draft and revise your paper on separate paper. Be sure that you complete all four steps in the writing process.

Name _____ Class _____ Date _____

Places to Know!

Map Skills Use the maps in this unit to identify the Places to Know! on the outline map. Before the name of each place below, write the letter that shows its location on the map.

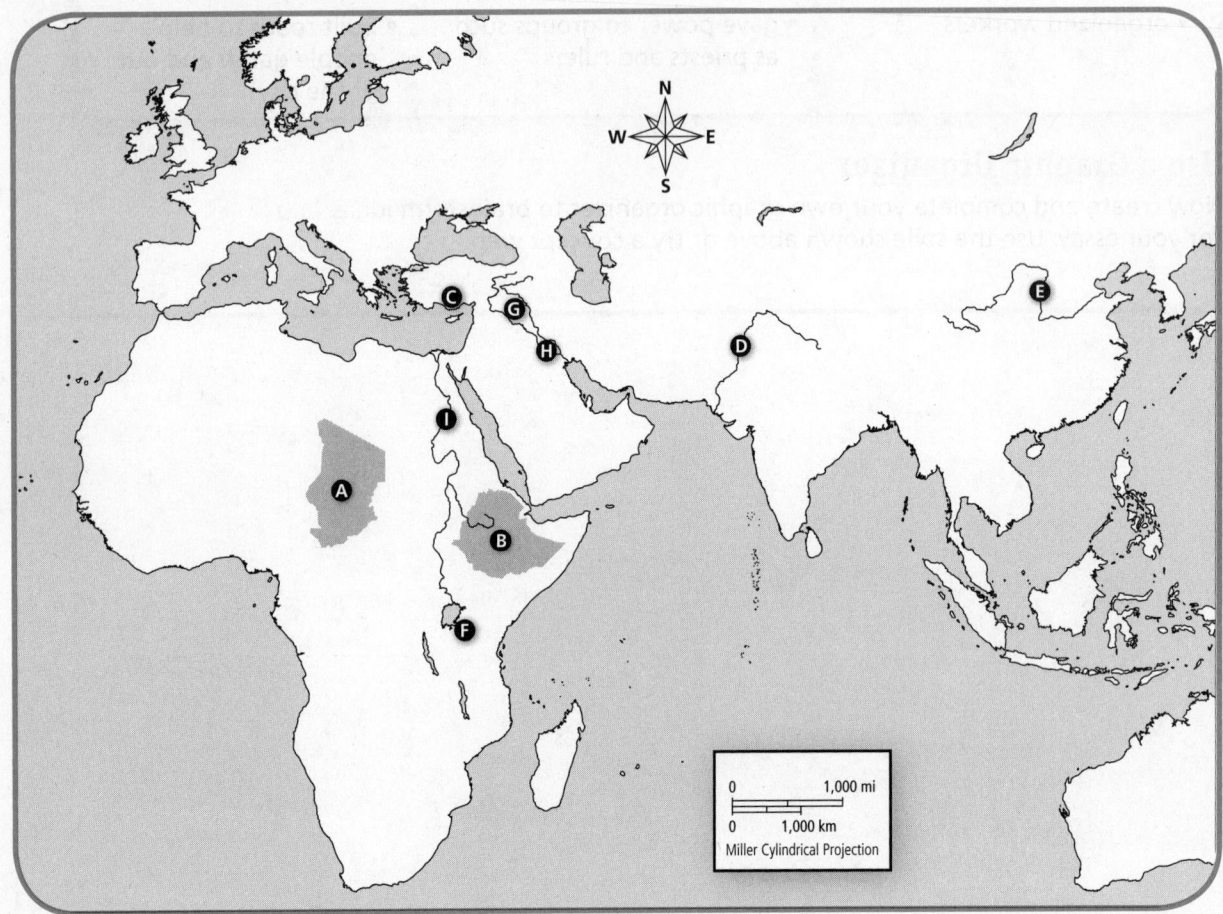

0   1,000 mi
0   1,000 km
Miller Cylindrical Projection

_____ Tigris and Euphrates rivers

_____ Olduvai Gorge

_____ Huang He

_____ Chad

_____ Nile River

_____ Çatalhöyük

_____ Uruk

_____ Ethiopia

_____ Indus River

Key Events

Timeline Use what you have read about human origins to complete the timeline below. Draw a line from each event to its correct position on the timeline. Then write a brief description of each event.

2.5 million years ago _____
_____

200,000 years ago _____
_____

100,000 years ago _____
_____

70,000–12,000 years ago _____
_____

3 million years ago

1 million years ago

100,000 years ago

20,000 years ago

10,000 years ago

5,000 years ago

A.D. 2050

10,000 years ago _____
_____

8,000 years ago _____
_____

6,000–7,000 years ago _____
_____

A.D. 1959 _____ in Africa.
_____

A.D. 2009 _____
_____

Name _____ Class _____ Date _____

What are the consequences of technology?

Preview Before you begin this chapter, think about the Essential Question. Understanding how the Essential Question connects to your life will help you understand the chapter you are about to read.

Connect to Your Life

① Think of a time you went on a journey. How did you get to your destination? What did you take with you?

_____

_____

② Think about a type of technology you used on your trip, how it affected you, and whether the effect was positive or negative. Fill in the table below with your ideas.

Technology I Used on My Journey		
Technology	**Its Effects**	**Positive or Negative?**
	•	•
	•	•
	•	•

Connect to the Chapter

③ Preview the chapter by skimming the chapter's heads, photographs, and graphics. In the table below, name a Mesopotamian technological advance for each category. Then predict how that technology contributed to Mesopotamia's development. Explain your answer.

	Technology	Prediction
Trade		
Agriculture		
Navigation		
Communication		

④ After reading the chapter, return to this page. Circle your predictions that were correct.

Name _____ Class _____ Date _____

Connect to myStory: Cyrus the Great: King of the World

(1) Think about how Cyrus conquered the Babylonians. Have you ever figured out a way to do something that was very difficult? How did you solve your problem?

_____

_____

(2) Using clues from Cyrus's story and images from the chapter, predict what life was like in the Fertile Crescent. Write your predictions in the table below.

Life in the Fertile Crescent	
Communication	
Education	
Government	
Agriculture	

Word Wise

Use a Word Bank Choose one word from the word bank to fill in each blank. When you have finished, you will have a short summary of important ideas from the section.

Word Bank

Fertile Crescent	irrigate
barter	ziggurats
Mesopotamia	city-states
polytheism	cuneiform

The _____ is a region of the Middle East that stretches

from the Persian Gulf to the Mediterranean Sea. This region includes

_____, where several independent states known as

_____ developed. As these communities developed, ancient

Sumerians used technology to improve agriculture. They learned how to

_____, or supply water to, their crops. They also exchanged

goods without using money in a trading system known as

_____. Sumerians practiced _____, or the

belief in more than one god. To honor their gods, they built pyramid-shaped

temples called _Ziggurats_. Sumerians also developed a writing

system in which scribes made wedge-shaped marks in wet clay. This writing

system was called _Cuneiform_.

Name _____ Class _____ Date _____

Take Notes

Identify Main Ideas and Details The column headings in the table below match the headings in your textbook. Reread each section. For each topic write the main idea and the details that support it. Use what you have read about the civilization of Sumer to complete the concept web below.

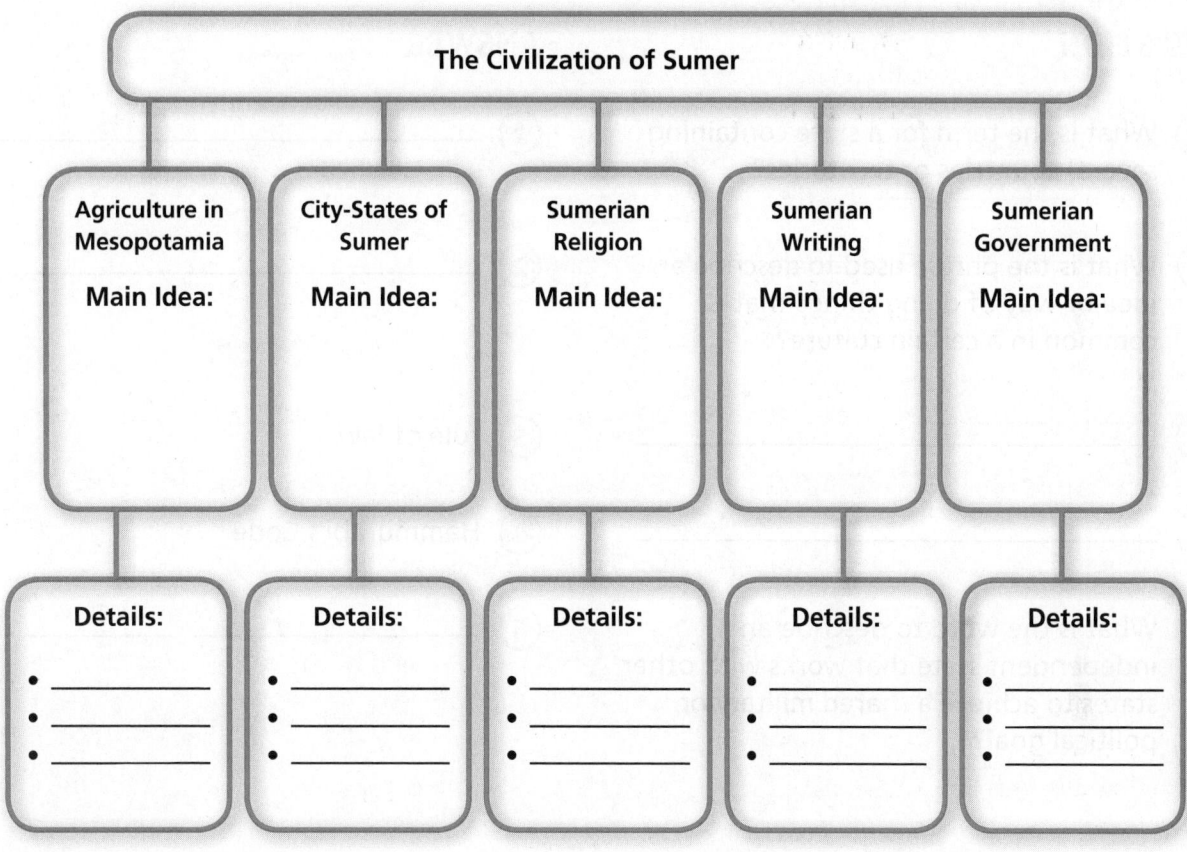

The Civilization of Sumer

Agriculture in Mesopotamia
Main Idea:

City-States of Sumer
Main Idea:

Sumerian Religion
Main Idea:

Sumerian Writing
Main Idea:

Sumerian Government
Main Idea:

Details:
- _____
- _____
- _____

Details:
- _____
- _____
- _____

Details:
- _____
- _____
- _____

Details:
- _____
- _____
- _____

Details:
- _____
- _____
- _____

Essential Question

How did technology help Sumerian civilization develop?

_____

_____

_____

Word Wise

Vocabulary Quiz Show Some quiz shows ask a question and expect the contestant to give the answer. In other shows, the contestant is given an answer and must supply the question. If the blank is in the Question column, write the question that would result in the answer in the Answer column. If the question is supplied, write the answer.

QUESTION	ANSWER
① What is the term for a state containing several countries or territories?	① _____
② What is the phrase used to describe an idea or way of doing things that is common in a certain culture?	② _____
③ _____	③ rule of law
④ _____	④ Hammurabi's Code
⑤ What is the word to describe an independent state that works with other states to achieve a shared military or political goal?	⑤ _____

Name _____ Class _____ Date _____

Take Notes

Analyze Cause and Effect In this section, you read how Sargon formed the world's first empire. Use what you have read about this event to complete the cause-and-effect chart below.

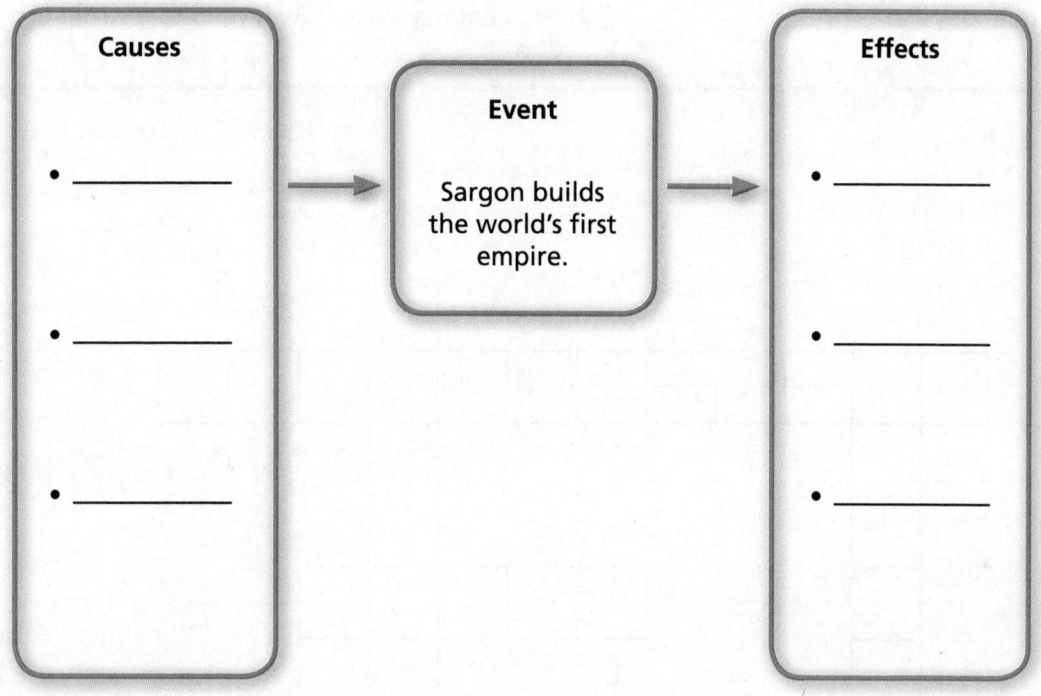

Causes

• _____

• _____

• _____

Event

Sargon builds the world's first empire.

Effects

• _____

• _____

• _____

Essential Question

How do you think Sumerian inventions and technologies might have helped later empires form and expand?

_____

_____

_____

Name _____ Class _____ Date _____

Word Wise

Crossword Puzzle The *Across* and *Down* clues are definitions of key terms from this section. Fill in the numbered *Across* boxes with the correct key terms. Then do the same with the *Down* clues.

Across	Down
2. a permanent army of professional soldiers	1. term for soldiers who fight while riding horses
4. a carved stone or pillar	3. payment made to show loyalty to a stronger power
5. money	

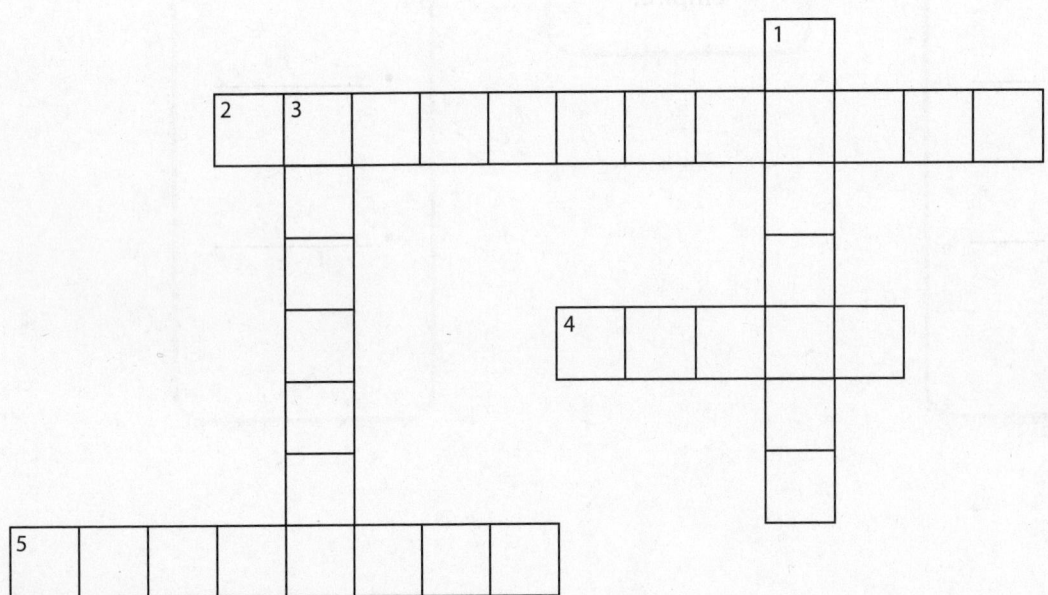

Name _____ Class _____ Date _____

Take Notes

Summarize Use what you have read about the Assyrian and Persian empires to fill in the key ideas from this section of the chapter in the table below.

The Assyrian and Neo-Babylonian Empires	Rise of the Persian Empire	Persia's Government and Religion	Arts of Mesopotamia
Key Ideas •	**Key Ideas** •	**Key Ideas** •	**Key Ideas** •
•	•	•	•
•	•	•	•

? Essential Question

How did Assyrian, Babylonian, and Persian rulers use technology to expand and unite their empires?

_____

_____

_____

Word Wise

Words in Context For each question below, write an answer that shows your understanding of the boldfaced key term.

(1) Why did Phoenician traders bring **imports** to their homeland? _____

_____

_____

(2) What items did Phoenician traders ship as **exports** to other regions?

_____

_____

(3) How did Phoenician sailors become experts at **navigation**? _____

_____

_____

(4) How did Phoenician trading stations develop into **colonies**? _____

_____

_____

(5) How did **cultural diffusion** help preserve the legacy of the Phoenicians?

_____

_____

(6) How did the Phoenician **alphabet** simplify writing? _____

_____

_____

Name _____ Class _____ Date _____

Take Notes

Summarize Use the web flowchart below to summarize what you've learned about the Phoenicians.

> ## The Phoenicians

The Phoenician People: _____

Phoenicians and the Sea: _____

Legacy of the Phoenicians: _____

 **Essential Question**

How did the Phoenician economy depend on technology? _____

_____

_____

Name _____ Class _____ Date _____

What are the consequences of technology?

Prepare to Write
Throughout this chapter, you have explored the Essential Question in your text, journal, and On Assignment at myworldhistory.com. Use your notes and what you've learned to write a five-paragraph essay describing how technology helped the development of civilizations in the Fertile Crescent.

Workshop Skill: Outline an Essay
Your essay will contain five paragraphs: an introduction, three body paragraphs, and a concluding paragraph. You will need to capture your reader's attention. Also, you will need to create a thesis statement.

The Hook Think about technology's role in the development of the Fertile Crescent. For example, the wheel and the discovery of how to make bronze were technologies that helped spread Sumerian culture. Then create a "hook" that will capture your reader's interest. For example, *How did the invention of the computer change our lives?* Notice how this makes the reader think about technology. On the lines below, write some hook ideas to generate interest in the technologies of the Fertile Crescent.

Hook idea 1: What would Sumer have done without the wheel?

Hook idea 2: _____

Hook idea 3: _____

The Thesis Statement Now state your thesis, which is the main idea of your essay. The thesis should state three ideas, in the form of topic sentences, that you will use to support your position. These ideas will be the focus of your body paragraphs.

In this case, the thesis statement is the last sentence in your introduction. Add your own ideas to the thesis statement given below.

Example *Technology was a key element in the development of ancient*

civilizations. The wheel and the invention of bronze helped Sumer become

the first great civilization. Later empires like the _____ and

the _____ built upon the Sumerian achievements. By the

time of the Phoenicians, the development of _____,

_____, and _____ had made technology

necessary for economic survival in a changing world.

The Introduction Your first paragraph is the introduction. This is how you will get your readers "hooked" on the topic and make them want to read more. The introduction includes your hook and thesis statement.

Body Paragraphs Your essay will include three body paragraphs, each with a topic sentence, main idea, supporting details, and conclusion. Use the chart below to piece together your three body paragraphs.

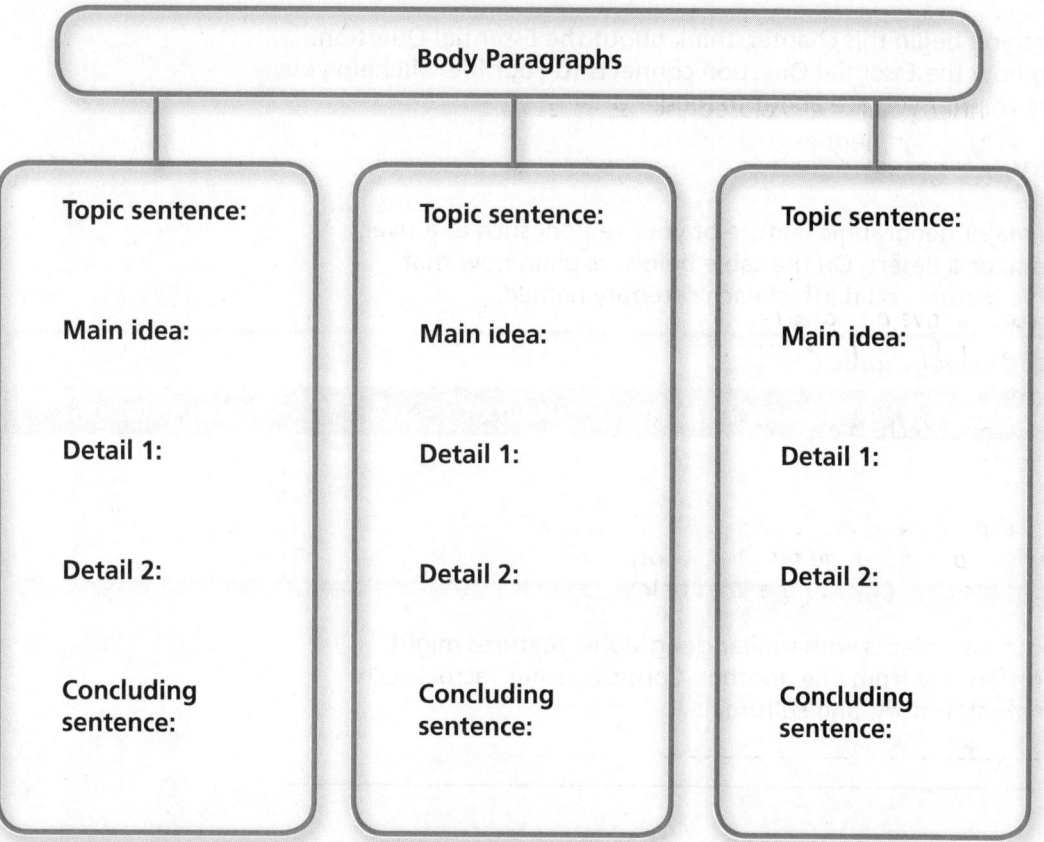

Body Paragraphs

Topic sentence:

Main idea:

Detail 1:

Detail 2:

Concluding sentence:

Topic sentence:

Main idea:

Detail 1:

Detail 2:

Concluding sentence:

Topic sentence:

Main idea:

Detail 1:

Detail 2:

Concluding sentence:

Conclusion Your last paragraph is your conclusion, in which you summarize the main ideas presented in your essay. This is your opportunity to get your point across to your readers. Review your big ideas and complete the conclusion below.

Example *The examples of Sumerian achievements in agriculture and*

metalwork and the use of Sumerian achievements by the

_____, _____, and _____

show how technology spreads. The success of the Phoenicians demonstrated

the importance of _____ *in a growing*

_____ .

Draft Your Essay

Review and revise your outline to be sure your thoughts are clearly presented. Then write your essay and proofread it with a writing partner.

Name _____ Class _____ Date _____

Essential Question

How much does geography affect people's lives?

Preview Before you begin this chapter, think about the Essential Question. Understanding how the Essential Question connects to your life will help you understand the chapter you are about to read.

Connect to Your Life

① Choose a major geographic feature of your region, such as a river, a mountain, or a desert. On the table below, explain how that geographic feature could affect each category named.

Effects of Geographic Feature			
Economy	• Outdoor Activities	• Climate	• Transportation
	•	•	•

② Think about why places with similar geographic features might develop differently from one another. Consider other factors such as government, history, and culture.

_____

_____

Connect to the Chapter

③ Preview the chapter. Skim the headings, photos, and graphics. In the table below, predict how you think geography affected ancient Egypt and Nubia.

Geographic Features of Ancient Egypt and Nubia	• Effect on Culture and • Everyday Life	• Effect on Economic • Activities and • Trade	• Effect on Building • Materials
Climate	•	•	•
Waterways	•	•	•
Deserts	•	•	•

④ After you have read the chapter, circle the predictions that were correct.

56

Connect to myStory: Hatshepsut: Taking Power With Style

1 Hatshepsut built monuments and dressed in traditional attire to convince her people that she could be a pharaoh. Suppose that you had to convince people that you could do something extraordinary. What would you do?

_____

_____

_____

2 Hatshepsut wanted to make Egypt strong and wealthy. To do this, she had to make up ways to rule as a woman. In the table below, write about what Hatshepsut did as the first woman king of Egypt. Then give some reasons why she had to act as she did.

Hatshepsut's Actions	Reasons for Her Actions

3 Think about the events from the story of Hatshepsut. Then write three predictions about things you will learn about Egypt and Nubia.

_____

_____

_____

Name _____ Class _____ Date _____

Word Wise

Word Map Follow the model below to make a word map. The key term *cataract* is in the center oval. Write the definition in your own words at the upper left. In the upper right, list Characteristics, which means words or phrases that relate to the term. At the lower left, list Non-Characteristics, which means words and phrases that would *not* be associated with it. In the lower right, draw a picture of the key term *or* use it in a sentence.

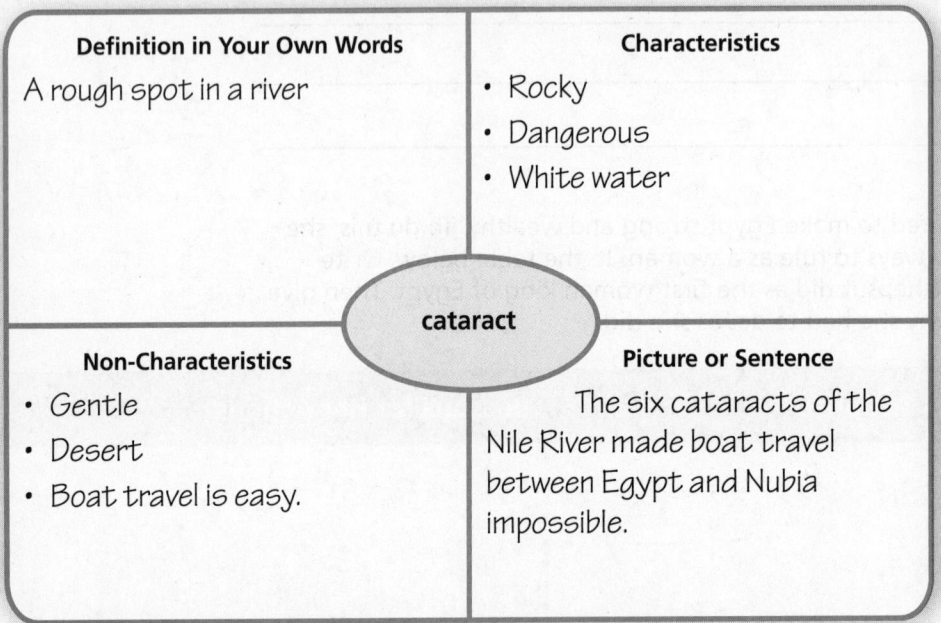

Definition in Your Own Words

A rough spot in a river

Characteristics

- Rocky
- Dangerous
- White water

cataract

Non-Characteristics

- Gentle
- Desert
- Boat travel is easy.

Picture or Sentence

The six cataracts of the Nile River made boat travel between Egypt and Nubia impossible.

Now use the word map below to explore the meaning of the word *pharaoh*. You may use your student text, a dictionary, and a thesaurus to complete each of the four sections.

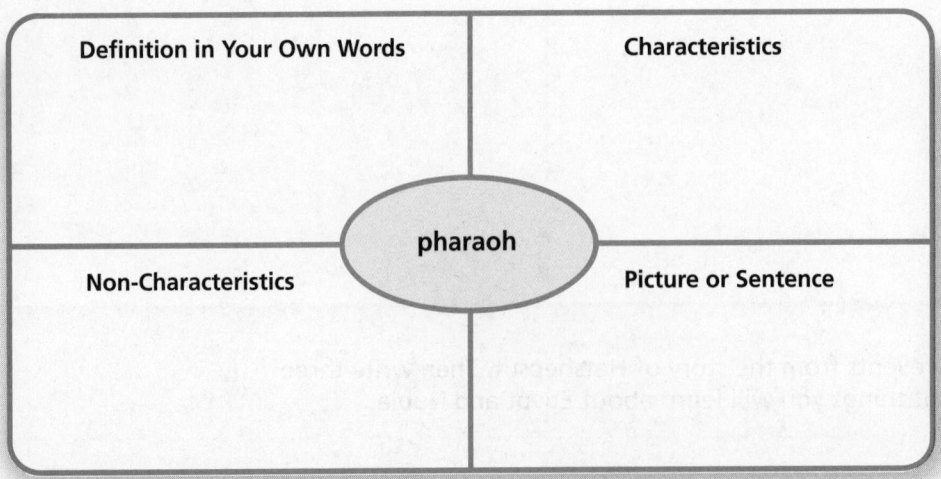

Definition in Your Own Words

Characteristics

pharaoh

Non-Characteristics

Picture or Sentence

Make word maps of your own on a separate piece of paper for these words: *mummy, bureaucracy, delta, artisan,* and *dynasty.*

58

Name _____ Class _____ Date _____

Take Notes

Identify Main Ideas and Details Use what you have read about Egypt and Nubia to complete the table. In each space at the top, write one main idea, using the heads in red in your textbook. Beneath each head write at least two details to support the main idea. Follow the example.

The Nile River Valley	Civilization Develops	Kingdoms of Egypt
World's longest river flows through it.		
Strip of fertile land between deserts		
Yearly flooding		

In the table below, use the remaining red heads from the section.

Essential Question

Which aspects of ancient Egyptian civilization were based on its geography? Which were not?

_____

_____

_____

Name _____ Class _____ Date _____

Word Wise

Words in Context For each question below, write an answer that shows your understanding of the boldfaced key term.

(1) How were **hieroglyphics** different from an alphabet?

use images = sounds = words

(2) What was **papyrus** made from and what was it used for?

Paper, rope, fabric

(3) How did Egyptians come to have such a good knowledge of **anatomy**?

mumify organs

(4) How did Egyptians make and use **sculptures**?

carving with stone

(5) What was the purpose of a **pyramid**?

pyramid to keep a pharaohs body safe

Name _____ Class _____ Date _____

Take Notes

Summarize Use what you have read about art, architecture, and learning in Egypt to complete the concept web below.

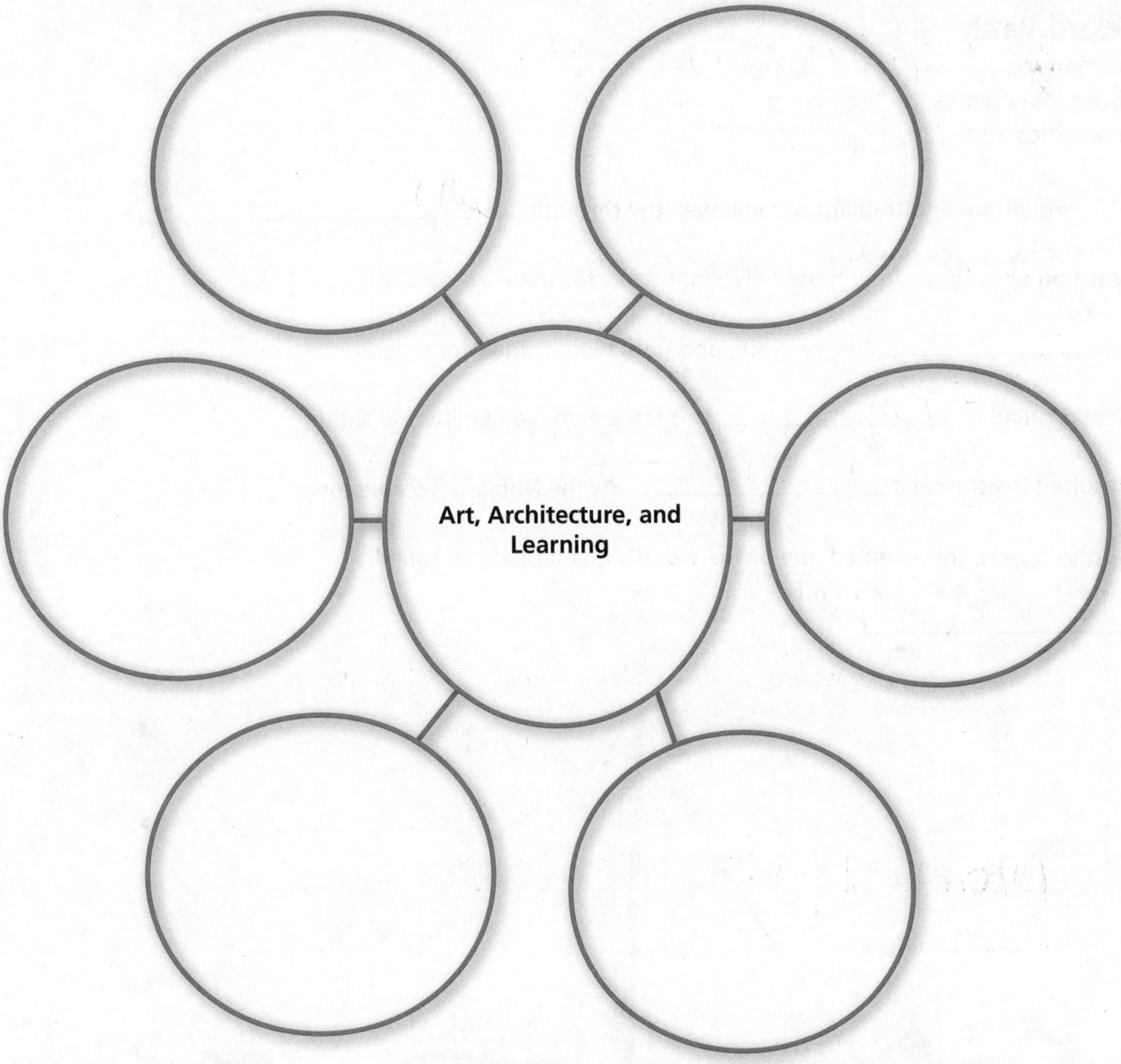

Art, Architecture, and Learning

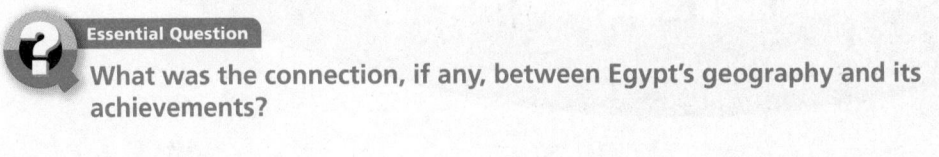

Essential Question

What was the connection, if any, between Egypt's geography and its achievements?

_____

_____

_____

Word Wise

Word Bank Choose one word from the word bank to fill in each blank. When you have finished, you will have a short summary of important ideas from the section.

Word Bank

~~commerce~~   ~~ebony~~
interdependence   ~~ivory~~
Meroitic script

Egyptians and Nubians became wealthy through _~~commerce~~_ **commerce**

with other nations. They traded elephant tusks for their

ivory. Ivory, cloth, and gold were traded for a dark

wood called _ebony_. This trade between Egypt and Nubia

resulted in economic _interdependence_. As the Nubians became more

sophisticated, they created one of the world's first alphabets, called

meroitic script

Name _____ Class _____ Date _____

Take Notes

Analyze Cause and Effect Use what you have read about Egypt and Nubia to complete the chart. Where there is a cause, provide the effect. If the effect is given, write the cause.

Cause	Effect

Egypt needed Nubia's gold, and Nubia needed Egypt's grain. →

→ Nubians adopted parts of the Egyptian religion.

→ Nubians had to pay tribute to the Egyptian pharaoh.

Egyptians destroyed Napata, the capital of Nubia. →

Essential Question

Give examples of how geography helped shape the civilization of Nubia.

_____

_____

_____

? Essential Question Writer's Workshop

How much does geography affect people's lives?

Prepare to Write

Throughout this chapter, you have explored the Essential Question in your text, in your journal, and On Assignment at myworldhistory.com. Use what you've learned to write an introduction and thesis statement about how much geography affects people's lives.

Workshop Skill: Write an Introduction and Thesis Statement

First, review the four essay types. Decide which type is best suited to the ideas you want to express. Which type of essay have you chosen?

_____

Develop your thesis, which is your response to the Essential Question. Begin by reviewing your notes. To help yourself decide whether to answer the question positively or negatively, list reasons that support each position in the table below.

Geography Affects People's Lives Positively by	Geography Affects People's Lives Negatively by

Write the position you have chosen below, along with the three strongest reasons that support it. Note at least one fact or example for each reason.

Position (Positive or Negative)	
Supporting Reasons	Facts and/or Examples

Write Your Thesis Statement

Your thesis statement states your position and three reasons that support it. The thesis statement will be the last sentence or sentences in your introductory paragraph. For example: *Geography affects people's lives positively by*

_____, _____, and _____.

If your sentence is too long, place your reasons in a second sentence. For example: *Geography affects people's lives positively. This is true because*

_____, _____, and _____.

Now write your thesis statement:

_____

Write Your Introduction

The first paragraph of an essay introduces the topic to the reader. An introduction has three parts.

1. A statement indicating what the essay is about

Example *Geography, no matter where we live, affects our lives positively*

by _____.

2. An indication of why the subject or issue is important

Example *By understanding the geography of an area, we can*

understand _____.

3. A thesis statement

Write your introductory sentence: _____.

State the issue's importance: _____.

Write your thesis statement, including three supporting arguments:

_____

_____

_____

Draft Your Essay

Introduction Rewrite your introductory paragraph on your own paper.
Body Paragraphs Develop each argument to support your position in a separate paragraph. Include details and examples.
Conclusion Summarize your arguments. When you have finished, proofread your essay.

Name _____ Class _____ Date _____

Essential Question

How are religion and culture connected?

Preview Before you begin this chapter, think about the Essential Question. Understanding how the Essential Question connects to your life will help you understand the chapter you are about to read.

Connect to Your Life

(1) Define the word *culture*. Think of ways a religion you know about has influenced culture. Then complete the table below. Fill in the name of the religion and what you observe about each cultural element.

Religion		
Elements of Local Culture	Description or Example	Influence of Religion
Attitude Toward the Elderly		
Holidays Celebrated		
Types of Food		

(2) Explain how one of the subjects in the chart might be different if religion did not influence it.

_____

_____

Connect to the Chapter

(3) Preview the chapter by skimming the photos, headings, and graphics. In the table below, predict how religion affected the culture of ancient Israel.

Elements of Jewish Culture	Description or Example	Influence of Religion
Government and Rulers		
Laws		
Food		

(4) After you finish reading the chapter, look at this chart again. Circle the predictions that were correct.

Name _____ Class _____ Date _____

Connect to myStory: The Story of Ruth

(1) Think about someone you know or have heard about who has a different set of beliefs from your own. In what ways do the person's religious beliefs affect his or her culture?

_____

_____

_____

(2) Ruth gave up her own people and religion to follow Naomi. She needed certain qualities to be able to do this. In the first column of the table below, write some of the qualities that enabled Ruth to do what she did. In the second column, write an action that shows each quality. In the third column, write the results of those actions.

Ruth's Qualities	Action That Shows the Quality	Results of Ruth's Actions

(3) Think about the events from the story of Ruth. Then write two predictions about things you will learn about the ancient Israelites and their religion, Judaism.

_____

_____

_____

_____

Word Wise

Use a Word Bank Choose one word from the word bank to fill in each blank. When you have finished, you will have a short summary of important ideas from the section.

Word Bank

commandments	covenant
ethics	Exodus
monotheism	Torah

Unlike many other religions that originated in the Fertile Crescent,

Judaism is the belief in only one God, or _____. The first

five books of the Bible, called the _____, tell how Judaism

began. These books describe how God told the Israelites to practice right

behavior, or _____. The Torah tells that God made a

_____ with Abraham, whom Jews consider to be the

founder of their religion. According to the Bible, the Israelites ended up in

Egypt, where they became slaves. Moses became their leader and helped

them in an escape from slavery called the _____. The Bible

describes how God told Moses to give the Israelites a series of ten

_____ to teach them how to act toward God and other

people.

Name _____ Class _____ Date _____

Take Notes

Summarize In this section you have learned about Abraham, the Exodus, the Ten Commandments, and the Return to the Promised Land. Use what you know from your reading to complete the chart below. In each empty box below a heading, summarize the information from the part of the section below that heading.

The Worship of One God	The Exodus	The Ten Commandments	Return to the Promised Land

Essential Question

Explain how religion helped shape the culture of the ancient Israelites, as presented in the Hebrew Bible.

_____

_____

_____

Name _____ Class _____ Date _____

Word Wise

Vocabulary Quiz Show Some quiz shows ask a question and expect the contestant to give the answer. In other shows, the contestant is given an answer and must supply the question. If the blank is in the Question column, write the question that would result in the answer in the Answer column. If the answer is supplied, write the appropriate question.

QUESTION	ANSWER
(1) _____	(1) Scripture
(2) What is a person called who is chosen by God to bring messages to the people?	(2) _____
(3) _____	(3) rabbi
(4) What is the name of a collection of teachings and commentaries about the Bible and Jewish law?	(4) _____
(5) _____	(5) righteousness
(6) What is another word for fair treatment for all?	(6) _____
(7) _____	(7) Sabbath

Name _____ Class _____ Date _____

Take Notes

Analyze Cause and Effect Use what you have read about Judaism to complete the chart below. In each box to the left, you will see a type of Jewish religious writing. In each box to the right, write ways in which that body of writings affected Jewish beliefs.

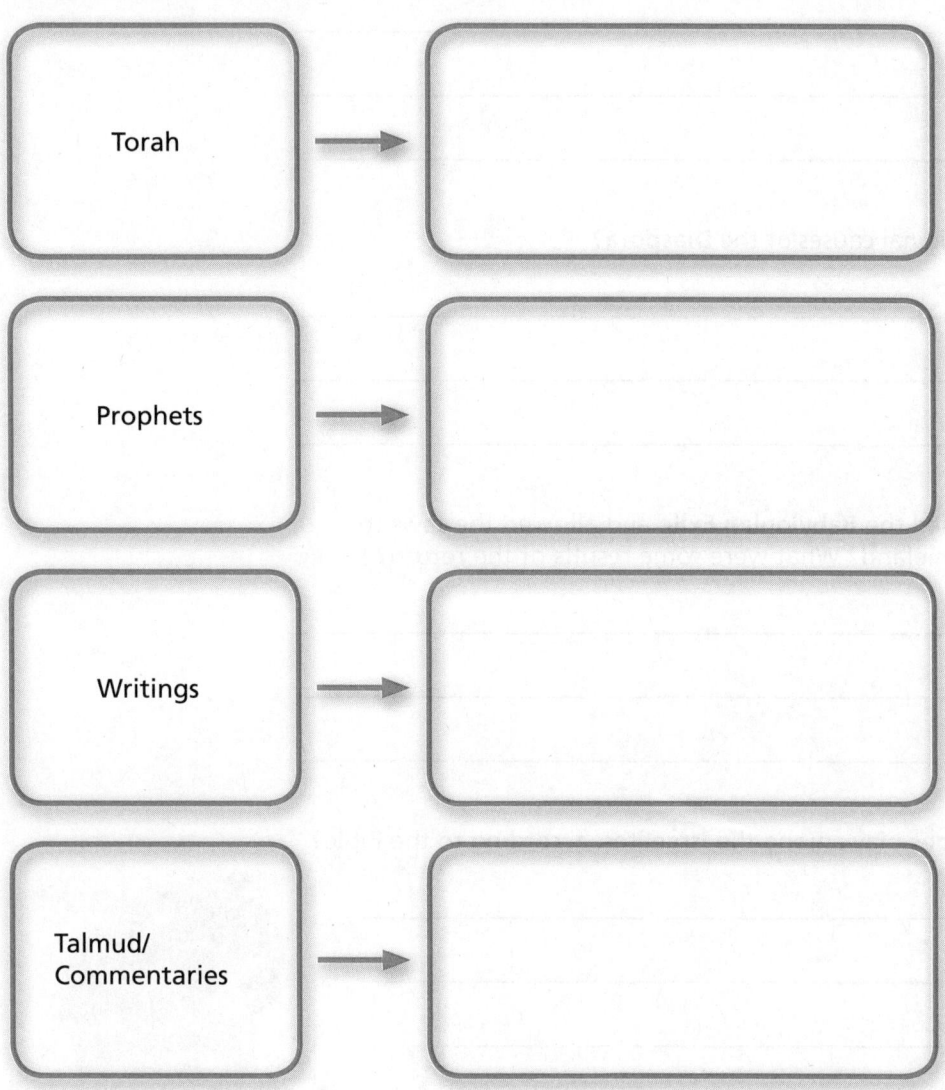

Torah →

Prophets →

Writings →

Talmud/ Commentaries →

Essential Question

Give examples of ways in which Judaism as a religion has shaped Jewish culture.

_____

_____

_____

Name _____ Class _____ Date _____

Word Wise

In Context For each question below, write an answer that shows your understanding of the boldfaced key term.

① What is a **synagogue** used for?

_____

_____

_____

② What were the original causes of the **Diaspora**?

_____

_____

_____

③ Which empire ended the **Babylonian Exile** and allowed the Jews to return to their homeland? What were some results of the return?

_____

_____

_____

④ What role did **judges** play among the Israelites, according to the Bible?

_____

_____

_____

Name _____ Class _____ Date _____

Take Notes

Sequence Use what you have read about the Jewish people to fill in the timeline below. In each box, write the event that occurred on that date.

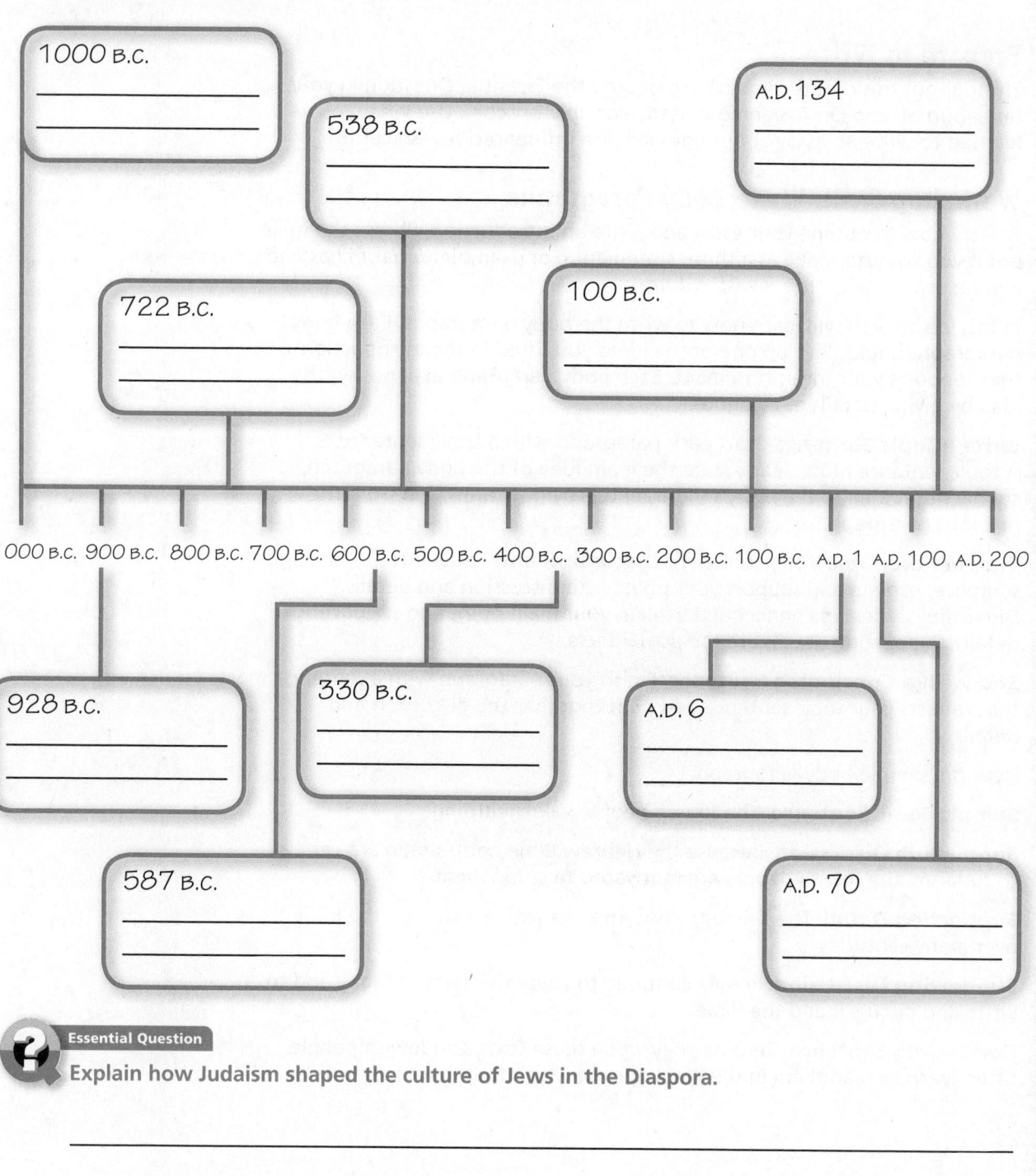

1000 B.C.
_____
_____

538 B.C.
_____
_____

A.D.134
_____
_____

722 B.C.
_____
_____

100 B.C.
_____
_____

1000 B.C. 900 B.C. 800 B.C. 700 B.C. 600 B.C. 500 B.C. 400 B.C. 300 B.C. 200 B.C. 100 B.C. A.D. 1 A.D. 100 A.D. 200

928 B.C.
_____
_____

330 B.C.
_____
_____

A.D. 6
_____
_____

587 B.C.
_____
_____

A.D. 70
_____
_____

Essential Question

Explain how Judaism shaped the culture of Jews in the Diaspora.

_____
_____
_____

Name _____ Class _____ Date _____

How are religion and culture connected?

Prepare to Write

Throughout this chapter, you have explored the Essential Question in your text, journal, and On Assignment at myworldhistory.com. Use what you've learned to write an essay about how religion influenced Jewish culture.

Workshop Skill: Write Body Paragraphs

Review how to outline your essay and write an introduction. Phrase the main point you want to make as a thesis statement. For example, *Judaism has had a great influence on the Jewish culture.*

In this lesson, you will learn how to write the body paragraphs. Each body paragraph should develop one of the ideas you listed in the introduction that supports your thesis statement. Each body paragraph expands on the idea by giving details or evidence.

Write a Topic Sentence Start each paragraph with a topic sentence. A topic sentence must clearly state the main idea of the body paragraph, connect that idea to the essay's thesis, and provide a transition from the previous paragraph.

Support the Topic Sentence with Discussion and Facts After your topic sentence, explain and support your point with discussion and details. Discussion sentences connect and explain your main point and supporting details. Supporting details are the actual facts.

End with a Concluding Sentence Finish your paragraph with a sentence that reflects your topic sentence and pulls together the discussion and details.

Here is a sample body paragraph:

Sample Topic Sentence The Jewish people value learning.

Supporting Discussion Because the Hebrew Bible and Talmud are central to Judaism, the Jewish people are motivated to study them.

Supporting Detail The Talmud was written as scholars studied the Bible over many centuries.

Supporting Discussion People continue to study the Talmud today and to write and discuss it and the Bible.

Concluding Sentence Because they value these texts, the Jewish people often learn to read them in the languages in which they were first written.

Topic Sentence

_____

_____

Supporting Discussion

_____

_____

_____

Supporting Detail

_____

_____

_____

Supporting Detail

_____

_____

_____

Supporting Discussion

_____

_____

_____

Concluding Sentence

_____

_____

Draft Your Essay

Use the body paragraph above in your complete essay written on your own paper. Be sure that each of your body paragraphs has a topic sentence, supporting details, and a concluding sentence.

Name _____ Class _____ Date _____

Places to Know!

Map Skills Use the maps in this unit to identify the Places to Know! on the outline map. Before the name of each place below, write the letter that shows its location on the map.

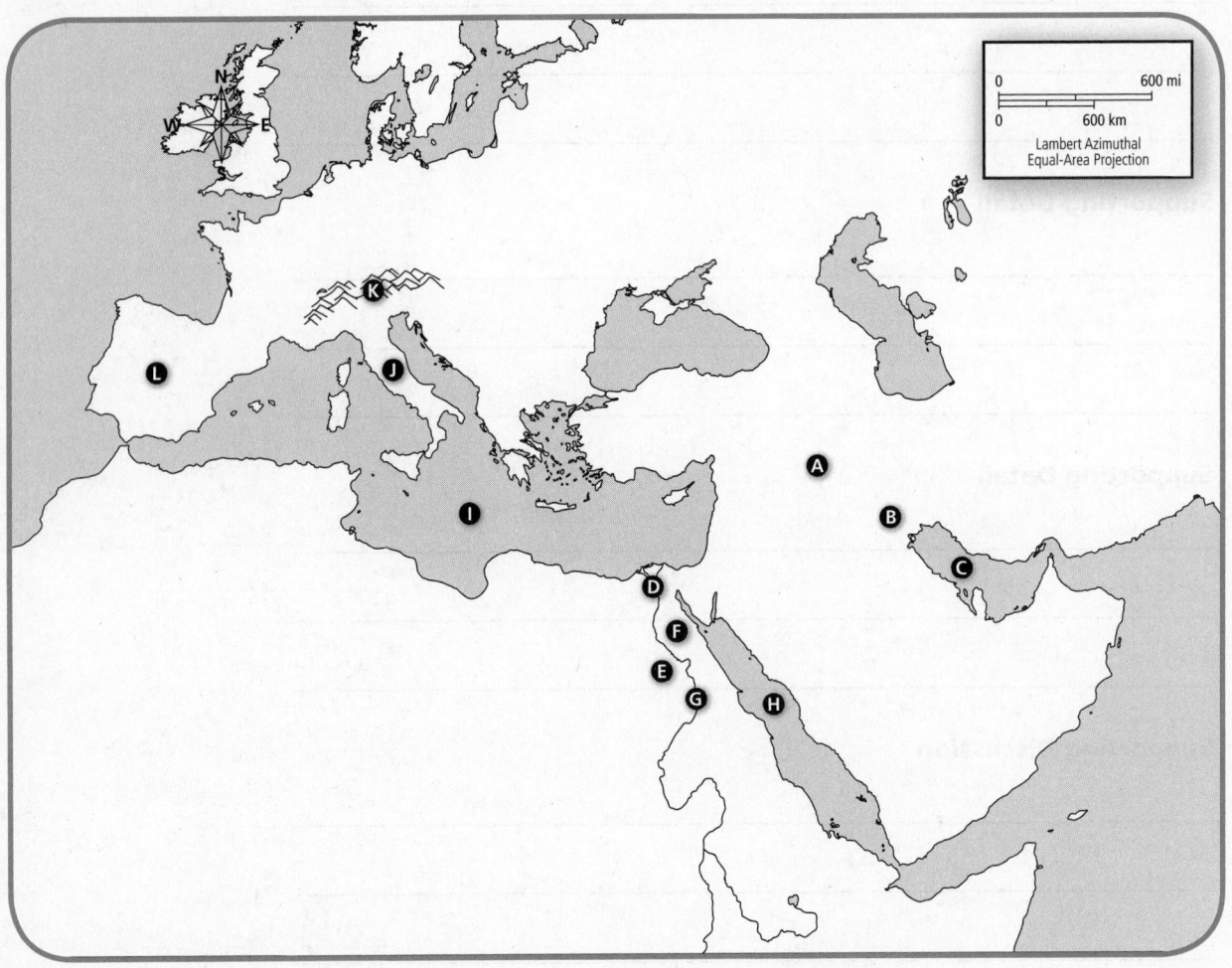

_____ Persian Gulf   _____ Alps

_____ Eastern Desert   _____ Mesopotamia

_____ Nile River   _____ Sumer

_____ Red Sea   _____ Lower Egypt

_____ Mediterranean Sea   _____ Upper Egypt

_____ Iberian Peninsula   _____ Italy

Key Events

Timeline Use what you have read about the ancient Near East to complete the timeline below. Draw a line from each event to its correct position on the timeline. Then write a brief description of each event.

3500 B.C.

3000 B.C.

2500 B.C.

2000 B.C.

1500 B.C.

1000 B.C.

500 B.C.

3500 B.C. _____
_____

2100 B.C. _____
_____

1700 B.C. _____
_____

1000 B.C. _____
_____

1475 B.C. _____
_____

1250 B.C. _____
_____

665 B.C. _____
_____

539 B.C. _____
_____

Name _____ Class _____ Date _____

Essential Question

How much does geography affect people's lives?

Preview Before you begin this chapter, think about the Essential Question. Understanding how the Essential Question connects to your life will help you understand the chapter you are about to read.

Connect to Your Life

(1) Think of the climate and physical features in your community. Describe these below.

Climate: _____

Waterways: _____

Landscape: _____

(2) Now consider how these geographic features affect economic activities and types of sports and recreation in your community. Fill in the table below with your ideas.

Geographic Features	• Effects of Geographic Features on Economic • Activities	• Effects of Geographic Features on Recreation • and Sports
Climate		
Waterways		
Landscape/Resources		

Connect to the Chapter

(3) Preview the chapter. Skim the headings, photos, and graphics. In the table below, predict how you think geography affected the Indus Valley civilization.

Geographic Features of the Indus Valley	• Effect on the • People	• Effect on Economic Activities and • Trade	• Effect on Building • Materials
Climate			
Waterways			
Landscape/Resources			

(4) After reading the chapter, return to this page. Circle your predictions that were correct.

Name _____ Class _____ Date _____

Connect to myStory: Amala and Trijata

1 Does your family's well-being rely on a consistent climate or rainfall? Explain why or why not.

_____

_____

_____

2 What climate event did Amala's family rely on?

_____

3 What will happen to Amala's family if this climate event does not occur? Write at least two predictions.

_____

_____

4 In the diagram below, describe three details the story provides about the Ganges River.

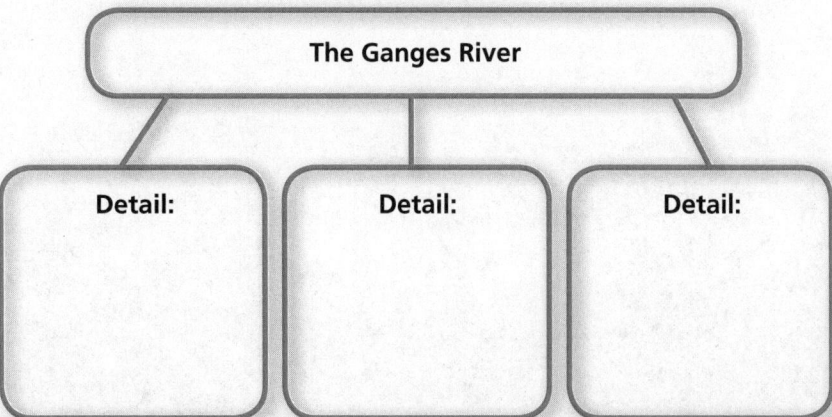

The Ganges River

Detail: Detail: Detail:

5 How important do you think the Ganges River is to India today? Provide reasons for your response.

_____

_____

Name _____ Class _____ Date _____

Word Wise

Vocabulary Quiz Show Some quiz shows ask a question and expect the contestant to give the answer. In other shows, the contestant is given an answer and must supply the question. If the blank is in the Question column, write the question that would result in the answer in the Answer column. If the question is supplied, write the answer.

QUESTION	ANSWER
(1) _____	(1) monsoon
(2) _____	(2) river system
(3) What is the name given to a large landmass that is set apart from the rest of a continent?	(3) _____
(4) _____	(4) citadel
(5) Where was surplus grain stored in Indus Valley cities?	(5) _____

Name _____ Class _____ Date _____

Take Notes

Identify Main Ideas and Details The topics in the diagram below match
the headings in Section 1. Reread the section. Use what you read about the
Indus Valley civilization to complete the diagram. For each topic, write the
main idea and the details that support it.

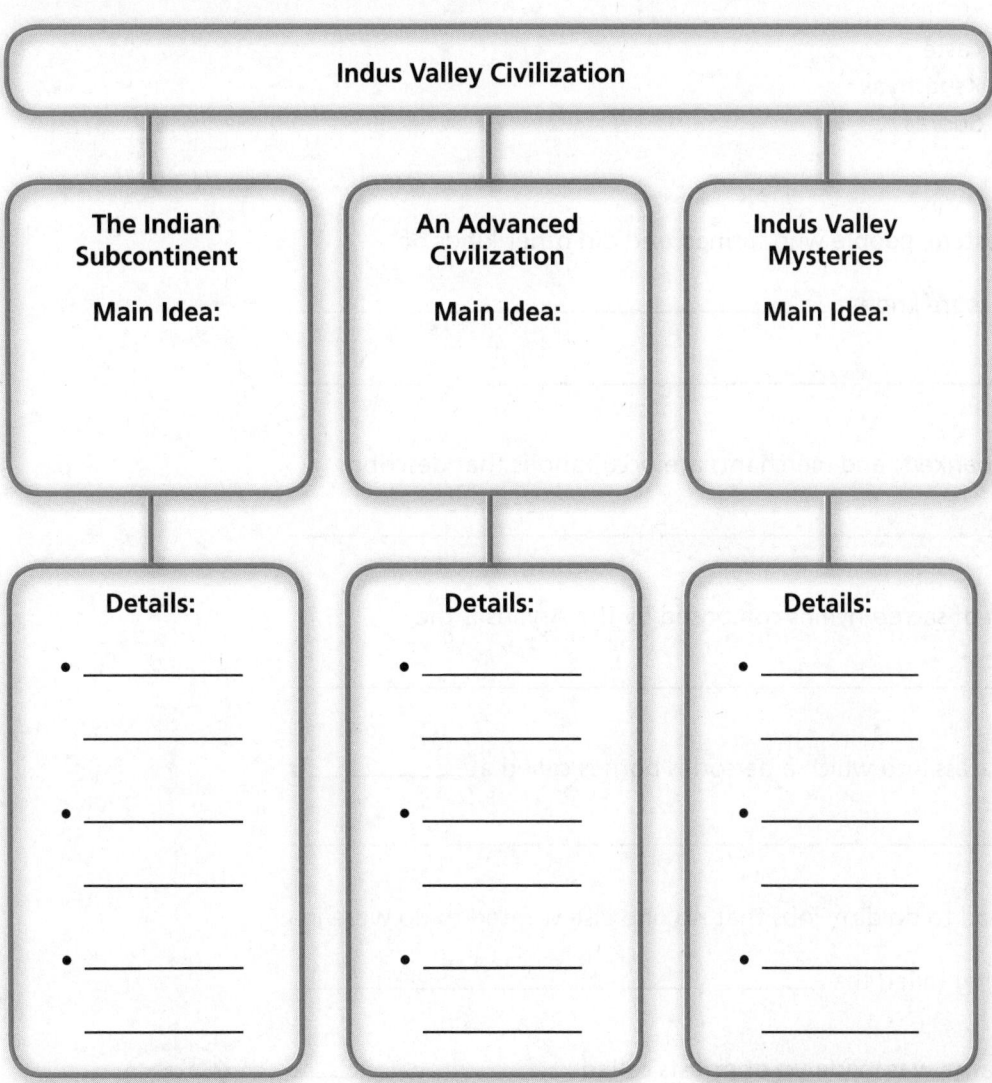

```
                    ┌─────────────────────────────────┐
                    │     Indus Valley Civilization     │
                    └─────────────────────────────────┘
```

The Indian Subcontinent	An Advanced Civilization	Indus Valley Mysteries
Main Idea:	**Main Idea:**	**Main Idea:**

Details:	Details:	Details:
• _____	• _____	• _____
_____	_____	_____
• _____	• _____	• _____
_____	_____	_____
• _____	• _____	• _____
_____	_____	_____

Essential Question

Give examples of how geography helped shape
the civilization of the Indus Valley.

_____

_____

_____

81

Name _____ Class _____ Date _____

Word Wise

Sentence Builder Finish the sentences below with a key term from this section. You may have to change the form of the words to complete the sentences.

Word Bank
Veda	caste
Brahmins	Kshatriyas
Vaishyas	Sudras
Dalits	

① In the caste system, people who farmed and did other kinds of

manual work were known as _____

_____

② Landowners, bankers, and merchants are occupations that describe

the varna _____

③ The collection of sacred hymns composed by the Aryans is the

_____

④ A fixed social class into which a person is born is called a _____

_____

⑤ People who had to do dirty jobs that no one else wanted to do were in

a caste grouping called the _____

⑥ The highest varna was made up of priests called _____

_____

⑦ In the caste system, rulers and warriors made up the second-highest

varna, the _____

Name _____ Class _____ Date _____

Take Notes

Summarize Use what you have read about India's Vedic age to fill in the key ideas from Section 2 in the two boxes below. Then use the key ideas to write a summary statement about India's Vedic age.

The Origins of the Indo-Aryans

Key Ideas:

- _____
  _____

- _____
  _____

- _____
  _____

- _____
  _____

- _____
  _____

The Caste System

Key Ideas:

- _____
  _____
  _____

- _____
  _____

- _____
  _____

- _____
  _____

Summary statement:

_____

_____

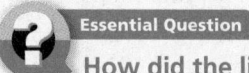
Essential Question

How did the lives of the Aryans change as they moved from the dry grasslands west of the Indus to the humid Ganges Plain?

_____

_____

_____

Word Wise

Words in Context For each question below, write an answer that shows your understanding of the boldfaced key term.

① What was **Brahmanism** based on? _____

_____

② How were **gurus** and their students in a sense the founders of

Hinduism? _____

_____

③ How do Hindus regard **Brahman**? _____

_____

④ According to Hinduism, what happens to one's soul when undergoing

reincarnation? _____

_____

⑤ What does good **karma** bring? _____

_____

⑥ What does it mean to follow one's **dharma**? _____

_____

⑦ How is the rule of **ahimsa** included in dharma? _____

_____

⑧ What happens when a person reaches **moksha**? _____

_____

Name _____ Class _____ Date _____

Take Notes

Sequence Use the diagram below to show how Brahmanism changed to become Hinduism. In the boxes on the left, list features of Brahmanism. In the boxes on the right, list features of Hinduism. Complete the box that follows with Hindu beliefs.

From Brahmanism to Hinduism

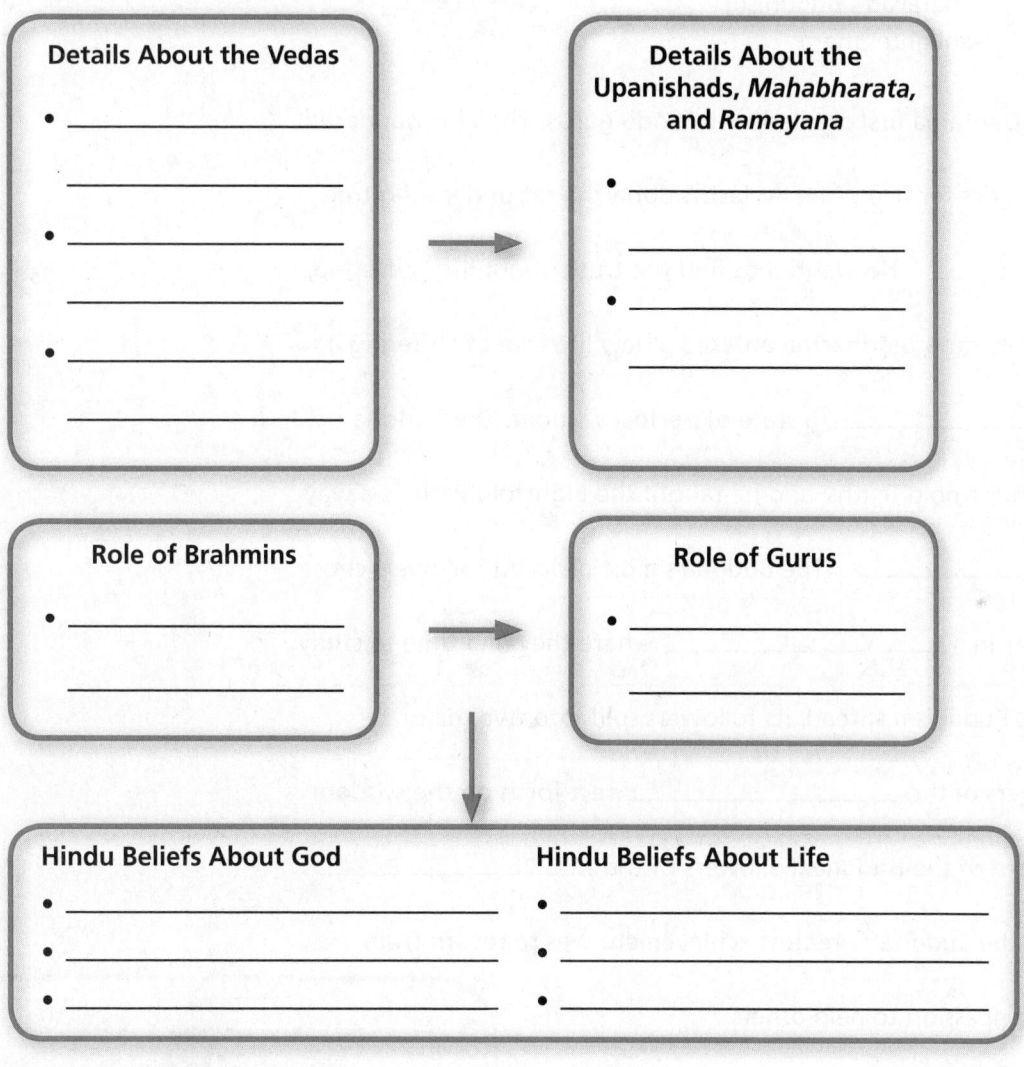

Details About the Vedas

- _____
  _____
- _____
  _____
- _____
  _____

Details About the Upanishads, *Mahabharata*, and *Ramayana*

- _____
  _____
- _____
  _____

Role of Brahmins

- _____
  _____

Role of Gurus

- _____
  _____

Hindu Beliefs About God

- _____
- _____
- _____

Hindu Beliefs About Life

- _____
- _____
- _____

Essential Question

How important is India's geography to the beliefs of Hinduism?

_____

_____

_____

Word Wise

Use a Word Bank Choose one word from the word bank to fill in each blank. When you have finished, you will have a short summary of important ideas from the section.

Word Bank

nirvana	Mahayana Buddhism
meditate	Theravada Buddhism
monastery	enlightenment

Siddhartha Gautama first studied with Hindu gurus. Then he wandered with religious ascetics for five years. At last, Siddhartha sat under a fig tree to _____. He wanted to find the truth about life, suffering, and death. After 49 days, Siddhartha entered a new life free of suffering and achieved _____, a state of perfect wisdom. The Buddha discovered the Four Noble Truths, and he taught the Eightfold Path as a way to reach _____. The Buddha's most devoted followers chose to live with others in a _____, where they had time to study and meditate. As Buddhism spread, its followers split into two major branches. Followers of the _____ sect focus on the wisdom and enlightenment of the Buddha. Followers of the _____ sect believe that the Buddha's greatest achievement was to return from nirvana out of compassion to help others.

Name _____ Class _____ Date _____

Take Notes

Compare and Contrast In the left side of the diagram below, list Buddhist beliefs. In the right side, list Hindu beliefs. Identify overlapping beliefs in the "Both" section of the diagram.

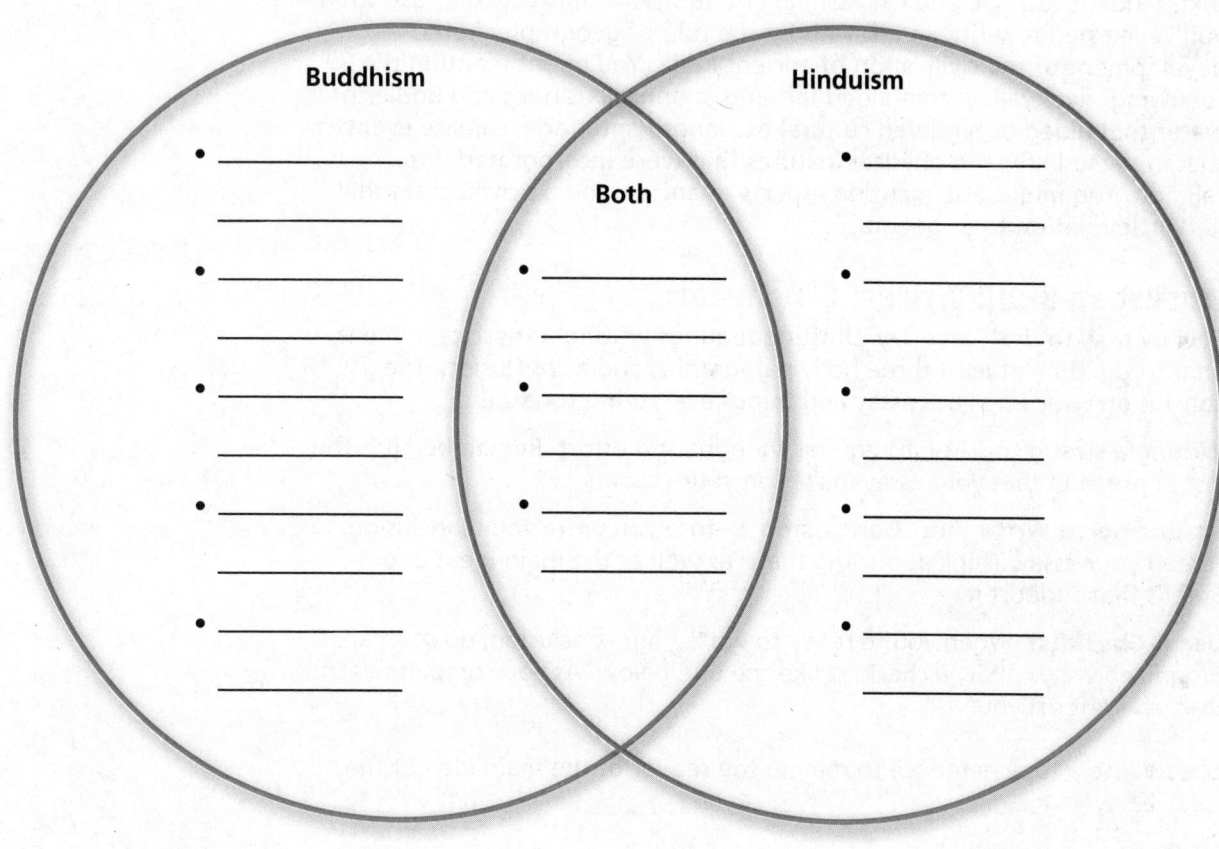

Buddhism

- _____
  _____
- _____
  _____
- _____
  _____
- _____
  _____
- _____
  _____

Both

- _____
  _____
- _____
  _____
- _____
  _____

Hinduism

- _____
  _____
- _____
  _____
- _____
  _____
- _____
  _____

Essential Question

Did geography affect the spread of Buddhism? If so, how?

_____

_____

_____

87

 **Essential Question**   Writer's Workshop

How much does geography affect people's lives?

Prepare to Write

Throughout this chapter, you have explored the Essential Question in your text, Student Journal, and On Assignment at myworldhistory.com. Use what you've learned to write an essay about the role of geography in the development of the civilization of ancient India. You might mention the following: river valleys that aided farming, mountain ranges and bodies of water that aided or hindered cultural exchanges and trade, climate events that impacted life, and physical features that were incorporated into religion. You might also mention aspects of ancient India's civilization that had little relation to its geography.

Workshop Skill: Write a Conclusion

Review how to draft an essay. Drafting requires writing a thesis statement, an introduction, at least three body paragraphs, and a conclusion. The conclusion wraps up your essay and brings everything together.

Writing a strong conclusion requires thought and effort. Remember, it is the last impression that your essay makes on your readers.

Preparing to Write Your Conclusion Before you write your conclusion, reread your essay. Think about the thesis as well as the main ideas and details that support it.

Use a Checklist When you're ready to write your conclusion, do so in an organized way. Follow a checklist like the one below. As you complete each task, check it off your list.

_____ Write a topic sentence to remind the reader of the main idea of the essay.

_____ Summarize the most important ideas.

_____ Restate your thesis in a way that is different from your introduction.

_____ Write a concluding sentence.

What Makes a Strong Conclusion? A strong conclusion should tie together the different strands of your essay. It should give your reader the feeling that everything adds up and makes sense.

Sample Conclusion Here are some sample sentences that could be used to form a cohesive conclusion.

- Sample topic sentence: Many factors contributed to the rise of India's civilization.

- Summary of an important idea: Flooding in the Indus Valley and Ganges Plain allowed farmers to raise ample food crops.

- Sample of thesis restatement: Geography shaped some, but not all aspects of ancient Indian civilization.

- Sample of concluding sentence: Ancient Indian civilization was shaped but not limited by its geography.

Write Your Conclusion

Now write your own concluding paragraph for your essay.

Topic Sentence _____

_____

Summary of an important idea _____

_____

Summary of another important idea _____

_____

Summary of an important idea _____

_____

Restate Your Thesis _____

_____

Concluding Sentence _____

_____

Draft Your Essay

Use the concluding paragraph above in your completed essay. Write your essay on another sheet of paper.

Name _____ Class _____ Date _____

How are religion and culture connected?

Preview Before you begin this chapter, think about the Essential Question. Understanding how the Essential Question connects to your life will help you understand the chapter you are about to read.

Connect to Your Life

1. Define *culture*. What elements are included in a culture?

_____

_____

2. In the table below, describe or give examples of elements of your local culture. Then note whether and how religion influences these elements.

Elements of Local Culture	Description or Example	Influence of Religion
Roles of Men and Women		
Holidays Celebrated		
Types of Food		

Connect to the Chapter

3. Preview the chapter. Skim the headings, photos, and graphics. In the table below, predict how you think religion affected the culture of Maurya and Gupta India.

Elements of the Culture of Maurya and Gupta India	Description or Example	Influence of Religion
Rulers		
Laws		
Music		

4. After reading the chapter, return to this page. Circle your predictions that were correct.

Name _____ Class _____ Date _____

Connect to myStory: Emperor Ashoka and the Gift of Dirt

1 What was a major turning point in your life or in the history of the United States?

_____

_____

2 How was the battle of Kalinga a turning point for Ashoka?

_____

_____

3 In the diagram below, identify five actions of Ashoka after he turned to Buddhism.

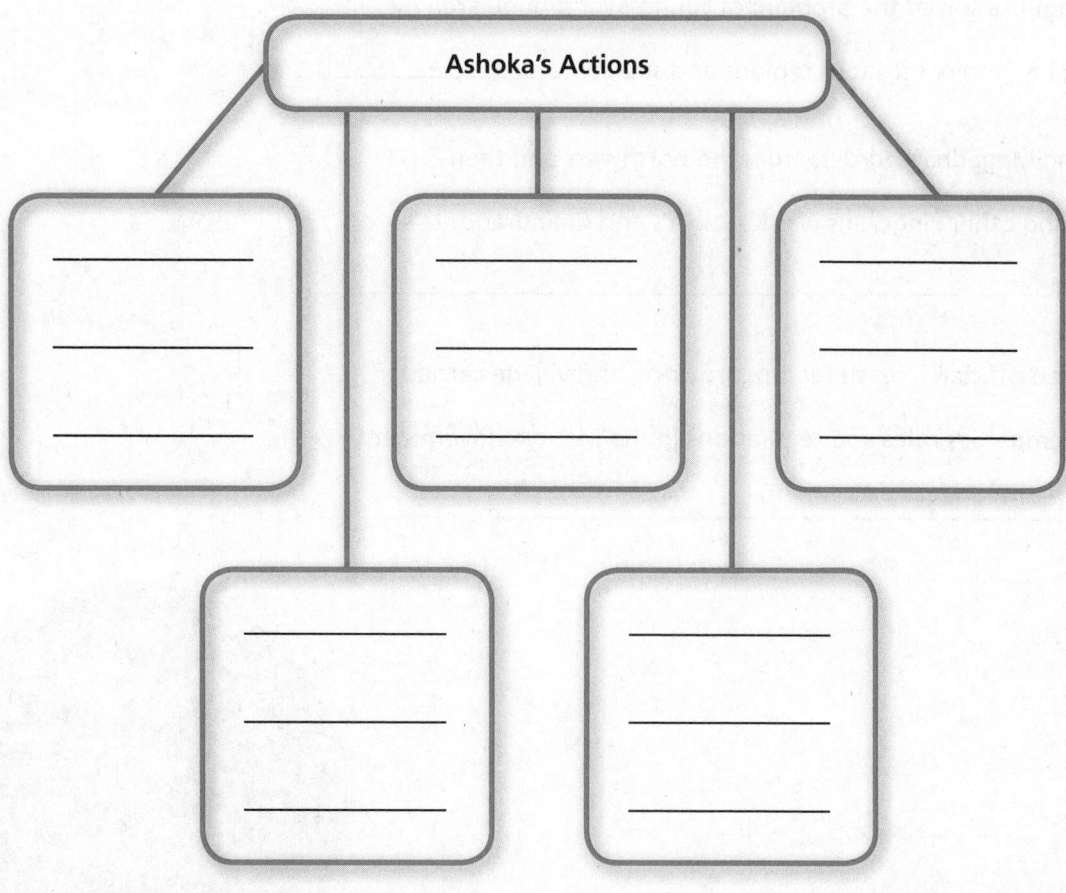

Ashoka's Actions

Word Wise

Sentence Builder Complete the sentences below with a key term from this section. You may have to change the form of the words to complete the sentences.

Word Bank
strategy   province
bureaucracy   subject
tolerance

① Ashoka's willingness to respect different beliefs and customs is known

   as _____.

② Chandragupta set up a huge spy network and gave no right to privacy

   or freedom of speech to his _____.

③ Chandragupta solved the problem of ruling over a huge area by

   dividing his empire into four regions and smaller _____.

④ Attacking Magadha's borders from the northwest and then

   conquering other kingdoms was Kautilya's and Chandragupta's

   long-term _____.

⑤ Appointed officials in each region, province, and village carried

   out the emperor's rules and regulations in the Maurya government

   _____.

Name _____ Class _____ Date _____

Take Notes

Analyze Cause and Effect Use what you have read about the Maurya empire to complete the activity below. For each cause given, write the effect or effects.

1. Cause: Greeks invade India, and many kingdoms divide the subcontinent.

2. Cause: Chandragupta faces the problem of ruling over a large area with many different needs.

3. Cause: Chandragupta needs to support a large army and a costly lifestyle.

4. Cause: Chandragupta lives in constant fear of his enemies.

5. Cause: The kingdom of Kalinga resists the conquest of Ashoka.

6. Cause: Ashoka is shocked by the suffering at the battle of Kalinga.

1. Effect(s): _____
_____
_____
_____

2. Effect(s): _____
_____
_____
_____

3. Effect(s): _____
_____
_____
_____

4. Effect(s): _____
_____
_____
_____

5. Effect(s): _____
_____
_____
_____

6. Effect(s): _____
_____
_____
_____
_____
_____
_____

Essential Question

What impact did religion have on the Maurya empire?

_____
_____
_____

Word Wise

Vocabulary Quiz Show Some quiz shows ask a question and expect the contestant to give the answer. In other shows, the contestant is given an answer and must supply the question. If the blank is in the Question column, write the question that would result in the answer in the Answer column. If the question is supplied, write the answer.

QUESTION

1. _____

2. _____

3. What is the counting system based on units of ten?

4. _____

ANSWER

1. citizenship

2. numeral

3. _____

4. metallurgy

Name _____ Class _____ Date _____

Take Notes

Summarize Use what you have read to fill in the key ideas from Section 2 in the correct places below. Then use the key ideas to write a summary statement about the Gupta empire.

Achievements in Literature and the Arts
- _____
  _____
- _____
  _____
- _____
  _____
- _____
  _____

Achievements in Mathematics and Astronomy
- _____
  _____
- _____
  _____
- _____
  _____
- _____
  _____

Gupta Emperors and Their Achievements
- _____
  _____
- _____
  _____
- _____
  _____
- _____
  _____

Achievements in Medicine and Metallurgy
- _____
  _____
- _____
  _____
- _____
  _____
- _____
  _____

Summary Statement:

_____

_____

Essential Question

Which aspects of Gupta civilization were connected to religion? Which were not?

_____

_____

_____

95

Essential Question Writer's Workshop

How are religion and culture connected?

Prepare to Write

Throughout this chapter, you have explored the Essential Question in your text, journal, and by going On Assignment at myworldhistory.com. Use what you have learned in this chapter to write an essay about how religion and culture were connected in Maurya and Gupta India.

Workshop Skill: Revise Your Work

This workshop focuses on revising your essay. Recall that the four major steps of the writing process include: (1) prewriting, (2) drafting, (3) revising, and (4) presenting. You have already prewritten and drafted your essay. During the revising step, you review your work to make sure your ideas are clear to your readers. Few people get everything right the first time. After you write a first draft, it is time to revise.

Steps to Follow Revision requires looking at the essay as a whole. It also involves a close look at each paragraph and sentence. Follow these steps to revise your essay in an organized way. As you complete each step, check it off the list.

Introduction and Thesis Statement

_____ The introduction of my essay is easy to understand and interesting.

_____ My thesis statement is clear and broad enough to support many details.

Paragraphs

_____ Each paragraph has a topic sentence and supporting sentences.

_____ The transitions between paragraphs make sense.

_____ My conclusion is based on information in my essay.

Sentence Structure

_____ Each sentence has a subject and a verb.

_____ My sentences vary in length and sentence types.

Proofread

_____ My sentences are free of errors in grammar, punctuation, and capitalization.

Proofreading Marks

C̲ capitalize	ℓ́ lowercase
ℓ delete	⌒ comma
ro⌃k insert	⊙ period

Here is an example of a short paragraph that has been proofread. Changes have been made to improve sentence variety, too.

When we think of religious art, we often think of paintings or sculpture.

In India, however˄ a special kind of dancing called Kuchipudi expressed

religious devotion. it is a form of dance based on story⌒ies from the hindu

religion. At first˄ the performers were men. Eventually˄ women were trained

in the art. The dances are amazingly ̶graceful, ̶but They are difficult to master.

In one, the dancer stands on a brass plate, swift⌒ly circling its rim, while

balancing a jug of water on her head.

Now revise the following paragraph. Use proofreading marks to correct the errors in capitalization, punctuation, and spelling.

Buddhist archetecture began during Ashokas reign. He ordered huge

pillars to be built, messages on the pilars urged people to lead moral lives.

Ashoka also was responsible for building huge *stupas*. These mounds of brick

honored the buddha. In western india, *stupas* were carved out of rock in the

mountainside.

Name _____ Class _____ Date _____

Copyright © Pearson Education, Inc., or its affiliates. All Rights Reserved.

Essential Question

How much does geography affect people's lives?

Preview Before you begin this chapter, think about the Essential Question. Understanding how the Essential Question connects to your life will help you understand the chapter you are about to read.

Connect to Your Life

(1) Imagine that you are an artist and have been asked to paint a landscape of your community. What physical features would this landscape painting include?

_____

_____

(2) Think about how physical features affect the types of jobs and the people in your community. Fill in the table below with your ideas.

Geographic Features	• Effects of Geographic • Features on Jobs	• Effects of Geographic • Features on Population
Climate		
Waterways		
Landscape/Resources		

Connect to the Chapter

(3) Preview the chapter. Skim the headings, photos, and graphics. In the table below, predict how you think geography affected the Shang and Zhou dynasties.

Geographic Features of Ancient China	• Effect on • Government	• Effect on Economic • Activities and Trade	• Effect on • Agriculture
Climate			
Waterways			
Landscape/Resources			

(4) After reading the chapter, return to this page. Circle your predictions that were correct.

Name _____ Class _____ Date _____

Connect to myStory: The Wisdom of Zhang Shi, Mother of Mencius

1 What traits do you think a person with "character" has? How can one gain these traits?

_____

_____

2 How did Zhang Shi support her son after her husband died?

_____

_____

3 What occupations are discussed in the myStory? Put them in the order of "most important" to "least important" according to Zhang Shi.

Occupations
a.
b.
c.
d.

4 Why did Zhang Shi move three times for her son?

_____

_____

5 Where did Zhang Shi and her son live? Fill in the table with the locations of his homes.

Location of Zhang Shi's Homes
a.
b.
c.

6 For what reason did Zhang Shi cut her weaving?

_____

_____

Name _____ Class _____ Date _____

Word Wise

Vocabulary Quiz Show Some quiz shows ask a question and expect the contestant to give the answer. In other shows, the contestant is given an answer and must supply the question. If the blank is in the Question column, write the question that would result in the answer in the Answer column. If the question is supplied, write the answer.

QUESTION

ANSWER

(1) What is a fine, dustlike material that can form soil?

(1) _____

(2) _____

(2) dike

(3) What are the earliest written records from China?

(3) _____

(4) _____

(4) pictographs

Name _____ Class _____ Date _____

Take Notes

Summarize Use information from Section 1 to summarize key ideas about Shang China into the diagram below.

Geography of China

River Systems

_____
_____
_____

Isolation (physical barriers)

_____
_____
_____

The Shang Dynasty

Rise of Shang

_____
_____

Shang Government

_____
_____
_____

Writing

_____
_____

Bronze Metalworking

_____
_____

? Essential Question

How did the Huang River affect the lives of the Chinese who settled along its banks?

_____
_____
_____

101

Name _____ Class _____ Date _____

Word Wise

Words In Context For each question below, write an answer that shows your understanding of the boldfaced key term.

1 How did the **Mandate of Heaven** justify the overthrow of a dynasty?

_____

_____

2 How did the actions of the Zhou kings lead to powerful **warlords**?

_____

_____

3 What caused China to enter an era of **chaos**?

_____

_____

4 What was life like in China during the **Warring States period**?

_____

_____

Name _____ Class _____ Date _____

Take Notes

Identify Main Ideas and Details Use what you read about the Zhou dynasty to complete the table below. For each main idea, write details that support it.

China Under the Zhou Dynasty	
Main Ideas	**Supporting Details**
The Zhou overthrew the Shang and established a new dynasty.	• _____ • _____ • _____
The Zhou expanded the boundaries of their kingdom.	• _____ • _____ • _____
The second part of the Zhou dynasty became a time of chaos.	• _____ • _____ • _____
The Zhou adopted some but not all Shang practices.	• _____ • _____ • _____
Both nobles and peasants had duties to fulfill.	• _____ • _____
Zhou achievements improved warfare, agriculture, and trade.	• _____ • _____ • _____ • _____

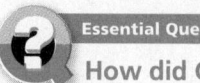

Essential Question

How did China's geography make it difficult for the Zhou kings to keep their large kingdom united?

_____

_____

Name _____ Class _____ Date _____

Word Wise

Sentence Builder Finish the sentences below with a key term from this section. You may have to change the form of the words to complete the sentences.

Word Bank

philosophy   ancestor worship
Confucianism   filial piety
Daoism

(1) The philosopher known as the "First Teacher" developed a set of

teachings called _____.

(2) The philosophy of following a simple life is _____.

(3) The practice of honoring the spirits of the dead is known

as _____.

(4) Confucians referred to the devotion of children to their parents

as _____.

(5) A set of beliefs about the world and how to live is called

a _____.

Name _____ Class _____ Date _____

Take Notes

Compare and Contrast In the diagram below, describe the beliefs of spirit and ancestor worship, Confucianism, and Daoism.

Spirit and Ancestor Worship

1. Kinds of spirits and where they dwelled

    _____

    _____

2. Why ancestors were honored

    _____

3. Rituals to honor ancestors

    _____

Confucianism

1. Founder

    _____

2. Goal

    _____

3. Name of work

    _____

4. Teachings

    _____

    _____

    _____

    _____

Daoism

1. Founder

    _____

2. Goal

    _____

3. Name of work

    _____

4. Teachings

    _____

    _____

    _____

    _____

Essential Question

How did Chinese geography have an influence on beliefs in ancient China?

_____

_____

_____

Name _____ Class _____ Date _____

Essential Question | Writer's Workshop

How much does geography affect people's lives?

Prepare to Write

Throughout this chapter, you have explored the Essential Question in your text, journal, and On Assignment at myworldhistory.com. Use what you have learned to write a formal letter telling the Zhou king how he should use resources of the Huang River valley to improve the lives of the people.

Workshop Skill: Write a Letter

There are two types of letters: formal and informal. If you are writing a letter to a newspaper, business, government leader, or other institution, follow the formal style. If you are writing a letter to a friend or family member, follow the informal style.

Today you will write a letter to the Zhou king. Your purpose is to help him maintain the Mandate of Heaven. In doing so, you will offer advice on ways that the Zhou ruler can use resources and geographical features of China to improve the lives of the people.

The Parts of a Letter Your letter will include the following elements: date, heading, greeting, body, conclusion, closing, and signature.

Date, Heading, and Greeting In a formal letter, the heading includes your return address and the date in the upper right corner, and the name and address of the recipient on the left. Skip a line and write the greeting. Most letters use "Dear" and the recipient's name. In a formal letter, use a title such as *Dr., Mrs., Senator,* or in this case, *Son of Heaven,* followed by the person's last name and a colon.

Body Use the body of the letter to explain your purpose. Why did you choose to write to this person? What ideas about the Mandate of Heaven do you want to express? For example, you might want to point out that natural disasters, such as flooding of the Huang River or a drought, would tell the people that heaven no longer supports the dynasty. Offer advice on ways that the ruler could prevent or minimize natural disasters, such as by building dams, canals, or irrigation channels.

Conclusion, Closing, and Signature Conclude by briefly restating your main point. If you want the recipient to take action, state that. Below the conclusion, skip a line, write a closing such as "Sincerely yours," or "Yours truly," followed by a comma. Sign your full name below it.

Draft Your Letter

Use the format below to write the first draft of your letter.

(your address and date; do not put your name) _____

_____

_____

_____   **Name and address of the recipient**

_____

_____

_____

Dear _____

Body _____

_____

_____

_____

_____

_____

_____

Conclusion _____

_____

_____

_____

Closing _____

Signature _____

Finalize Your Letter

Remember to follow the steps of the writing process to revise and edit your letter. Then neatly copy it onto a clean sheet of paper.

Name _____ Class _____ Date _____

Essential Question

What should governments do?

Preview Before you begin this chapter, think about the Essential Question. Understanding how the Essential Question connects to your life will help you understand the chapter you are about to read.

Connect to Your Life

(1) What are three things that government can do better than individuals?

a. _____

b. _____

c. _____

(2) Think about how governing bodies and laws affect your life. Complete the table below with your ideas.

Government's Role			
In My School	In My Home	In My Community	Beyond My Community

Connect to the Chapter

(3) Preview the chapter. Skim the headings, photos, and graphics. In the table below, predict how you think the Qin and Han emperors will influence life in China during their dynasties.

Government's Role in Qin and Han China				
	Defense	Laws	Economy	Family Life
Qin				
Han				

(4) After reading the chapter, return to this page. Circle your predictions that were correct.

Name _____ Class _____ Date _____

Connect to myStory: An Emperor in This Life and the Next

(1) What would you like people to remember about you 2,000 years from now?

_____

_____

(2) What made Qin Shi Huangdi different from the kings that came before him?

_____

_____

(3) In the diagram below, identify three of Shi Huangdi's achievements mentioned in the myStory.

Shi Huangdi's Achievements

(4) Why did Shi Huangdi order such a grand tomb and thousands of terra-cotta soldiers to be built?

_____

_____

(5) Do you think China's first emperor should be remembered for his accomplishments or his cruelty? Explain your answer.

_____

_____

Word Wise

Vocabulary Quiz Show Some quiz shows ask a question and expect the contestant to give the answer. In other shows, the contestant is given an answer and must supply the question. If the blank is in the Question column, write the question that would result in the answer in the Answer column. If the question is supplied, write the answer.

QUESTION	ANSWER
① _____	① Great Wall
② _____	② standardize
③ What system of governing has strong laws and harsh punishments?	③ _____
④ _____	④ censor

Name _____ Class _____ Date _____

Take Notes

Identify Main Ideas and Details The topics in the diagram below are headings in Section 1. Use what you have read about the Qin dynasty to complete the diagram. For each topic, write the main idea and the details that support it.

Unity Under the Qin

Main Idea:

Uniting Warring States	Defending the Empire	Uniform Standards	Organizing the Empire
Details:	Details:	Details:	Details:
_____	_____	_____	_____
_____	_____	_____	_____
_____	_____	_____	_____
_____	_____	_____	_____

Rule of the First Emperor

Main Idea:

A Legalist Government	Harsh Laws	Thought Control	The Fall of the Qin Dynasty
Details:	Details:	Details:	Details:
_____	_____	_____	_____
_____	_____	_____	_____
_____	_____	_____	_____
_____	_____	_____	_____
_____	_____	_____	_____

Essential Question

What did the Legalists think the role of government should be?

_____

_____

_____

Name _____ Class _____ Date _____

Word Wise

Sentence Builder Finish the sentences below with a key term from this section. You may have to change the form of the words to complete the sentences.

Word Bank
official   civil service
Silk Road   envoy
cuisine

1. The network of trade routes connecting China to Central Asia and the Middle East was known as the _____.

2. In the Han dynasty, many layers of government existed between the villages at the bottom and the emperor at the top, and these layers included people assigned to their positions, or _____.

3. Various types of food traded along the Silk Road enriched Chinese _____.

4. Government officials who were selected based on skills and knowledge made up the _____.

5. The Han created trade relations with kingdoms to the east by sending representatives of the emperor known as _____.

Name _____ Class _____ Date _____

Take Notes

Analyze Cause and Effect Use what you have read about the Han dynasty to complete the activity below. For each cause given, write the effect or effects.

1. **Cause:** To Learn how to govern, Liu Bang consulted with Confucian scholars.
   EFFECTS:
   _____
   _____

2. Han emperors wanted to avoid the disunity the Zhou dynasty had faced.
   EFFECTS:
   _____
   _____

3. Emperor Wudi wanted to find talented officials.
   EFFECTS:
   _____
   _____

4. Emperor Wudi needed allies to fight against the nomadic Xiongnu.
   EFFECTS:
   _____
   _____

5. Zhang Qian described exotic lands and horses that sweat blood.
   EFFECTS:
   _____
   _____

6. Han Emperors made it illegal to export silk worms from China.
   EFFECTS:
   _____
   _____

7. The Silk Road became a path for the exchange of products and ideas.
   EFFECTS:
   _____
   _____

 Essential Question

You must make an exam for officials in the U.S. government. What knowledge should government officials have?

_____
_____
_____

Word Wise

Crossword Puzzle The *Across* and *Down* clues are definitions of key terms from this section. Fill in the numbered *Across* boxes with the correct key terms. Then do the same with the *Down clues*.

Across	Down
4. a single group controls the production of a good or service	1. tool to detect earthquakes
5. a protective coating made from the sap of a special tree	2. therapy that uses needles to cure sickness and stop pain
	3. the art of beautiful writing

Name _____ Class _____ Date _____

Take Notes

Summarize Use what you have read about Han society and achievements to fill in the key ideas from Section 3 in the diagram below. Then use the key ideas to write a summary statement about Han China.

Han Society	Economic Life	Han Achievements
The Social Order _____ _____ _____ _____ _____ _____	**Agriculture** _____ _____ _____ _____ _____ _____	**China's Traditional Arts** _____ _____ _____ _____ _____ _____
Family Life _____ _____ _____ _____	**Industry** _____ _____ _____ _____	**Advances in Science** _____ _____ _____ _____
The Role of Women _____ _____ _____ _____	**Controlling Production and Prices** _____ _____ _____ _____	**Chinese Inventions** _____ _____ _____ _____

Summary Statement:

Essential Question

One way Han emperors raised money was by taking over the iron and salt industries. What is another way that governments can get funds?

_____

_____

_____

Essential Question Writer's Workshop

What should governments do?

Prepare to Write

Throughout this chapter, you have explored the Essential Question in your text, Student Journal, and On Assignment at myworldhistory.com. Use what you've learned to write an essay about the actions of the Qin and Han emperors. You might mention Shi Huangdi's role in defending Qin borders, standardization, the legal system, and censorship. You might also describe Wudi's creation of civil service exams, establishment of the Silk Road, and making state monopolies of the iron and salt industries. Other topics may include the official Bureau of Music, scientific inventions sponsored by government, and Han production of paper.

Workshop Skill: Understand the Four Types of Essays

First you must decide what type of essay you want to write. There are four essay types: narrative, expository, research, and persuasive.

Narrative Essay This essay is similar to a story. It has characters, a setting, and a plot.
- The characters are the people that the story is about, and the setting is the time and place in which the story happens.
- The plot is the sequence of events that take place. Plots include conflict and lead up to a climax, which is the turning point of the story.

Expository Essay This essay has a main idea supported by evidence and examples.
- An introductory paragraph opens with a thesis statement that high-lights the main idea.
- The introduction is followed by body paragraphs. Each one discusses a point that supports the main idea. Evidence and examples show that the supporting points are true.
- The conclusion sums up the essay by restating the thesis and supporting points.

Research Essay This essay has the same structure as an expository essay. The difference lies in the type of evidence used to prove supporting points.
- Evidence and examples should come from a broad range of reliable sources.
- Writers use quotations, footnotes, and a bibliography to show where they located the evidence used in the essay.

Persuasive Essay This essay is written when the author wants to convince readers to adopt an opinion or take action.
- The introduction tells why the topic is important. Then the thesis state-ment explains what the writer wants readers to think or do.
- In the body paragraphs, the writer uses both arguments and evidence to prove the supporting points.
- The conclusion reviews the main points and urges the reader to adopt the opinion or take the action mentioned.

Identify Essay Types

Read the four descriptions in the table below. In the column on the right, write if the essay described is narrative, expository, research, or persuasive.

Essay Description	Type
1. The essay urges governments today to follow the example of the Han emperor. It offers examples of how the people prospered during the Han dynasty.	_____
2. The essay examines the role of government during the Qin and Han dynasties. It contains graphs, statistics, and quotations. Sources are listed in footnotes.	_____
3. The essay states that censorship during the Qin dynasty hurt the people. It explains three general ways that this occurred.	_____
4. The essay tells a story about the Qin emperor burning books during his reign. The story ends when Shi Huangdi needs help but cannot find a book that provides the information.	_____

Plan Your Essay

Answering these questions will help you make decisions about your essay.

1 What do I want to say about the role of Qin and Han government?

_____

_____

2 Do I want to tell a story, explain an idea, present evidence, or persuade others about something?

_____

_____

3 What type of essay will best help me accomplish my goal?

_____

_____

Organize Your Essay

Now that you have chosen an essay type, outline your essay. Remember to have an introductory paragraph, three body paragraphs, and a conclusion.

Draft Your Essay

Write your essay using the outline you created. When you have finished, proofread your essay.

Places to Know!

Map Skills Use the maps in this unit to identify the Places to Know! on the outline map. Before the name of each place below, write the letter that shows its location on the map.

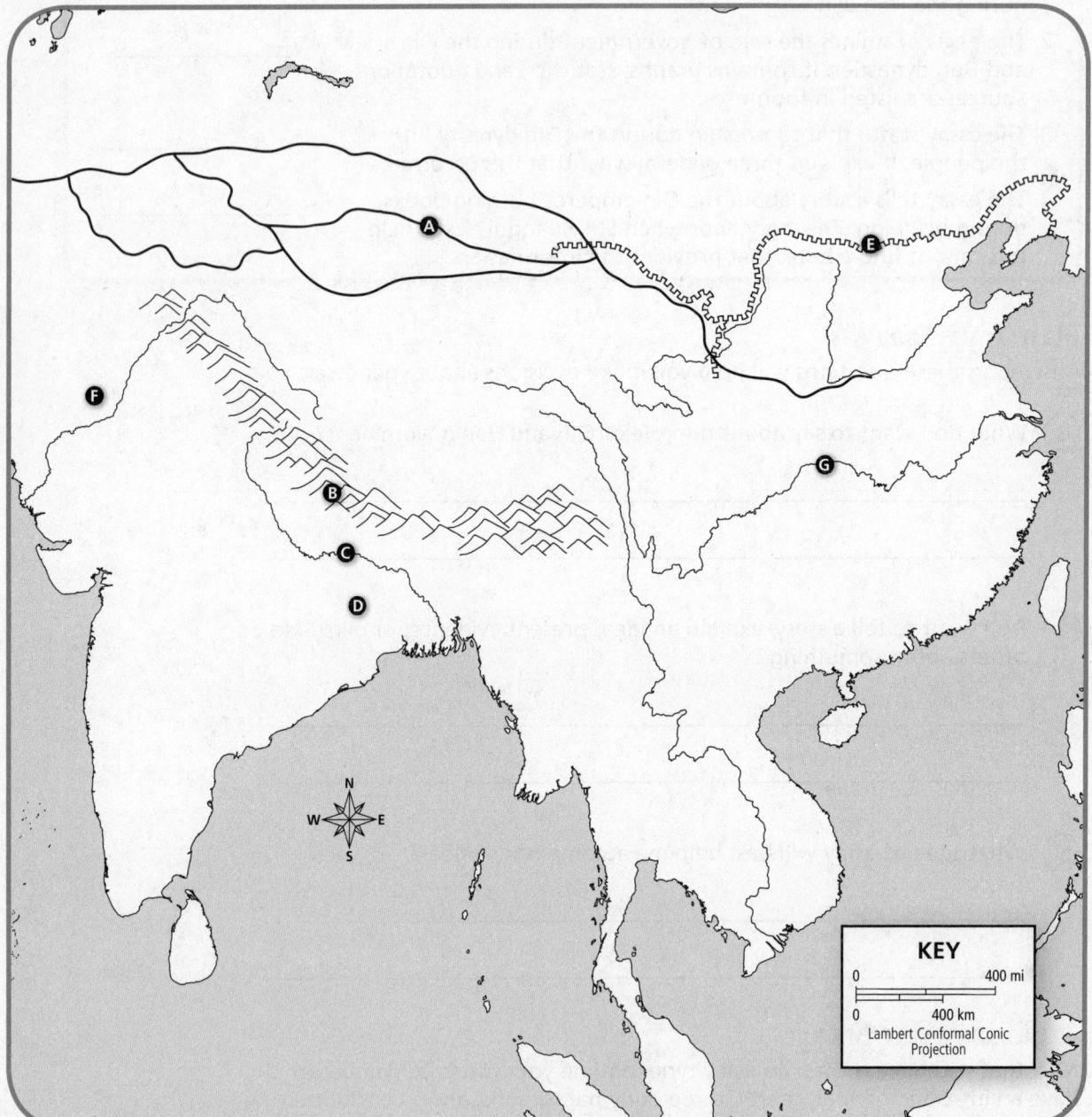

_____ Magadha

_____ Chang River

_____ Himalayas

_____ Harappa

_____ Ganges River

_____ Silk Road

_____ Great Wall

Name _____ Class _____ Date _____

Key Events

Timeline Use what you have read about ancient India and China to complete the timeline below. Draw a line from each event to its correct position on the timeline. Then write a brief description of each event.

3000 B.C.

2600 B.C. _____
_____

321 B.C. _____
_____

2500 B.C.

2000 B.C.

1800 B.C. _____
_____

221 B.C. _____
_____

1500 B.C.

1000 B.C.

500 B.C. _____
_____

206 B.C. _____
_____

500 B.C.

A.D. 1

400 B.C. _____
_____

A.D. 320 _____
_____

A.D. 500

A.D. 1000

What is power? Who should have it?

Preview Before you begin this chapter, think about the Essential Question. Understanding how the Essential Question connects to your life will help you understand the chapter you are about to read.

Connect to Your Life

(1) What are some synonyms of the word *power*? _____

_____

(2) List at least four members or groups who are active in your school community. Place the letter next to the person or group on the line below to show where each falls on the power scale below, from little power to great power.

- a _____

- b _____

- c _____

- d _____

Little Power _____ **Great Power**

Connect to the Chapter

(3) Skim the chapter text, subheads, and visuals and look for information about the division of power in ancient Greece. Use the information to complete the second row of the table below.

Division of Power in Ancient Greece				
Who holds power?	Power goes to the wealthiest.	Power goes to the strongest.	Power goes to the most experienced.	Power goes to all citizens.
Where or when?				

(4) After reading the chapter, return to this page. Change any answers that were incorrect.

Name _____ Class _____ Date _____

Connect to myStory: Pericles: Calm in the Face of Danger

(1) If you were Pericles, how would you have reacted as the Persians came closer to Athens?

_____
_____
_____

(2) In the myStory, why do the Athenians flee instead of remaining to fight the Persians on land?

_____
_____

(3) What motivated the Athenians to join other Greeks against the Persians?

_____
_____

(4) How was power in Athens handled differently than power in Persia?

_____
_____

(5) What happened at Salamis in 480 B.C.?

_____
_____

(6) What lesson did Pericles learn from the battle of Salamis?

_____
_____

Word Wise

Vocabulary Quiz Show Some quiz shows ask a question and expect the contestant to give the answer. In other shows, the contestant is given an answer and must supply the question. If the blank is in the Question column, write the question that would result in the answer in the Answer column. If the question is supplied, write the answer.

QUESTION	ANSWER
① _____	① polis
② _____	② citizens
③ Where were temples and public buildings located in Greek city-states?	③ _____
④ _____	④ politics
⑤ What term means "rule by the best people"?	⑤ _____

Name _____ Class _____ Date _____

Take Notes

Analyze Cause and Effect Use what you read about the rise of Greek city-states to complete the table below. For each cause given, write the effect. For each effect given, write the cause.

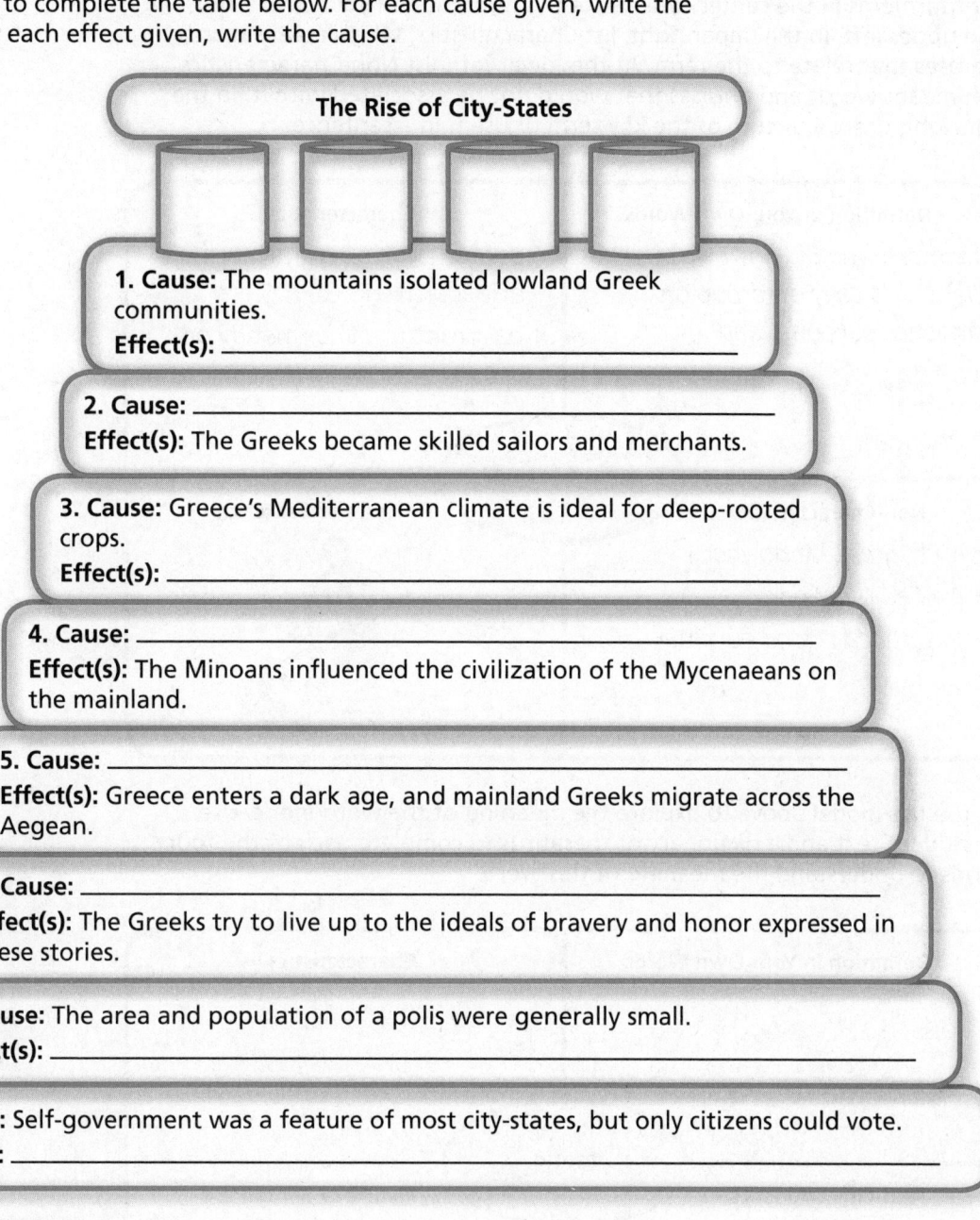

The Rise of City-States

1. Cause: The mountains isolated lowland Greek communities.
Effect(s): _____

2. Cause: _____
Effect(s): The Greeks became skilled sailors and merchants.

3. Cause: Greece's Mediterranean climate is ideal for deep-rooted crops.
Effect(s): _____

4. Cause: _____
Effect(s): The Minoans influenced the civilization of the Mycenaeans on the mainland.

5. Cause: _____
Effect(s): Greece enters a dark age, and mainland Greeks migrate across the Aegean.

6. Cause: _____
Effect(s): The Greeks try to live up to the ideals of bravery and honor expressed in these stories.

7. Cause: The area and population of a polis were generally small.
Effect(s): _____

8. Cause: Self-government was a feature of most city-states, but only citizens could vote.
Effect(s): _____

Essential Question

Who held political power in Greek city-states?

_____

_____

_____

Word Wise

Word Map Follow the model below to make a word map. The key term *tenant farmer* is in the center oval. Write the definition in your own words at the upper left. In the upper right, list Characteristics, which means words or phrases that relate to the term. At the lower left, list Non-Characteristics, which means words and phrases that would *not* be associated with it. In the lower right, draw a picture of the key term *or* use it in a sentence.

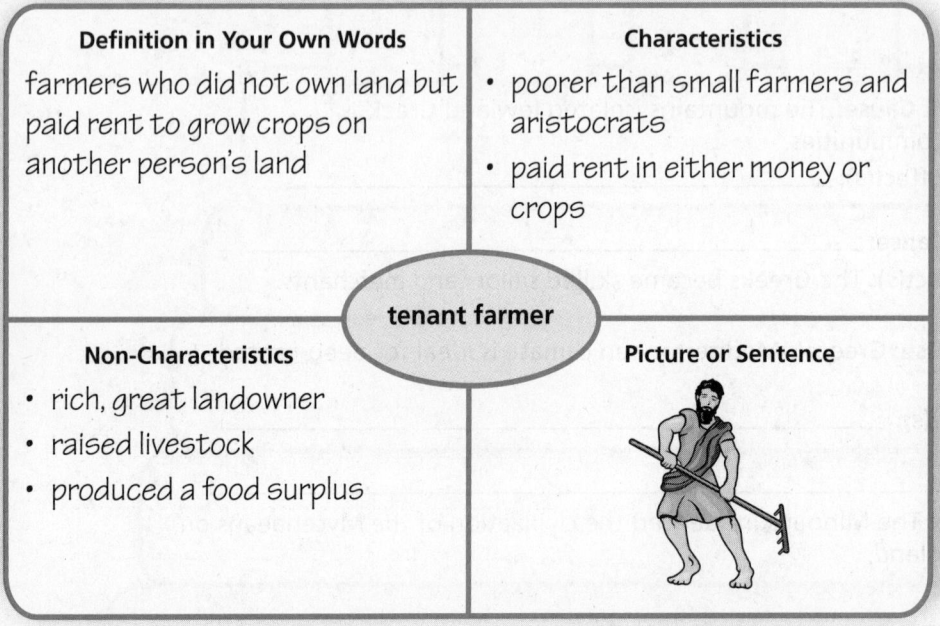

Definition in Your Own Words
farmers who did not own land but paid rent to grow crops on another person's land

Characteristics
• poorer than small farmers and aristocrats
• paid rent in either money or crops

tenant farmer

Non-Characteristics
• rich, great landowner
• raised livestock
• produced a food surplus

Picture or Sentence

Now use the model above to explore the meaning of the word *metic*. Use your student text and a dictionary or thesaurus to complete each of the four sections to understand the meaning of this word.

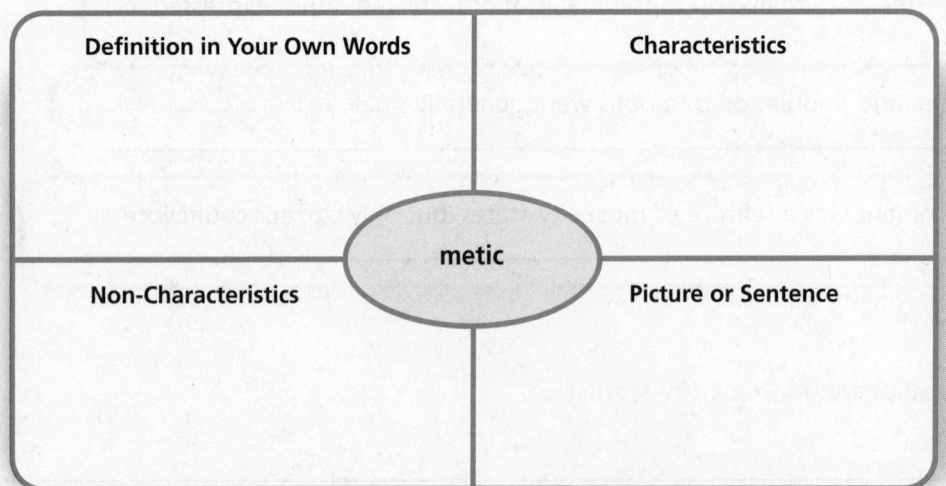

Definition in Your Own Words

Characteristics

metic

Non-Characteristics

Picture or Sentence

Make a word map of your own on a separate piece of paper for the following word: *slavery.*

Name _____ Class _____ Date _____

Take Notes

Identify Main Ideas and Details Use what you read about the Greek society and economy to complete the diagram below. For each main idea, write details that support it.

Greek Society and Economy	
Main Ideas	**Supporting Details**
In the Greek world, women had different rights and roles.	• _____ • _____ • _____ • _____ • _____ • _____
Ancient Greek society had a complex class system.	• _____ • _____ • _____ • _____ • _____
The population of Greek city-states increased, and the Greeks had to find ways to feed the people.	• _____ • _____ • _____
Greek colonization affected both trade and culture.	• _____ • _____ • _____ • _____

Essential Question

Who held the most power in the Greek family?

_____

_____

Word Wise

Sentence Builder Finish the sentences below with a key term from this section. You may have to change the form of the words to complete the sentences.

Word Bank

oligarchy   phalanx
tyranny   democracy
citizenship   direct democracy
representative democracy

① Many city-states moved toward rule by the many, a form of government

called _____.

② People have rights and responsibilities when they gain membership in a

community, or _____.

③ A political system in which citizens elect others to represent them in

government is called a(n) _____.

④ Political power is held by a small group of people in a(n)

_____.

⑤ A political system in which citizens participate directly in decision

making is called a(n) _____.

⑥ A formation of heavily armed foot soldiers who moved together as a

unit was called a(n) _____.

⑦ A government run by a strong ruler was known as a(n)

_____.

Name _____ Class _____ Date _____

Take Notes

Summarize Use what you have read to fill in key ideas about the topics in Section 3 in the boxes below. Then use the key ideas to write a summary statement about democracy in Athens.

Before Democracy	Power of the People	Athenian Democracy at Work
Oligarchies _____ _____ _____ _____ _____ **The Phalanx** _____ _____ _____ _____ **Tyrannies** _____ _____ _____ _____	**Solon** _____ _____ _____ _____ **Cleisthenes** _____ _____ _____ **Pericles** _____ _____ _____ _____ **Idea of Citizenship** _____ _____ _____ _____	**The Assembly** _____ _____ _____ _____ **The Boule** _____ _____ _____ _____ **The Courts** _____ _____ _____ _____ **Limited Direct Democracy** _____ _____ _____ _____

Summary Statement: _____

_____

Essential Question

How did citizens gain power in Athens?

_____

_____

_____

Word Wise

Words in Context For each question below, write an answer that shows your understanding of the boldfaced key term.

(1) How did **ephors** give the Spartan assembly an important power?

_____

_____

(2) How were **helots** different from slaves?

_____

_____

(3) Why did Sparta become a **military state**?

_____

_____

(4) Why did Spartan males live in **barracks**?

_____

_____

Name _____ Class _____ Date _____

Take Notes

Compare and Contrast The left side of the chart below gives information about Athens. For each item about Athens, identify how Sparta was different.

Athens	Sparta
• City near the coast	• _____
• Used coins as money	• _____
• Naval power	• _____
• Democracy	• _____
• Led by boule (one-year terms)	• _____
• Powerful assembly that passed laws	• _____
• Valued luxury and beauty	• _____
• Well-rounded education for boys	• _____
• Goal: to become good citizens	• _____
• Wealthier women stayed indoors	• _____
• Women had few rights	• _____
• Valued individual expression	• _____
• Valued new ideas	• _____
• Democracy evolved over time	• _____

Essential Question

Who held the most power in Spartan society?

_____

_____

_____

What is power? Who should have it?

Prepare to Write

Throughout this chapter, you have explored the Essential Question in your text, journal, and by going On Assignment at myworldhistory.com. Use what you have learned in this chapter to write an expository essay about power and who held it in ancient Greece.

Workshop Skill: Use the Writing Process

This workshop focuses on the writing process. The writing process involves brainstorming, writing, revising, editing, and presenting your work. The steps are not always in exact order. You might want to revise as you write, for example.

Prewrite The prewriting stage is important. It involves gathering ideas and details and putting them in order. At this point, you brainstorm, do research, and take notes. You can reread the chapter looking for ideas.

After you have assembled all your facts, create an outline. Your essay should have five paragraphs: an introduction, three body paragraphs, and a conclusion.

Write Your Essay At this point, you should be able to write your essay. Consider the main point you want to make and open your essay with it. For example: Power was distributed differently in early Greek history and in the city-states of Athens and Sparta.

Each body paragraph should discuss who held the power in each of the three examples: early Greek history, Athens, and Sparta. Your conclusion should sum up your points. Restate your opening in a new way and briefly identify your three points again.

Revise and Edit Your Essay It is usually helpful to read an essay aloud when revising it. That way you can hear whether the sentences flow together. If you find that you have repeated the same sentence patterns over and over, make some changes. Vary the sentences. Make sure that your word choice expresses exactly what you mean. Always look for errors in punctuation, spelling, and grammar.

Ask someone to listen to you as you read your essay. He or she can point out places where your essay is unclear or where you have failed to connect ideas. Listen to what the person says.

Present Your Essay Rewrite your essay on a clean sheet of paper. Be sure to include your name, the date, and an essay title.

Take Notes

Taking notes is an important part of writing. Reread the chapter, looking for examples of people and groups who held power in ancient Greece. Use the chart as a guide.

Place	Who Held Power?
Early City States	
Democratic Athens	
Sparta	

Draft Your Essay

Draft your essay on another sheet of paper. Follow the steps you learned in this workshop to improve and revise your draft

Name _____ Class _____ Date _____

Essential Question

How should we handle conflict?

Preview Before you begin this chapter, think about the Essential Question. Understanding how the Essential Question connects to your life will help you understand the chapter you are about to read.

Connect to Your Life

(1) What are some synonyms of the word *conflict*? _____

_____

(2) Complete the table below with examples of conflicts you have observed in various settings.

	Type of Conflict	Source of Conflict
School		
Sporting Events		
Other		

Connect to the Chapter

(3) Skim this chapter's text, subheads, and visuals and look for information about conflicts in ancient Greek civilization. In the table below, use the information to make predictions about those conflicts.

	Who?	Sources of Conflict?
Conflict Within Greece		
Conflict With Outsiders		

(4) After reading the chapter, return to this page. Change any predictions that were incorrect.

Name _____ Class _____ Date _____

Connect to myStory: A Prophecy Fulfilled

1. Do you know what you want to be when you grow up? What have you done to help steer yourself in that career direction?

   _____

   _____

2. In the myStory, what did Alexander believe his destiny would be?

   _____

   _____

3. How did Alexander's upbringing prepare him to fulfill his destiny?

   _____

   _____

4. Where did Alexander meet Darius III's forces the first time? What happened?

   _____

   _____

5. How did Alexander quickly solve the problem of the Gordian knot?

   _____

6. How do you think Alexander the Great viewed conflict?

   _____

7. What conflict arose between Alexander and his own men? Why? How was it resolved?

   _____

   _____

Name _____ Class _____ Date _____

Word Wise

Words in Context For each question below, write an answer that shows your understanding of the boldfaced key term.

1 Why was the **Battle of Marathon** significant?

_____

_____

_____

2 What happened at the **Battle of Salamis**?

_____

_____

_____

3 What was the **Delian League,** and why was it formed?

_____

_____

_____

4 Who made up the **Peloponnesian League,** and why did its members resent Athens?

_____

_____

_____

Name _____ Class _____ Date _____

Take Notes

Compare and Contrast   Use what you have read about the Persian Wars and Peloponnesian War to list each war's opposing sides, reasons for conflict, and outcomes in the diagram below.

First Persian War

Opposing Sides:
_____
_____
_____

Reasons for Conflict:
_____
_____
_____
_____
_____

What Happened?
_____
_____
_____
_____
_____

Second Persian War

Opposing Sides:
_____
_____
_____

Reasons for Conflict:
_____
_____
_____
_____

What Happened?
_____
_____
_____
_____

Peloponnesian War

Opposing Sides:
_____
_____
_____

Reasons for Conflict:
_____
_____
_____
_____

What Happened?
_____
_____
_____
_____
_____

Essential Question

Why were the Greeks able to unite during the Persian Wars?

_____

_____

_____

Word Wise

Use a Word Bank Choose one word from the word bank to fill in each blank. When you have finished, you will have a short summary of important ideas from the section.

Word Bank

Alexandria   Hellenistic
sarissa

Philip of Macedonia gained control of Greece with powerful,

disciplined troops, each of whom was armed with a _____.

After Philip was assassinated, his son Alexander gained the throne.

Alexander secured control of Greece and then captured cities in Asia and

along the Mediterranean coast. He freed Egypt from the Persians and

founded _____ on the Nile delta. After defeating the

Persian empire, Alexander moved east into India. Everywhere he went,

Alexander founded Greek-style cities from which emerged

_____ culture. After he died, his huge empire was divided

into kingdoms.

Name _____ Class _____ Date _____

Take Notes

Sequence Use what you have read in this section to add details to the timeline below.

The Rise of Macedonia and Alexander's Empire

359 B.C.	1. _____ _____
	• Philip's powerful army defeats the Illyrians.
338 B.C.	2. _____ _____
	• Philip is assassinated.
	3. _____ _____
334 B.C.	4. _____ _____
	• Alexander frees the Egyptians from the Persians.
330 B.C.	5. _____ _____
	• Alexander leads his army into Afghanistan and India.
	6. _____ _____
323 B.C.	7. _____ _____

Essential Question

Why did the Greeks rebel after Philip's death?

_____

_____

_____

Word Wise

Vocabulary Quiz Show Some quiz shows ask a question and expect the contestant to give the answer. In other shows, the contestant is given an answer and must supply the question. If the blank is in the Question column, write the question that would result in the answer in the Answer column. If the question is supplied, write the answer.

QUESTION	ANSWER
(1) _____	(1) polytheism
(2) _____	(2) mythology
(3) Which famous sports event took place every four years and honored Zeus?	(3) _____
(4) What was the priestess of the temple of Apollo known as?	(4) _____
(5) _____	(5) lyric poetry
(6) _____	(6) chorus

Name _____ Class _____ Date _____

Take Notes

Identify Main Ideas and Details The column headings below match the topics in Section 3 of your textbook. Under each column heading, write the main idea of the topic and details that support it.

Greek Religion and Mythology	The Arts of Ancient Greece	Literature
Main Idea	**Main Idea**	**Main Idea**
_____	_____	_____
_____	_____	_____
_____	_____	_____
_____	_____	_____
_____	_____	
Details	**Details**	**Details**
• _____	• _____	• _____
_____	_____	_____
_____	_____	_____
• _____	• _____	• _____
_____	_____	_____
• _____	• _____	• _____
_____	_____	_____
• _____	• _____	• _____
_____	_____	_____
• _____	• _____	• _____
_____	_____	_____
• _____	• _____	• _____
_____	_____	_____

Essential Question

What sort of conflicts did Greek drama explore?

_____

_____

_____

Word Wise

Sentence Builder Finish the sentences below with a key term from this section. You may have to change the form of the words to complete the sentences.

Word Bank
Academy   Hippocratic oath
hypothesis   Socratic method

① A question-and-answer method of teaching is called the

_____.

② Plato's famous school of philosophy was the _____.

③ After making observations of a natural event, Greek scholars

explained their observations by forming a logical guess called a(n)

_____.

④ When promising to use their knowledge only in ethical ways, doctors

state the _____.

Name _____ Class _____ Date _____

Take Notes

Summarize Use what you have read in Section 4 to fill in key ideas about the topics in the table below.

Topics	Key Ideas
Greek Philosophy	
History and Politics	
Science and Technology	
Mathematics and Medicine	
Hellenistic Learning	

Essential Question

Why might Greek historians have written about conflicts?

_____

_____

_____

Essential Question Writer's Workshop

How should we handle conflict?

Prepare to Write

Throughout this chapter, you have explored the Essential Question in your text, journal, and by going On Assignment at myworldhistory.com. Use what you have learned in this chapter to write an outline about conflict in ancient Greece. Consider the Persian Wars, the Peloponnesian War, and Alexander the Great's conquests.

Workshop Skill: Outline an Essay

This workshop focuses on outlining an essay, or getting your thoughts in order before you begin to write. You need to consider these items as you prepare to write your essay: the "hook," the thesis statement, three body paragraphs, and the conclusion.

The Hook Your opening statement should catch the reader's attention. This is the hook. Think about Alexander the Great and his spectacular conquests. An example of a hook for an essay about Alexander could take the form of a question. For example: *What do you have to do to get "the Great" added to your name?* Notice how this question creates personal interest in the reader. On the lines below, write some hook ideas about conflict in ancient Greece.

_____

_____

The Thesis Statement Your thesis, or the main idea of your essay, comes after the hook. Your thesis should state three ideas you will use to support your position. These ideas will be the focus of your three body paragraphs. Read the sample introductory paragraph below. In this case, the thesis statement is the last sentence in the introduction.

Example *What do you have to do to get "the Great" added to your name?*

First, you need to be told from birth that you are descended from the god

Hercules. Then, you need to be given military training to become a great

leader. Finally, your teacher needs to be Aristotle, one of the greatest minds

in history. With this background, Alexander the Great was destined to

become one of the greatest conquerors of all time.

Organize Your Essay

Paragraph 1: Introduction Remember your hook ideas? Begin your introductory paragraph with one of those and end it by clearly stating your thesis.

Paragraph 2: Body Paragraph A In the sample thesis, three ideas were given to explain why Alexander the Great was the greatest conqueror. In your thesis, you will state three ideas about conflict in ancient Greece. State one of these ideas in body paragraph A and use at least two details to support it.

Topic Sentence _____

Detail 1 _____

Detail 2 _____

Concluding Sentence _____

Paragraph 3: Body Paragraph B Review your thesis and note your idea for the second topic, which will be the focus of body paragraph B. Try to make a smooth transition as you begin a new paragraph.

Topic Sentence _____

Detail 1 _____

Detail 2 _____

Concluding Sentence _____

Paragraph 4: Body Paragraph C Follow the steps given for body paragraphs A and B to write body paragraph C.

Topic Sentence _____

Detail 1 _____

Detail 2 _____

Concluding Sentence _____

Paragraph 5: Conclusion For the conclusion, summarize the ideas you presented in your thesis.

Draft Your Essay

Write your essay and then proofread it with a writing partner.

Places to Know!

Map Skills Use the maps in this unit to identify the Places to Know! on the outline map. Before the name of each place below, write the letter that shows its location on the map.

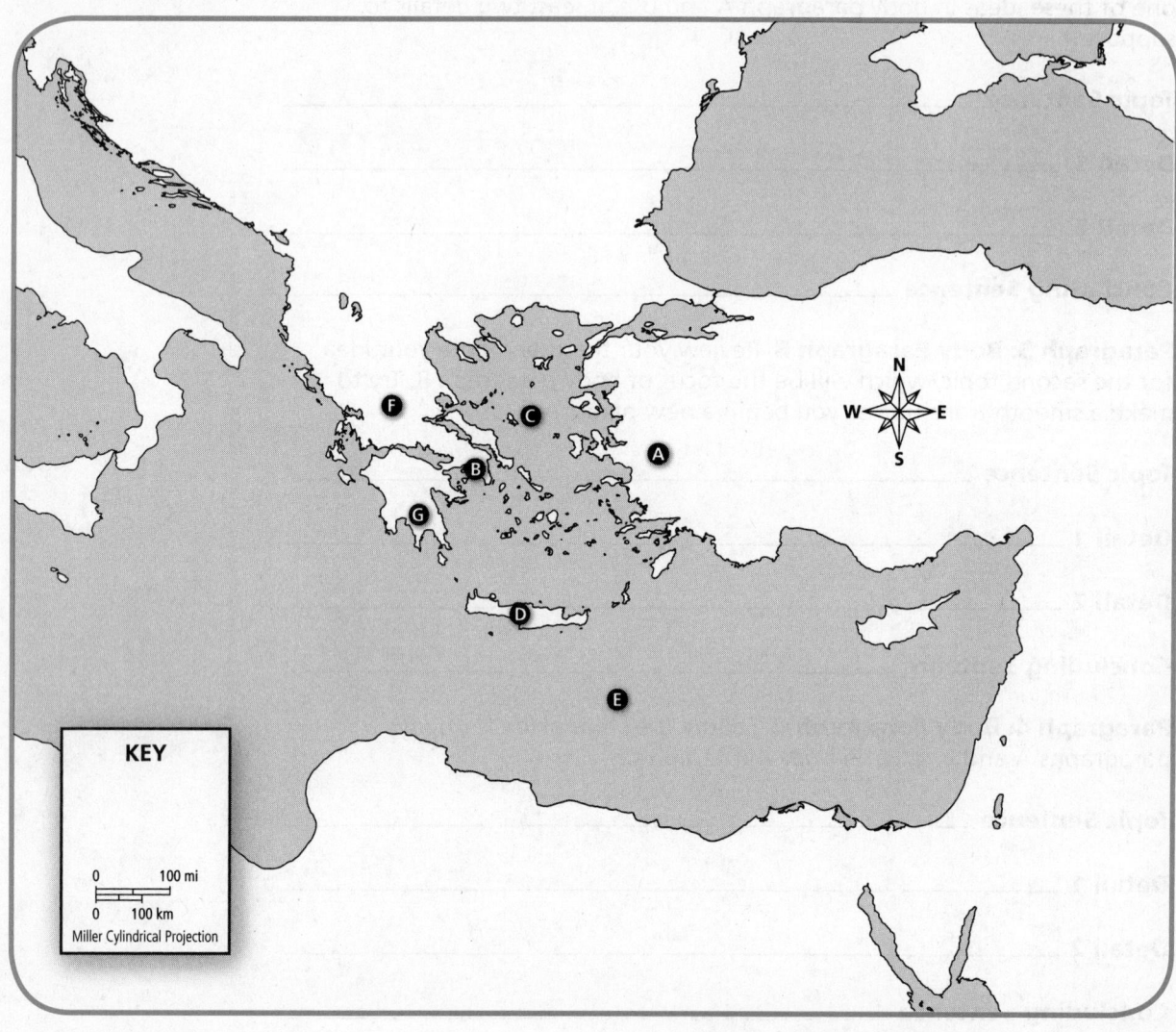

KEY

0   100 mi

0   100 km

Miller Cylindrical Projection

_____ **Greece**

_____ **Crete**

_____ **Athens**

_____ **Sparta**

_____ **Mediterranean Sea**

_____ **Aegean Sea**

_____ **Ionia**

Key Events

Timeline Use what you have read about ancient Greece to complete the timeline below. Draw a line from each event to its correct position on the timeline. Then write a brief description of each event.

1500 B.C.

1600 B.C. _____
_____

480 B.C. _____
_____

1250 B.C.

1450 B.C. _____
_____

431 B.C. _____
_____

1000 B.C.

1100 B.C. _____
_____

750 B.C.

404 B.C. _____
_____

700s B.C. _____
_____

500 B.C.

334 B.C. _____
_____

594 B.C. _____
_____

250 B.C.

Name _____ Class _____ Date _____

Essential Question

What should governments do?

Preview Before you begin this chapter, think about the Essential Question. Understanding how the Essential Question connects to your life will help you understand the chapter you are about to read.

Connect to Your Life

1. In the table below, each box tells about something government does. Under each heading for private citizens, write something that citizens like you or your family should do, such as volunteer work.

Government's Role and My Role			
School	**Home**	**In My Community**	**Beyond My Community**
Government: Funds school sports programs.	**Government:** Makes rules for protecting environment.	**Government:** Maintains public parks.	**Government:** Legislative branch makes laws.
Private citizens: _____ _____	**Private citizens:** _____ _____	**Private citizens:** _____ _____	**Private citizens:** _____ _____

2. Now think about how you and your government can work together. Which kinds of problems should government solve? Which should be the responsibility of citizens like you and your family?

_____

_____

Connect to the Chapter

3. Preview the chapter by skimming the chapter's heads, photographs, and graphics. Then predict which services the Roman government provided. List your ideas in the table below.

Roman Government			
Defense	**Laws**	**Economy**	**Public Services**

4. Read the chapter. Then update your table, adding new ideas, moving ideas to different columns, or crossing out ideas that no longer make sense to you.

146

Name _____ Class _____ Date _____

Connect to myStory: Tullia's Father Saves the Republic

1 Think about ways in which your life is like Tullia's. In what ways are you involved in shaping your community? How do you learn about current events? What adults do you admire for their efforts in the community?

_____

_____

_____

2 Use this Venn diagram to compare your experiences with Tullia's. Think about actions that shape a community or teach you about current events. Identify people you admire for their efforts in these areas.

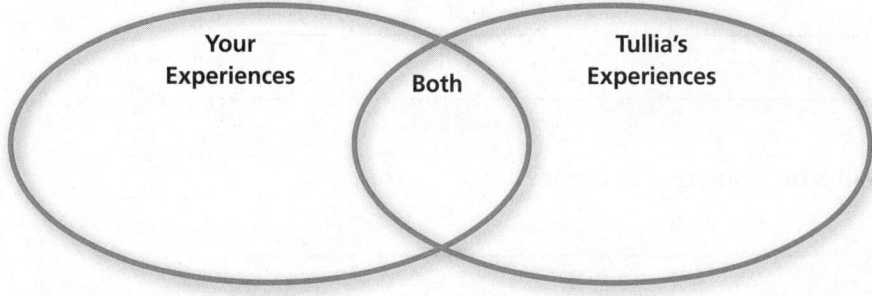

Your Experiences   Both   Tullia's Experiences

3 How important was government in the lives of the Romans? Write two predictions.

_____

_____

Word Wise

Words In Context For each question below, write an answer that shows your understanding of the boldfaced key term.

(1) What are some activities that might take place in the **forum** of ancient Rome?

_____

_____

_____

(2) How did Rome's government change when the **republic** replaced the monarchy?

_____

_____

_____

(3) What advantages did a **maniple** have in battle?

_____

_____

_____

(4) Approximately how many soldiers made up a **legion,** and what kind of soldiers were they?

_____

_____

_____

Name _____ Class _____ Date _____

Take Notes

Analyze Cause and Effect Both geography and previous cultures helped shape the Roman republic. As you read, record ways that each factor affected the Roman republic.

Causes   **Effects**

Geography

→

Greek and Etruscan Cultures

→

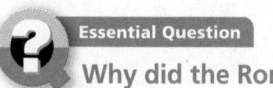 **Essential Question**

Why did the Romans overthrow their king and form a new system of government?

_____

_____

_____

Word Wise

Vocabulary Quiz Show Some quiz shows ask a question and expect the contestant to give the answer. In other shows, the contestant is given an answer and must supply the question. If the blank is in the Question column, write the question that would result in the answer in the Answer column. If the question is supplied, write the answer.

QUESTION

1. What do you call the highest officials in the Roman republic?

2. _____

3. What happens when one part of government stops or cancels the action of another part?

4. _____

5. What is the name for the garment that adult male Roman citizens wore?

ANSWER

1. _____

2. constitution

3. _____

4. magistrates

5. _____

Name _____   Class _____   Date _____

Take Notes

Identify Main Ideas and Details In this section, you read about how power was shared in the Roman government. In the web below, record details about each part or role in the Roman government. Tell about the responsibilities of this part of government and who can serve in it.

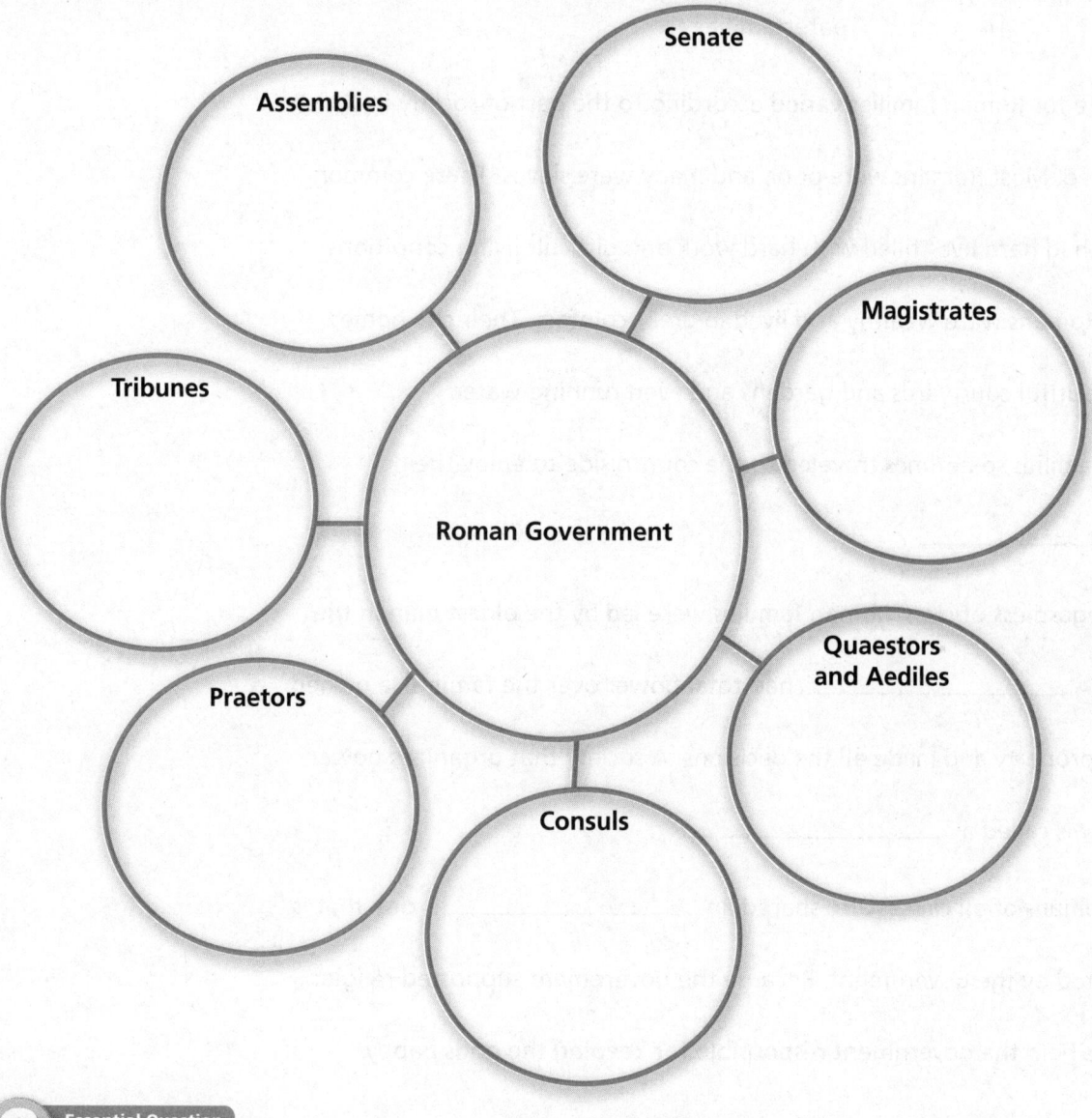

Essential Question

What are some benefits of dividing the government into three branches with separate or different powers?

_____

_____

_____

Word Wise

Word Bank Choose one word from the word bank to fill in each blank. When you have finished, you will have a short summary of important ideas from the section.

patriarchal society   established religion
villas   paterfamilias

Life for Roman families varied according to the part of society in which

they lived. Most Romans were poor, and many were slaves. These common

people had hard lives filled with hard work and difficult living conditions.

A few Romans were wealthy and lived in great comfort. Their city homes

had beautiful courtyards and gardens and even running water.

These families sometimes traveled to the countryside to enjoy their

_____.

Regardless of class, Roman families were led by the oldest man in the

family. A _____ had total power over the family. He owned

all the property and made all the decisions. A society that organizes power

this way is called a _____.

Romans of all classes also shared an _____, one that is

supported by the government. Because the government supported religion,

Romans held the government responsible for keeping the gods happy.

Reconstructed View of the
Villa Rūstica of the *Cornēliī*

Name _____ Class _____ Date _____

Take Notes

Compare and Contrast In this section, you learned about the way that
Roman society was divided by gender and class. In the table below, describe
the difference between each pair of groups. Then use the fourth column to
identify rights or responsibility shared by specific groups.

Men vs. Women	Slaves vs. Free	Rich vs. Poor	Overlaps
			All men except slaves could _____ _____ _____ _____ All women had to _____ _____ _____ No women were allowed to _____ _____ _____

Essential Question

What was the role of government in Roman religion?

_____

_____

_____

Word Wise

Word Map Follow the model below to make a word map. The key term *province* is in the center oval. Write the definition in your own words at the upper left. In the upper right, list Characteristics, which means words or phrases that relate to the term. At the lower left, list Non-Characteristics, which means words and phrases that would *not* be associated with it. In the lower right, draw a picture of the key term *or* use it in a sentence.

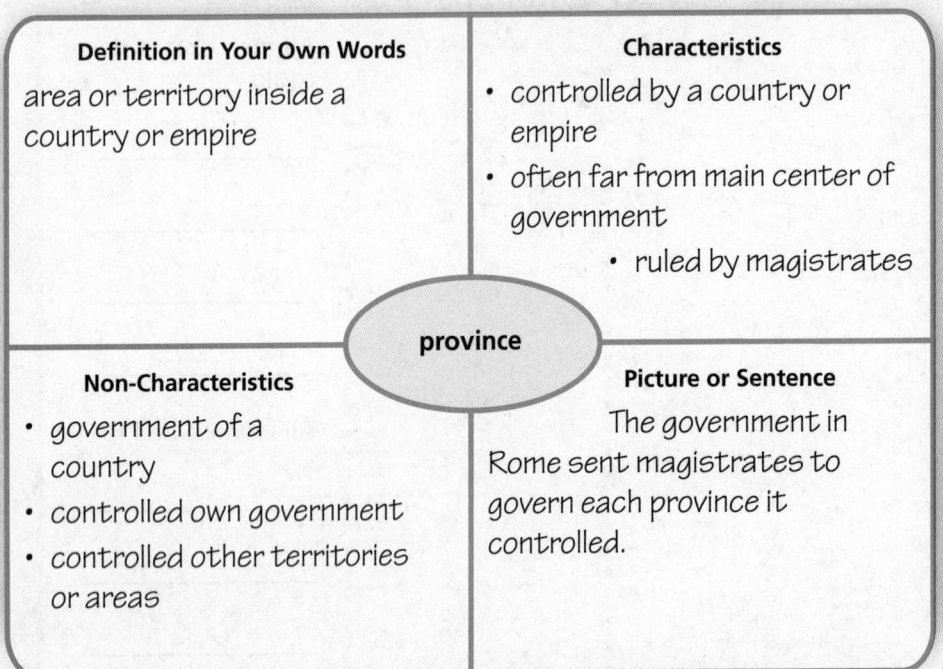

Definition in Your Own Words
area or territory inside a country or empire

Characteristics
- controlled by a country or empire
- often far from main center of government
  - ruled by magistrates

province

Non-Characteristics
- government of a country
- controlled own government
- controlled other territories or areas

Picture or Sentence
The government in Rome sent magistrates to govern each province it controlled.

Now use the word map below to explore the meaning of the word *civil war*. You may use your student text, a dictionary, and/or a thesaurus to complete each of the four sections.

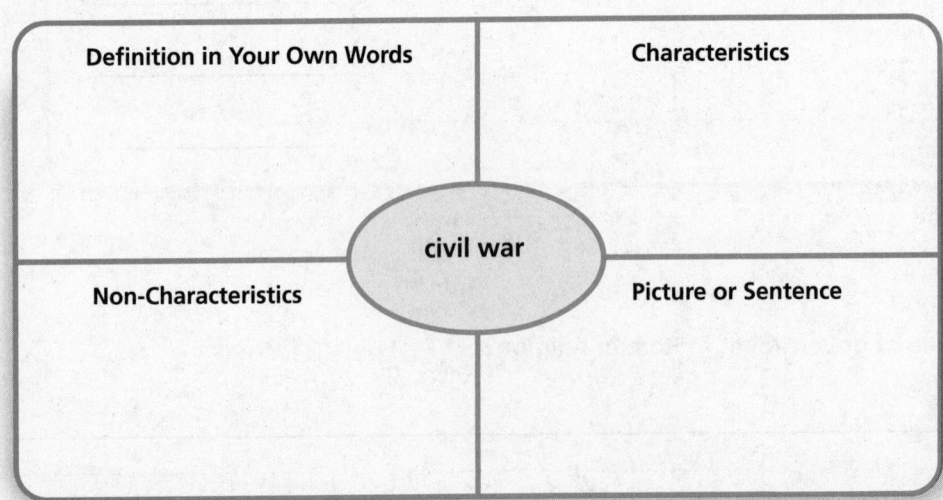

Definition in Your Own Words

Characteristics

civil war

Non-Characteristics

Picture or Sentence

Make word maps of your own on a separate piece of paper for these key terms: *Augustus* and *empire*.

Take Notes

Summarize In this section you read about events at the end of the Roman republic. In the flowchart below, briefly explain the weaknesses of the republic in the box on the left. Describe the actions of those responsible for the republic's crisis in the box on the right. Then summarize the effects of these problems during the republic's final crisis.

Weaknesses of the Republic	Actions of Politicians and Military Commanders
Corruption _____ _____ _____	**Marius and Sulla** _____ _____ _____ _____ _____
Urban Poor _____ _____ _____	**Pompey and Caesar** _____ _____ _____ _____
Power of the Army _____ _____ _____ _____	

Final Crisis

_____

_____

_____

Essential Question

How did Rome's increasing wealth and power help bring about the collapse of the Roman republic?

_____

_____

_____

What should governments do?

Prepare to Write

Throughout this chapter, you have explored the Essential Question in your text, journal, and by going On Assignment at myworldhistory.com. Use what you learned to write an essay about the feature of the Roman government that you think is the most important. Describe it and take a position on how it either helped the Roman republic to grow or contributed to its crisis and end.

Workshop Skill: Write an Introduction and Thesis Statement

In this lesson, you will learn more about how to develop a thesis and introduction for your essay. A thesis is the main point you want to make in your essay. It is not a topic. It is not a title. It is an idea that you will share and explain. Writers state a thesis in an introduction. This first paragraph is like a road map to your essay. It tells readers what your main point is and briefly lists the arguments you will make to support that point.

Determine the Essay Type Your first step is always to decide which kind of essay you are writing. To do this, look for signal words in the essay question. For example, the words *you think,* and *take a position* tell you that you are to write a persuasive essay. Your essay should express your opinion and try to convince the reader that it is correct. You will describe the feature of the Roman republic that you have chosen. Then you will explain why it is so important. You will need examples to support your explanation.

Write a Thesis Statement Consider the main point you want to make in your essay and phrase it as a thesis statement. For example: *Separation of powers, the most important feature of the Roman republic's government, contributed to both its growth and its final crisis.* Notice that this statement is specific to the question. It mentions only one feature of the government, and it refers to both its growth and its final crisis.

The body of the essay should describe *how* the division of power contributed to the republic's growth and crisis. Most important, it should explain *why* this factor contributed more than any other. You may put your thesis at the beginning or at the end of your introduction.

Build the Introduction An introduction tells readers what your essay will be about and also why they should care about your topic. This means you have to give readers a little background about the topic. For example, you might explain why the Romans started a republic and how the division of power related to those reasons. You should briefly summarize the main points you will make, perhaps in a single sentence. Finally, suggest to readers why your ideas are important.

Revise Your Thesis as You Write Sometimes as you explain your arguments, you may find that they do not exactly support the thesis. You may also change your topic a little bit. That is why it is important to check and revise your thesis often as you write.

As you revise your thesis, remember that it must
- fit the essay assignment.
- be clearly stated and easy to understand.
- be supported by evidence, such as facts and logic.

Sample Introduction Here is a sample thesis and introduction:

Separation of powers, the most important feature of the Roman republic's government, contributed to both its growth and its final crisis. In 509 B.C., the founders of the republic provided for separation of powers among many officials. In the 500 years that the republic flourished, the system succeeded in controlling those who were greedy for power. Over time, however, struggles over power weakened the republic. In 30 B.C. Rome once again became a monarchy. Understanding the success and failure of separation of powers in ancient Rome is important. It helps us recognize the need to protect the separation of powers in our own government.

Create Your Thesis and Introduction
Now write your own thesis and introduction.

Sample thesis _____

_____

Background _____

_____

Main Point 1 _____

_____

Main Point 2 _____

_____

Why It Matters _____

_____

Draft Your Essay
Use the thesis and introduction in your essay, which will be written on another paper. Complete your essay, and proofread it with a partner.

Name _____ Class _____ Date _____

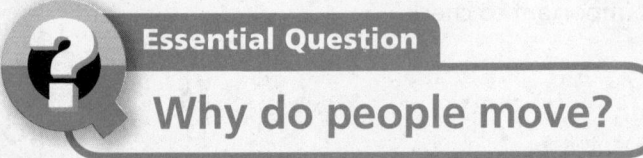

Essential Question

Why do people move?

Preview Before you begin this chapter, think about the Essential Question. Understanding how the Essential Question connects to your life will help you understand the chapter you are about to read.

Connect to Your Life

(1) Think about the reasons that people move. Some people move by choice and others move because they have to. Brainstorm some reasons, and then organize them by specific category. List your ideas in the table.

Reasons Why People Move				
Personal	• Geographic	• Business	• Political	• Military
	•	•	•	•
	•	•	•	•
	•	•	•	•
	•	•	•	•

(2) Consider all the ways that choice plays a role in the moves you have listed. How is moving by choice different from moving without choice? How is it the same?

_____

_____

Connect to the Chapter

(3) Preview the chapter by skimming the chapter's heads, photographs, and graphics. Then make predictions about how movement has affected nations and cultures throughout history. List your ideas in the table below.

Effects of Movement on Communities, Cultures, Nations				
Languages	• Values/Beliefs	• Culture	• Laws	• Infrastructure
	•	•	•	•
	•	•	•	•
	•	•	•	•
	•	•	•	•

(4) Read the chapter. Then review your ideas, and write *P* for positive changes and *N* for negative changes.

Name _____ Class _____ Date _____

Connect to myStory: Paul's Shipwreck

① Paul encouraged and inspired those who felt panic in the storm. Have you ever felt fear like the people on the ship? Tell about someone in your life who inspired you when you were afraid.

_____

_____

② Use this Venn diagram to compare your experience with that of the people on Paul's ship. Think about what was said that reassured you. Then think about what reassured the people on the ship.

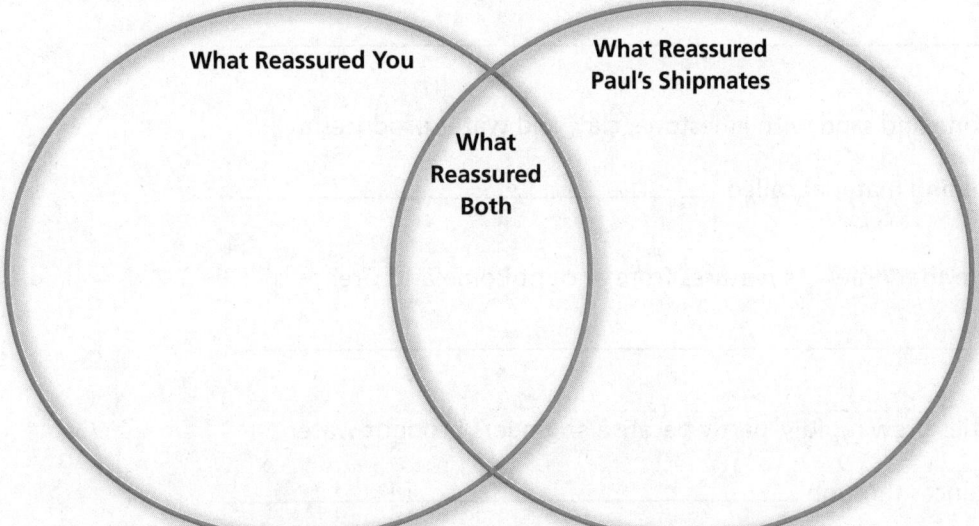

What Reassured You

What Reassured Paul's Shipmates

What Reassured Both

③ In the first box of the table below, list the challenges that Paul faced on his journey and the ways his commitment to his ideas helped him meet those challenges.

Challenges on the Journey	Role of Commitment

④ How do you think religious faith affected the people of Rome as they faced the challenges of a growing empire?

_____

_____

Name _____ Class _____ Date _____

Word Wise

Sentence Builder Complete the sentences using the information you learned in this section. You may have to change the form of the words to complete the sentence.

deify   Pax Romana
aqueduct   concrete
Greco-Roman

(1) Emperors who are worshipped as if they are gods have been

_____.

(2) Romans experienced a long period of peace and prosperity during the

_____.

(3) Mixing stone and sand with limestone, clay, and water produces a

useful building material called _____.

(4) The culture that draws its features from ancient Rome and Greece is

called _____.

(5) Roman cities grew rapidly, partly because engineers brought water

great distances through _____.

Name _____ Class _____ Date _____

Take Notes

Analyze Cause and Effect Many factors helped the Roman empire grow. As you read, record ways that each factor contributed to the Roman empire's growth.

Cause	Effects
Rule by Emperors	
Pax Romana	
Rome's Practical Achievements	
Roman Military	

Essential Question

If you traveled to Roman cities all across the empire in A.D.100, what similar buildings would you see wherever you went?

_____

_____

Word Wise

Vocabulary Quiz Show Some quiz shows ask a question and expect the contestant to give the answer. In other shows, the contestant is given an answer and must supply the question. If the blank is in the Question column, write the question that would result in the answer in the Answer column. If the question is supplied, write the answer.

QUESTION	ANSWER
① What do you call men who fight each other as part of public entertainment?	① _____
② _____	② mosaic
③ What kind of literature makes fun of its subject?	③ _____
④ _____	④ oratory
⑤ What category of languages includes Spanish, French, and Portuguese?	⑤ _____

Name _____ Class _____ Date _____

Take Notes

Identify Main Ideas and Details In this section, you read how Rome's culture blossomed during the Pax Romana. In the web below, record details about each aspect of that culture.

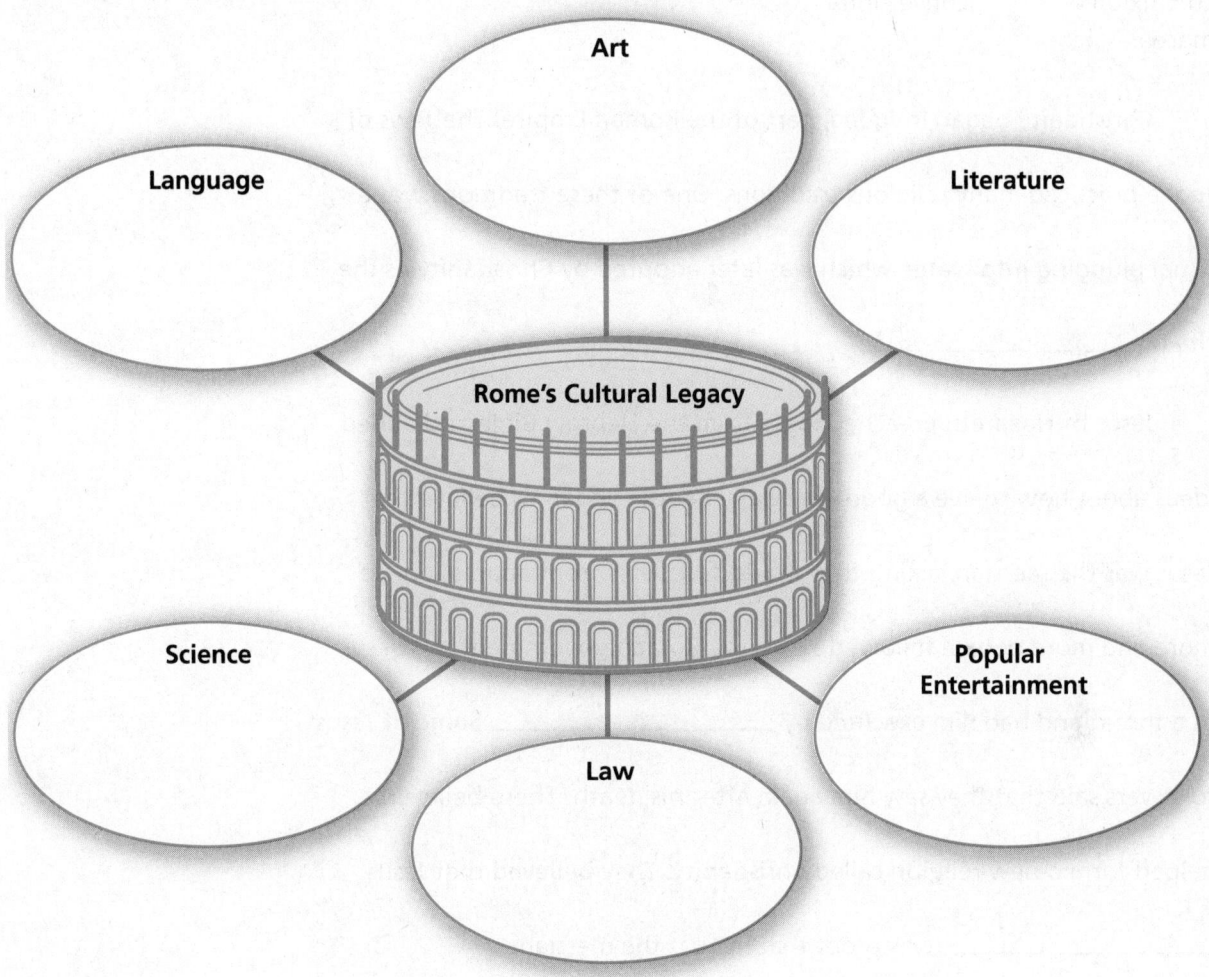

Art

Language

Literature

Rome's Cultural Legacy

Science

Law

Popular Entertainment

Essential Question

What important discovery did Galen make about how things move inside people's bodies?

_____

_____

_____

Word Wise

Word Bank Choose one word from the word bank to fill in each blank. When you have finished, you will have a short summary of important ideas from the section.

baptism   resurrection
crucifixion   conversion
martyr

Christianity began in Judea, part of the Roman Empire. The Jews of

Judea practiced many religious traditions. One of these traditions was a

ritual plunging into water, which was later adopted by Christianity as the

rite of _____.

Jesus of Nazareth preached ideas from the Hebrew Bible and added

ideas about how to live a good life. Many people began to believe that

Jesus was the messiah, a king that would save Jews from oppression. As

more and more people followed Jesus, the Roman government saw Jesus

as a threat and had him executed by _____. Some of Jesus'

followers said that they saw him again after his death. These believers

helped form a new religion called Christianity. They believed that Jesus'

_____ was proof that he was the messiah.

After Jesus' death, some of his followers worked to spread his

teachings. One was Paul, who opposed Christianity until he experienced a

_____ that changed his views. As Christianity spread, many

Roman emperors responded with persecution. Many Christians died for their

beliefs. Such people are called _____.

Name _____   Class _____   Date _____

Take Notes

Sequence In this section, you learned about the way that Christianity grew from Judaism into a separate religion that spread far and wide. On the timeline below, tell what happened at each of the dates listed.

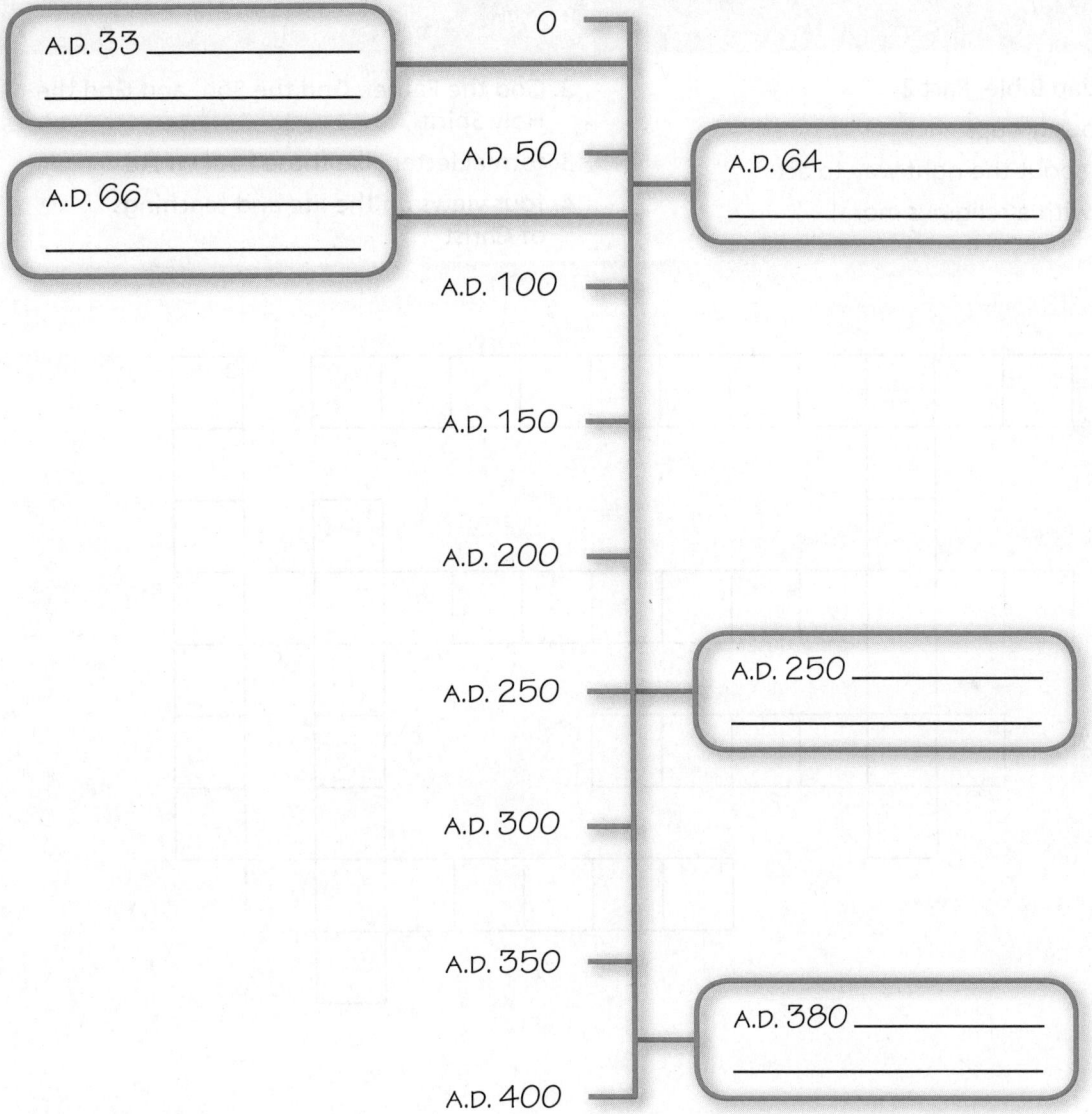

A.D. 33 _____
_____

0

A.D. 50

A.D. 64 _____
_____

A.D. 66 _____
_____

A.D. 100

A.D. 150

A.D. 200

A.D. 250

A.D. 250 _____
_____

A.D. 300

A.D. 350

A.D. 380 _____
_____

A.D. 400

Essential Question

How did the actions of the Roman government help allow the spread of Christianity and other ideas?

_____

_____

_____

Name _____ Class _____ Date _____

Word Wise

Crossword Puzzle The *Across* and *Down* clues are definitions of key terms from this section. Fill in the numbered *Across* boxes with the correct key terms. Then do the same with the *Down* clues.

Across	Down
1. Christian Bible, Part 2	2. God the Father, God the Son, and God the Holy Spirit
5. religious groups	3. formal letter, like those Paul wrote
6. ideas about the right way to act	4. four views on the life and teachings of Christ
7. story with a religious moral	

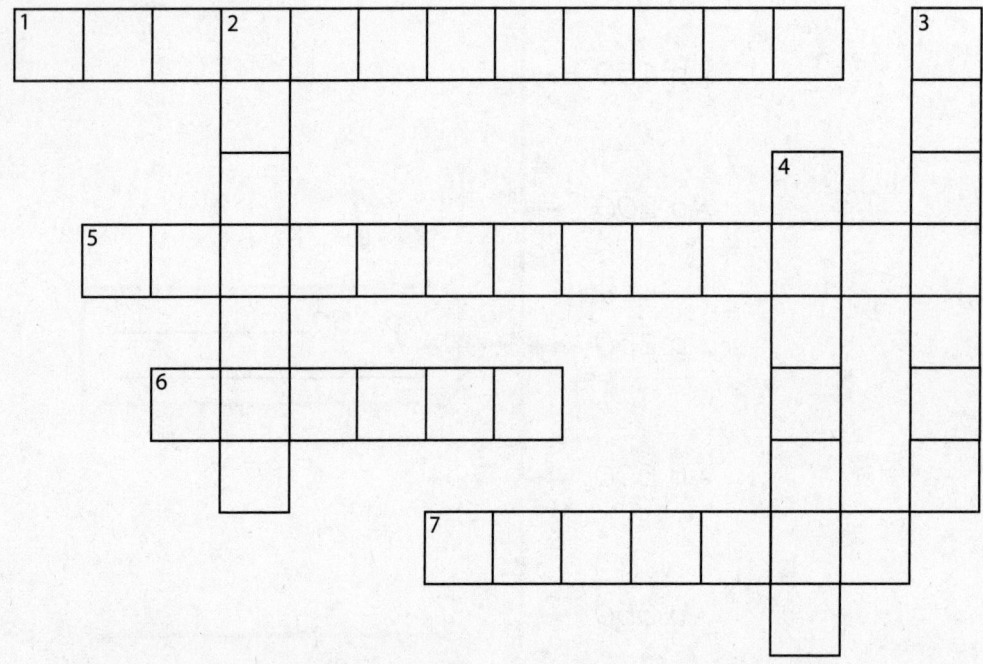

Name _____ Class _____ Date _____

Take Notes

Summarize In this section you read about the beliefs of Christianity. In the top boxes of the flowchart below, list the main ideas from each red heading in your text. Then write a brief statement to explain how the beliefs of Christianity, along with those of Judaism, shaped the Western world.

Christian Bible

Beliefs About God

Practicing Christianity

The Judeo-Christian Tradition

Summary Statement:

_____

_____

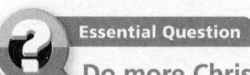

Essential Question

Do more Christians today live in Asia, where Christianity was founded, or on other continents?

_____

_____

_____

Word Wise

Words In Context For each question below, write an answer that shows your understanding of the boldfaced key term.

(1) What are problems that people might have in a time of **inflation**?

_____

_____

_____

(2) According to the Romans, why were the Germans **barbarians**?

_____

_____

_____

(3) How did the emperor Theodosius show his support for Christian **orthodoxy**?

_____

_____

_____

(4) What role did **mercenaries** play in the Roman empire's fight to survive?

_____

_____

_____

Name _____ Class _____ Date _____

Take Notes

Analyze Cause and Effect In this section you read about the decline of the Roman empire. As you read, think about the reasons for that decline. Then complete the flowchart below.

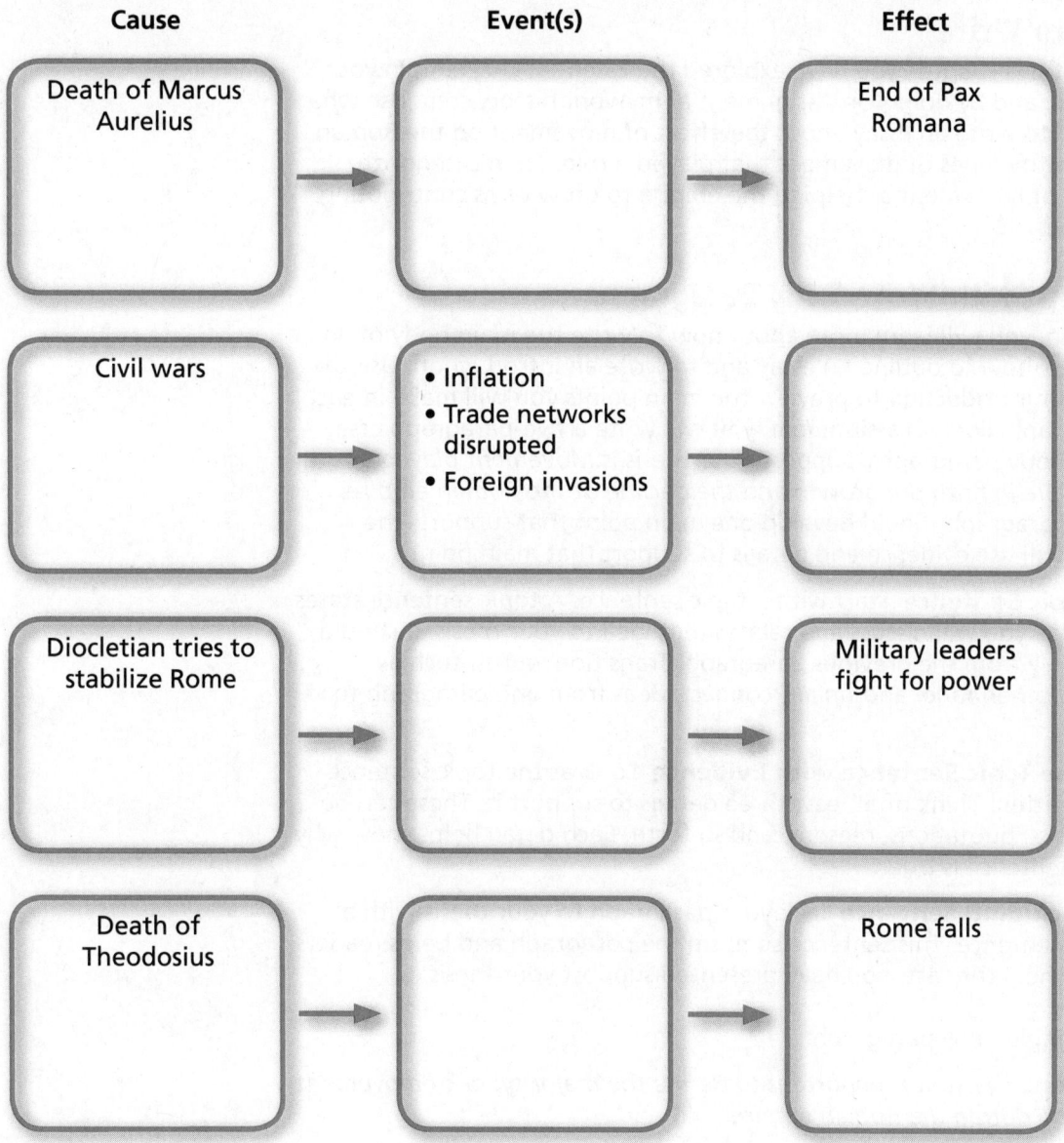

Cause	Event(s)	Effect
Death of Marcus Aurelius		End of Pax Romana
Civil wars	• Inflation • Trade networks disrupted • Foreign invasions	
Diocletian tries to stabilize Rome		Military leaders fight for power
Death of Theodosius		Rome falls

? Essential Question

How did the movement of the Huns affect the Roman empire?

_____

_____

_____

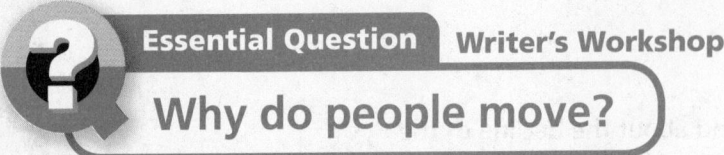

Essential Question   Writer's Workshop

Why do people move?

Prepare to Write
Throughout this chapter, you have explored the Essential Question in your text, journal, and by going On Assignment at myworldhistory.com. Use what you learned to write an essay about the effect of movement on the Roman empire. Identify types of movement that played a role. Then categorize these types of movement as helping the empire to grow or as contributing to its decline.

Workshop Skill: Write Body Paragraphs
In this lesson, you will learn more about how to write the main body of an essay. Review how to outline an essay and to write an introduction. Use the thesis in your introduction to preview the main points you will make in each body paragraph. For this assignment, you will write a five-paragraph essay with three body paragraphs. Suppose your thesis is *Movement played an important role in both the growth and the decline of the Roman empire*. Each body paragraph should develop one main point that supports the thesis. You will use evidence and details to support that main point.

Write a Topic Sentence Start with a topic sentence. A topic sentence states the main idea you will discuss and relates that idea to your thesis. It should flow smoothly from the previous paragraph. Transition words, such as *first, on the other hand,* and *finally,* connect ideas from one paragraph to the next.

Support the Topic Sentence with Evidence Look at the topic sentence you have written. Think of at least three details to support it. These can be facts, statistics, quotations, reasons, and so forth. Each detail helps show why your topic sentence is true.

Add a Concluding Sentence Link your paragraph to your thesis with a concluding sentence. This sentence sums up the paragraph and helps readers understand how the facts you have presented support your thesis

Here is a sample body paragraph:

Topic sentence *First, it is important to define the major types of movement that occurred during the Roman empire.*

Supporting detail *Military movement occurred when Roman soldiers traveled great distances to conquer new lands for the empire.*

Supporting detail *Trade was another kind of movement, as Roman merchants took goods to faraway places and returned with other goods.*

Supporting Detail *A third important category is movement of ideas. Some idea movement was deliberate, such as when Jesus and his followers traveled to spread Christian ideas. Other movement of ideas occurred as a result of trade or military conquest.*

Concluding sentence *Each type of movement played a role in both the growth and the decline of the Roman empire.*

Write a Body Paragraph

Now write your body paragraph for your essay.

Topic sentence

_____

_____

Supporting detail

_____

_____

Supporting detail

_____

_____

Supporting detail

_____

_____

Concluding sentence

_____

_____

Draft Your Essay

Use the body paragraph above in your essay, which will be written on another paper. Check that each body paragraph includes a topic sentence, supporting details, and a concluding sentence.

Name _____ Class _____ Date _____

Places to Know!

Map Skills Use the maps in this unit to identify the Places to Know! on the outline map. Before the name of each place below, write the letter that shows its location on the map.

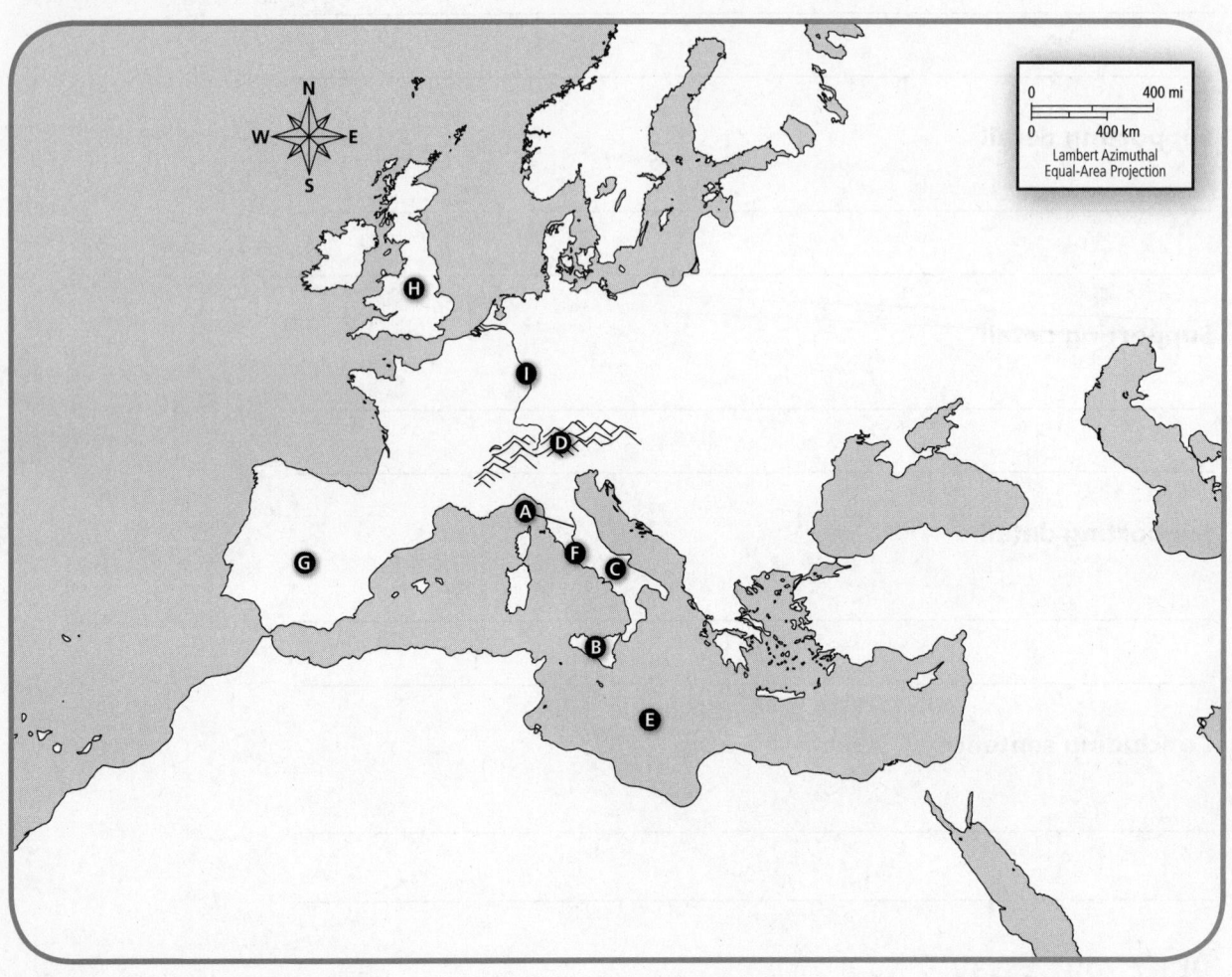

_____ **Mediterranean Sea**

_____ **Tiber River**

_____ **Rhine River**

_____ **Alps**

_____ **Rome**

_____ **Italy**

_____ **Sicily**

_____ **Britain**

_____ **Spain**

Key Events

Timeline Use what you have read about ancient Rome to complete the timeline below. Draw a line from each event to its correct position on the timeline. Then write a brief description of each event.

1000 B.C.

Around 800 B.C. _____
_____

A.D. 146 _____
_____

750 B.C.

500 B.C. _____
_____

A.D. 180 _____
_____

500 B.C.

44 B.C. _____
_____

A.D. 235–284 _____
_____

A.D. 1

A.D. 33 _____
_____

A.D. 380 _____
_____

A.D. 250

A.D. 476 _____
_____

A.D. 500

Name _____ Class _____ Date _____

Essential Question

What distinguishes one culture from another?

Preview Before you begin this chapter, think about the Essential Question. Understanding how the Essential Question connects to your life will help you understand the chapter you are about to read.

Connect to Your Life

(1) Think about what defines culture. For example, culture can be art, religion, or government. Identify as many elements as you can. Then list some examples of ways that these factors affect your life. List at least one example in each column.

How Culture Affects Me			
Science	• Technology	• Family Traditions	• Other (art, language)

(2) Think about some of the differences in culture you and your classmates have identified. Why might a culture change over time?

_____

_____

Connect to the Chapter

(3) Explore ways that national cultures can change. Preview the chapter by skimming the chapter's headings, photographs, and graphics. In the table below, list your predictions about how Byzantine culture changed over time.

	• When Western Roman Empire Collapsed	• During Byzantine Empire
Government/Laws		
Art		
Religion		

(4) Read the chapter. Then review your predictions. Circle those that were correct.

Name _____ Class _____ Date _____

Connect to myStory: The Nika Riot: Theodora's Great Victory

(1) Theodora had a decision to make. She could either run for her life, or she could fight for her position. What would you have done if you had to make such a choice? Explain your answer.

_____

_____

(2) Use this Venn diagram to compare your experiences with Theodora's. Think about angry or unpleasant situations and the ways you have dealt with them.

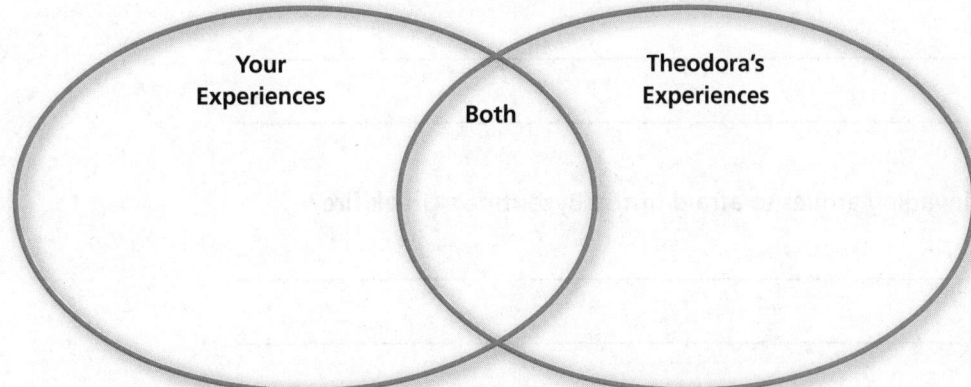

Your Experiences   Both   Theodora's Experiences

(3) In the table below, list the challenges that Theodora faces as empress and the qualities she has that help her deal with those challenges.

Challenges as Empress	Useful Qualities

(4) How do you think believing passionately in ideas could help people establish and expand the Byzantine empire? How might it help to be good at explaining those ideas to others?

_____

_____

Name _____ Class _____ Date _____

Word Wise

Words In Context For each question below, write an answer that shows your understanding of the boldfaced key term.

(1) Why did historians need a new name for the **Byzantine** empire?

_____

_____

_____

(2) How does a **moat** help a city defend itself?

_____

_____

_____

(3) Why were invading armies so afraid of the Byzantine's **Greek fire**?

_____

_____

_____

(4) What were the advantages to Constantinople of its location on a **strait**?

_____

_____

_____

Name _____ Class _____ Date _____

Take Notes

Analyze Cause and Effect Many factors affected the growth and spread of the Byzantine empire. As you read, give details to describe each factor on the left. Then explain its effect on the right.

Factors That Affected the Byzantine Empire

Effects on Byzantine Empire

Geography

Economy

Defense

Justinian's Leadership

Expansion

Civilization

Justinian's Death

Stability

Essential Question

How was the Byzantine empire different from the ancient Roman empire?

_____

_____

Name _____ Class _____ Date _____

Word Wise

Sentence Builder Complete the sentences using the information you learned in this section. You may have to change the form of the words to complete the sentence.

creed   icon
iconoclast   pope
Great Schism

(1) Church leadership was the most important issue between Eastern

Orthodox and Roman Catholic churches in the _____.

(2) The leader of the Roman Catholic church, and the bishop of Rome, was

the _____.

(3) Many Christians believed it was wrong to worship holy images called

_____.

(4) Constantine ordered Church officials to create a clear set of religious

beliefs, which was stated as a _____.

(5) Byzantines who went into churches and destroyed holy images were

called _____.

Name _____ Class _____ Date _____

Take Notes

Compare and Contrast In this section, you read how the Christian Church became divided. List features that the Roman Catholic Church and the Eastern Orthodox Church shared and features that made each church unique.

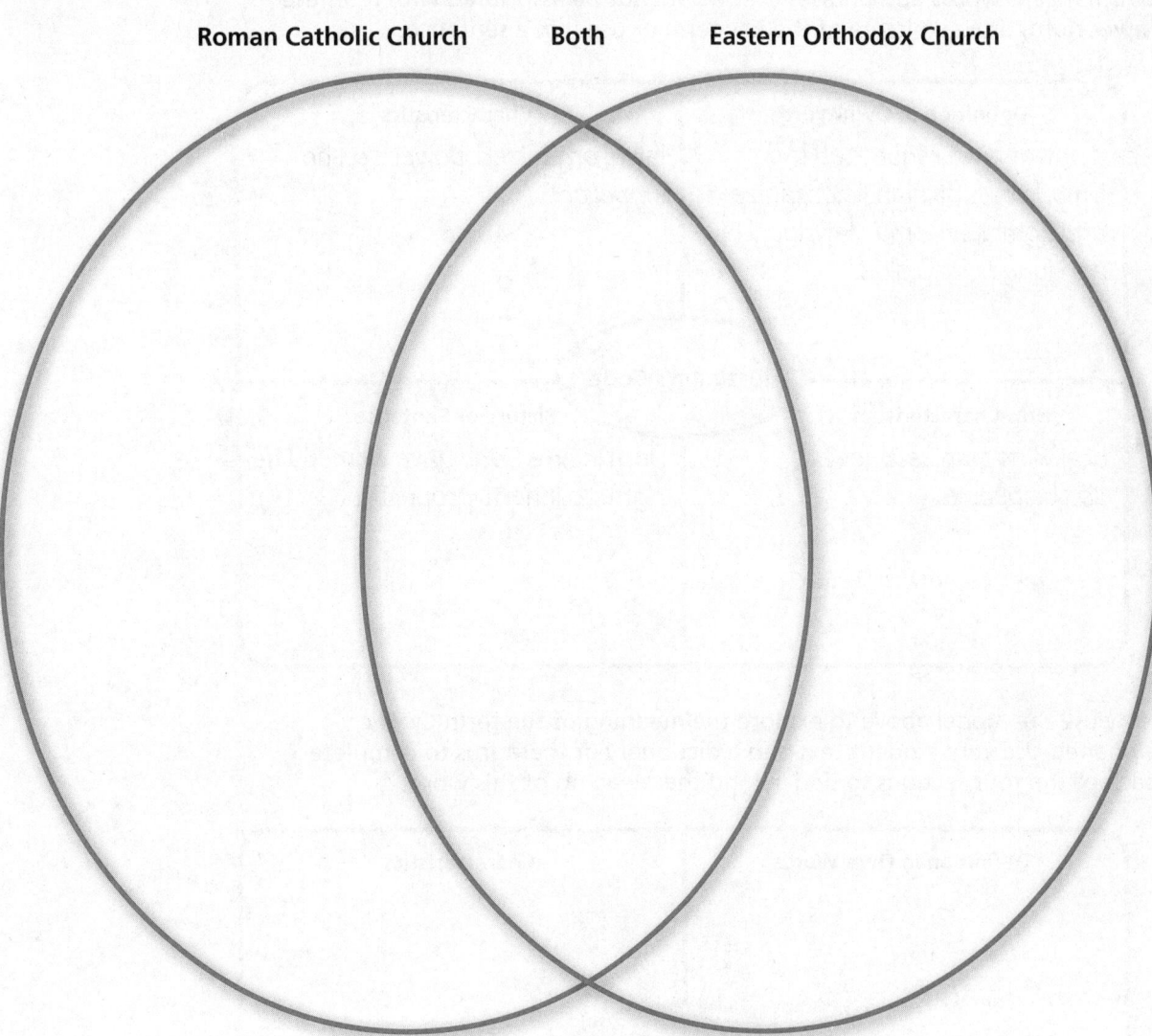

Roman Catholic Church   Both   Eastern Orthodox Church

Essential Question

What is one way in which culture set the Eastern Orthodox and Roman Catholic churches apart?

_____

_____

_____

Word Wise

Word Map Follow the model below to make a word map. The key term *Justinian's Code* is in the center oval. Write the definition in your own words at the upper left. In the upper right, list Characteristics, which means words or phrases related to the term. At the lower left, list Non-Characteristics, which means words and phrases that would *not* be associated with it. In the lower right, draw a picture of the key term *or* use it in a sentence.

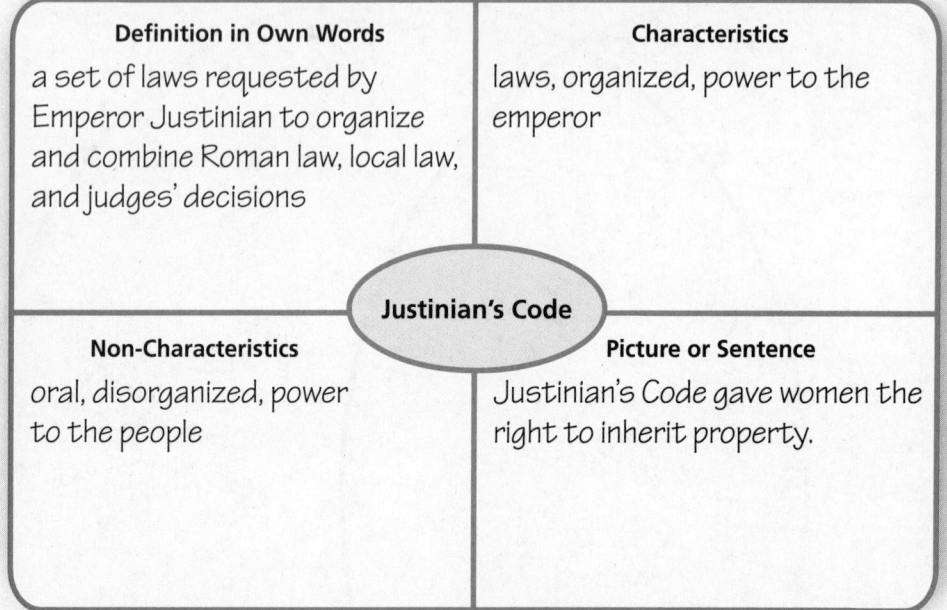

Definition in Own Words

a set of laws requested by Emperor Justinian to organize and combine Roman law, local law, and judges' decisions

Characteristics

laws, organized, power to the emperor

Justinian's Code

Non-Characteristics

oral, disorganized, power to the people

Picture or Sentence

Justinian's Code gave women the right to inherit property.

Now use the model above to explore the meaning of the term *Cyrillic alphabet*. Use your student text and a dictionary or thesaurus to complete each of the four sections to understand the meaning of this word.

Definition in Own Words

Characteristics

Cyrillic alphabet

Non-Characteristics

Picture or Sentence

Make word maps of your own on a separate piece of paper for the word *missionary*.

Name _____ Class _____ Date _____

Take Notes

Summarize In this section, you read about Byzantine civilization and its influence on the world. In each box below, write a main idea and two details about each subheading in the text. Then write a sentence summarizing the effect of the Byzantine empire on the world around it.

A Unique Culture	The Empire's Influence	Early Russia
Main Idea	**Main Idea**	**Main Idea**
Detail	**Detail**	**Detail**
Detail	**Detail**	**Detail**

Summary:

_____

_____

Essential Question

How did the Byzantine empire change the cultures of the Slavic peoples of Eastern Europe?

_____

_____

_____

Name _____ Class _____ Date _____

What distinguishes one culture from another?

Prepare to Write

Throughout this chapter, you have explored the Essential Question in your text, journal, and On Assignment at myworldhistory.com. Use what you learned to write a compare and contrast essay on how Byzantine culture differed from the Roman culture from which it arose. Consider the following aspects of culture: ethnic, religious, legal, art and architecture, and even location.

Workshop Skill: Write a Conclusion

Review how to write an essay. Consider the main point you want to make in your essay and phrase it as a thesis statement. For example: *The culture of the Byzantine empire continued many features of Roman culture, but also developed its own unique features.* In your introduction, list and briefly describe three aspects of culture that you will compare and contrast. In each body paragraph, explain how an aspect of culture is shared by both cultures or unique to one. Use details and evidence to support the comparison. For example, you might say that Christianity both united and divided the Byzantine and Roman cultures. Then you would give specific examples.

In this lesson, you will learn more about how to complete your compare and contrast essay with a conclusion. The conclusion of a compare and contrast essay has three goals. It must restate your main thesis. It must briefly mention exceptions to your thesis or main points. Finally, it must give readers a way to move beyond the essay, perhaps to a larger topic or one of more current importance.

Restate and Connect Start with a sentence that recalls your topic and thesis. Then add a sentence that uses vivid language to help readers visualize the comparison. For example, you might describe Byzantine architecture.

Mention Exceptions Next, imagine you are answering questions about your essay. What holes or gaps might someone question in your comparison and contrast? In one or two sentences, identify one of these holes or gaps and explain why it isn't important to the overall comparison.

Connection Beyond Finish your conclusion by connecting your comparison to the larger Essential Question *and* to contemporary issues, answering the question: Why should this comparison matter to your readers? Discuss ways that people can understand their world today by understanding this issue in history.

Here is a sample conclusion:

Sample Restatement As comparison of these features show, Byzantine art, religion, and legal systems had a great deal in common with Roman culture, and yet they had several unique features. For example, Byzantine churches shape the skyline with domes that highlight differences between the two churches.

Sample Exception Discussion It is true that early iconoclasts were Byzantine. However, in time this view was isolated to Western Christians, and Eastern Orthodox Christians became free to use icons as they wished in the practice of their religion.

Sample Connection Beyond These two great cultures—and their religions—were as similar as they were different. In the same way, today's great cultures can find common ground while respecting one another's differences.

Draft Your Essay

Now write your own conclusion for your essay.

Restatement _____

_____

_____

Exception Discussion _____

_____

_____

_____

Connection Beyond _____

_____

_____

_____

Use the conclusion above in your complete essay (written on other paper). Check your conclusion for a thesis restatement, discussion of an exception, and a clearly stated connection beyond the essay.

Essential Question

How are religion and culture connected?

Preview Before you begin this chapter, think about the Essential Question. Understanding how the Essential Question connects to your life will help you understand the chapter you are about to read.

Connect to Your Life

(1) Think about the connection between religion and culture. How can you tell that people in your community practice religion?

_____

_____

(2) Now think about the way that religion affects culture. In the table below, describe elements of your local culture and explore ways that religion influences these elements.

Elements of Local Culture	Description or Example	Influence of Religion
Importance of Study		
Roles of Men and Women		
Regular Shared Rituals		

Connect to the Chapter

(3) Before you read the chapter, preview its headings, images, and captions. Then complete the table by making predictions about ways that religion might have affected the culture of Islamic civilization.

Elements of the Culture of Islamic Civilization	Description or Example	Influence of Religion
Government and Rulers		
Regular Rituals		
Art and Architecture		

(4) Read the chapter, then circle and revise predictions that were not correct.

_____

_____

_____

Name _____ Class _____ Date _____

Connect to myStory: Ibn Battuta's Voyage

(1) Think about ways your life is like Ibn Battuta's. What have you learned from visiting new places or meeting new people?

_____

_____

(2) Use this Venn diagram to compare your experiences with Ibn Battuta's. Think about regular travels, interactions with new people and places, and lessons that were learned.

Your Experiences   **Both**   **Ibn Battuta's Experiences**

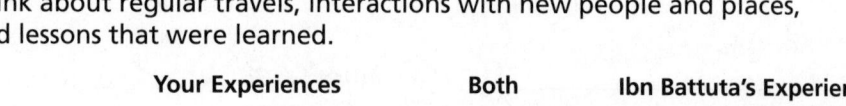

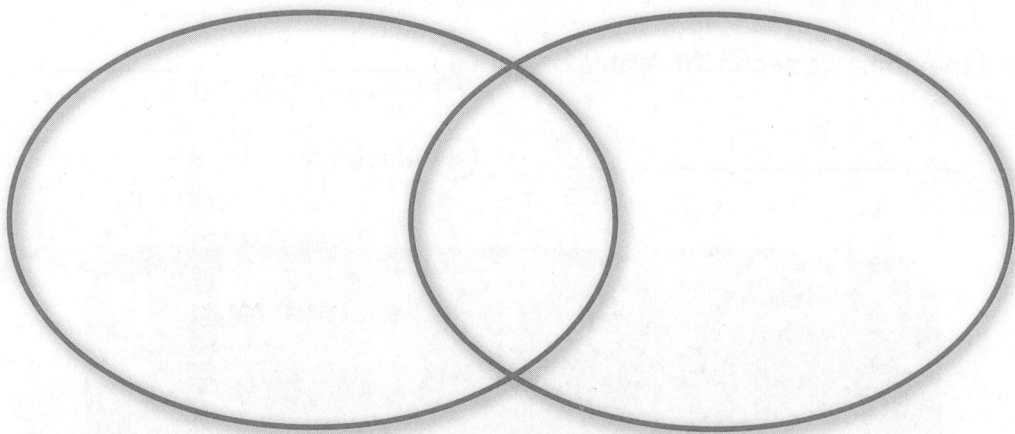

(3) What personal qualities did Ibn Battuta possess that caused him to make such a long journey?

_____

_____

Word Wise

Vocabulary Quiz Show Some quiz shows ask a question and expect the contestant to give the answer. In other shows, the contestant is given an answer and must supply the question. If the blank is in the Question column, write the question that would result in the answer in the Answer column. If the question is supplied, write the answer.

QUESTION

ANSWER

(1) Where is a place in the desert that water can be found?

(1) _____

(2) _____

(2) hijra

(3) Who are the nomadic people of Arabia?

(3) _____

(4) _____

(4) Kaaba

Name _____ Class _____ Date _____

Take Notes

Identify Main Ideas and Details In this section, you read about the geography and culture in Arabia both before and after the rise of Islam. Now list important ideas for each part of the text, along with two details for each main idea.

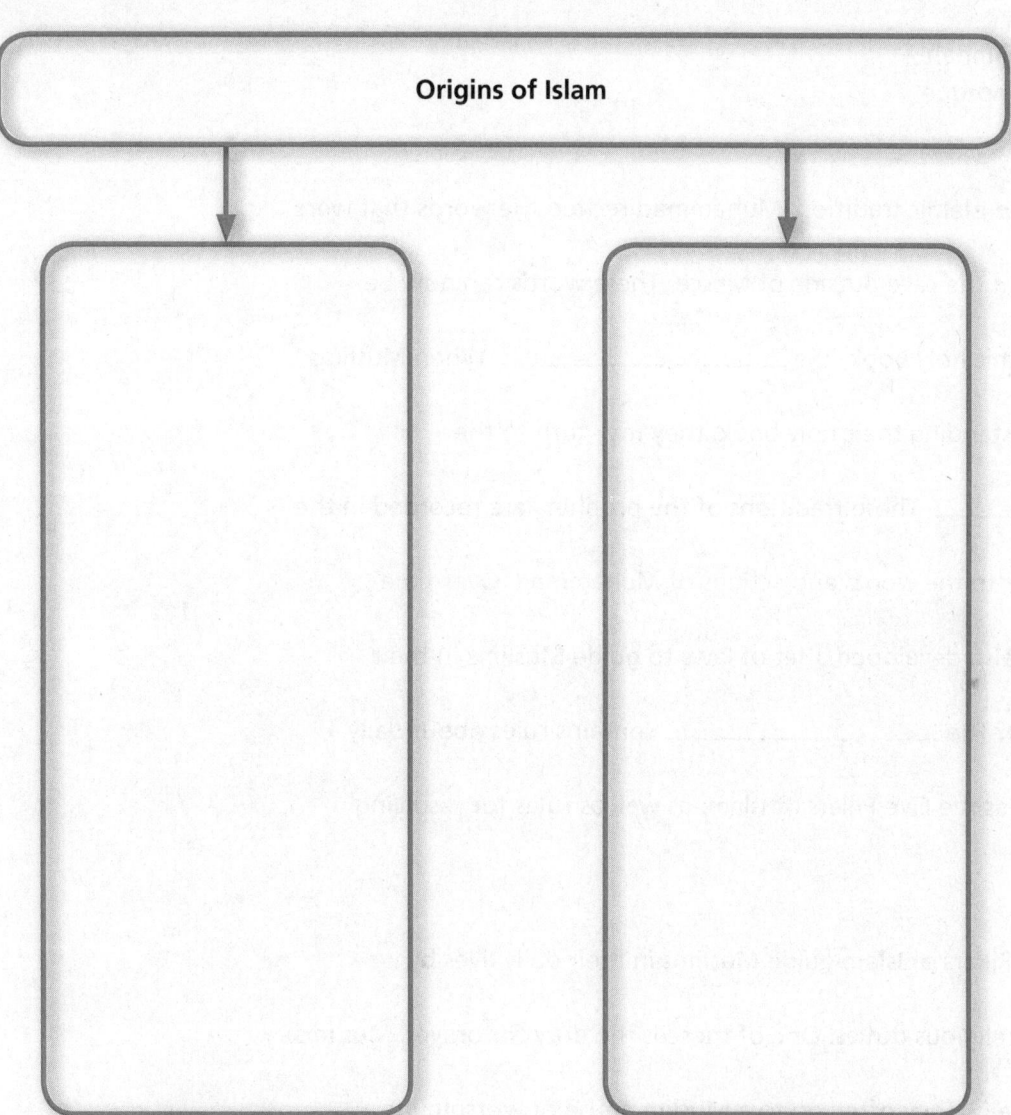

Origins of Islam

Essential Question

How did the coming of Islam change what religious activities took place at the Kaaba?

_____

_____

Word Wise

Use a Word Bank Choose one word from the word bank to fill in each blank. When you have finished, you will have a short summary of important ideas from the section.

Word Bank

Quran	Sunnah
hajj	mosque
Sharia	

According to Islamic tradition, Muhammad recited the words that were revealed to him in the cave outside of Mecca. These words can now be found in the Islamic holy book, the _____. When Muslims need help understanding their holy book, they may turn to the _____. These traditions of the prophets are recorded in the Hadith, and refer to the words and actions of Muhammad. Over time, Muslim scholars also developed a set of laws to guide Muslims in their personal conduct. The _____ contains rules about daily obligations such as the Five Pillars of Islam, as well as rules for resolving family issues.

The Five Pillars of Islam guide Muslims in their daily lives by describing their religious duties. One of these is the duty for prayer. Muslims pray five times daily. They often go to a Muslim house of worship, or _____. The fifth pillar is for pilgrimage. This obligation calls on Muslims to travel to Mecca at least once in their lives. Making the _____ to the shrines of the holy city brings Muslims together from around the world.

Name _____ Class _____ Date _____

Take Notes

Summarize In the table below, record important words or phrases that summarize each aspect of Islamic belief. Then write a brief paragraph summarizing these beliefs.

Sources of Islamic Teachings	• Beliefs About • God	• The Five Pillars • of Islam	• Prayer, Pilgrimage, • and Law

Summary

_____

_____

_____

_____

_____

_____

_____

Essential Question

How does the hajj help strengthen the community of Muslims around the world?

_____

_____

_____

Name _____ Class _____ Date _____

Word Wise

Words In Context For each question below, write an answer that shows your understanding of the boldfaced key term.

(1) What was the job of both early and later **caliphs,** and how did Muslim ideas apply to those jobs?

_____

_____

_____

(2) According to the **Sunnis,** what characteristics did a Muslim leader need?

_____

_____

_____

(3) What would a **Shia** Muslim have looked for in a leader?

_____

_____

_____

(4) In what states would you find **sultans,** and how would sultans be the same as or different from caliphs?

_____

_____

_____

Name _____ Class _____ Date _____

Take Notes

Sequence In this section, you learned about different Muslim empires and states. On the flowchart below, describe the main empires in historical order.

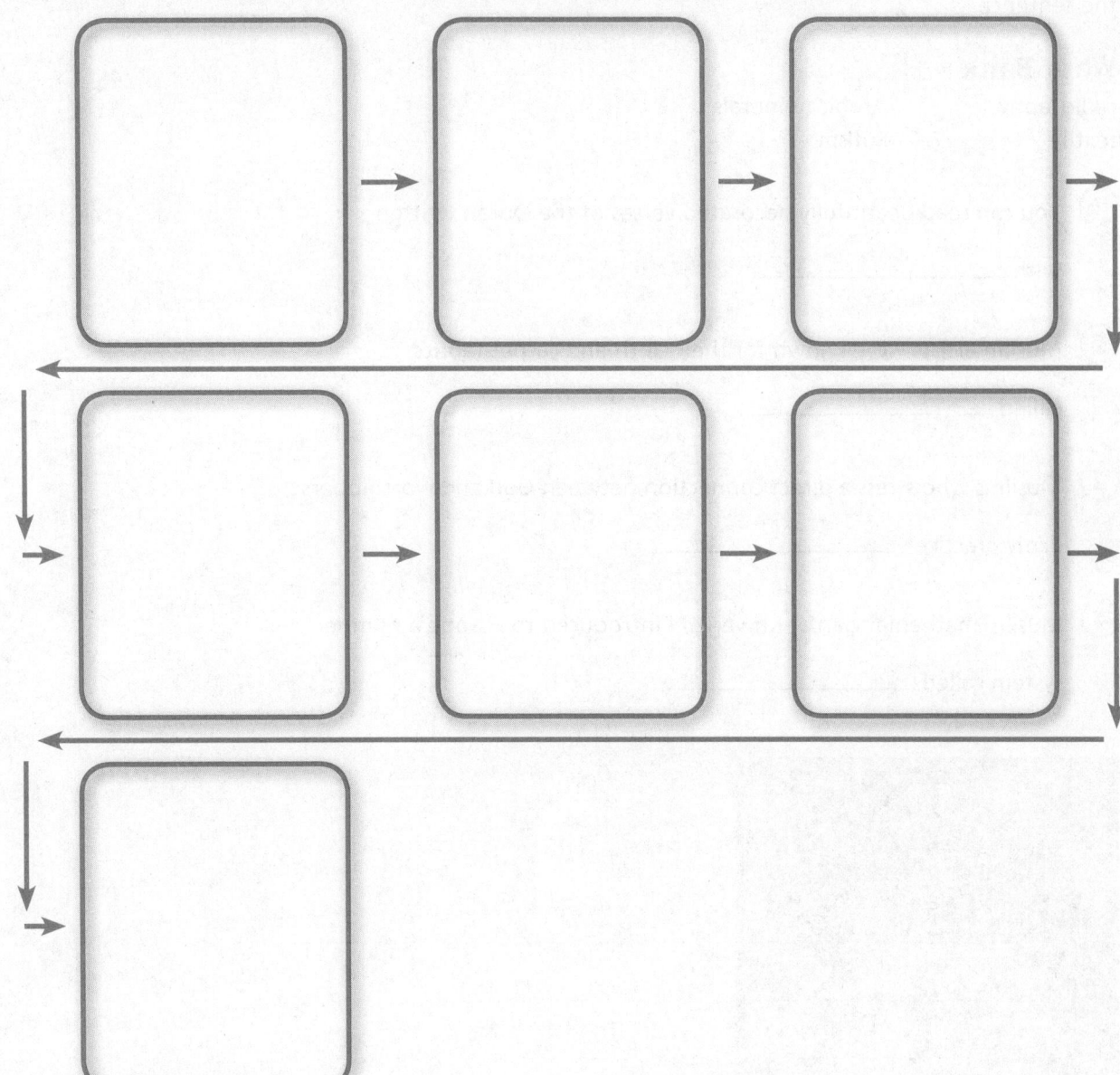

Essential Question

What changed about Persian culture after the Arab Islamic conquest of Persia? What did not change?

_____

_____

_____

Word Wise

Sentence Builder Complete the sentences using the information you learned in this section. You may have to change the form of the words to complete the sentence.

Word Bank

calligraphy   Arabic numerals

textile   Sufism

① You can read beautifully decorated verses of the Quran written

with _____.

② Muslim artists were known for their cloth and carpet fabrics

called _____.

③ Muslims who stress a direct connection between God and worshippers

likely practice _____.

④ Muslim mathematician al-Khwarizmi introduced to Europe a number

system called _____.

Name _____ Class _____ Date _____

Take Notes

Analyze Cause and Effect In Sections 1–3, you read about ways that Islamic civilization expanded. In the web below, describe some achievements that this expansion created in different areas.

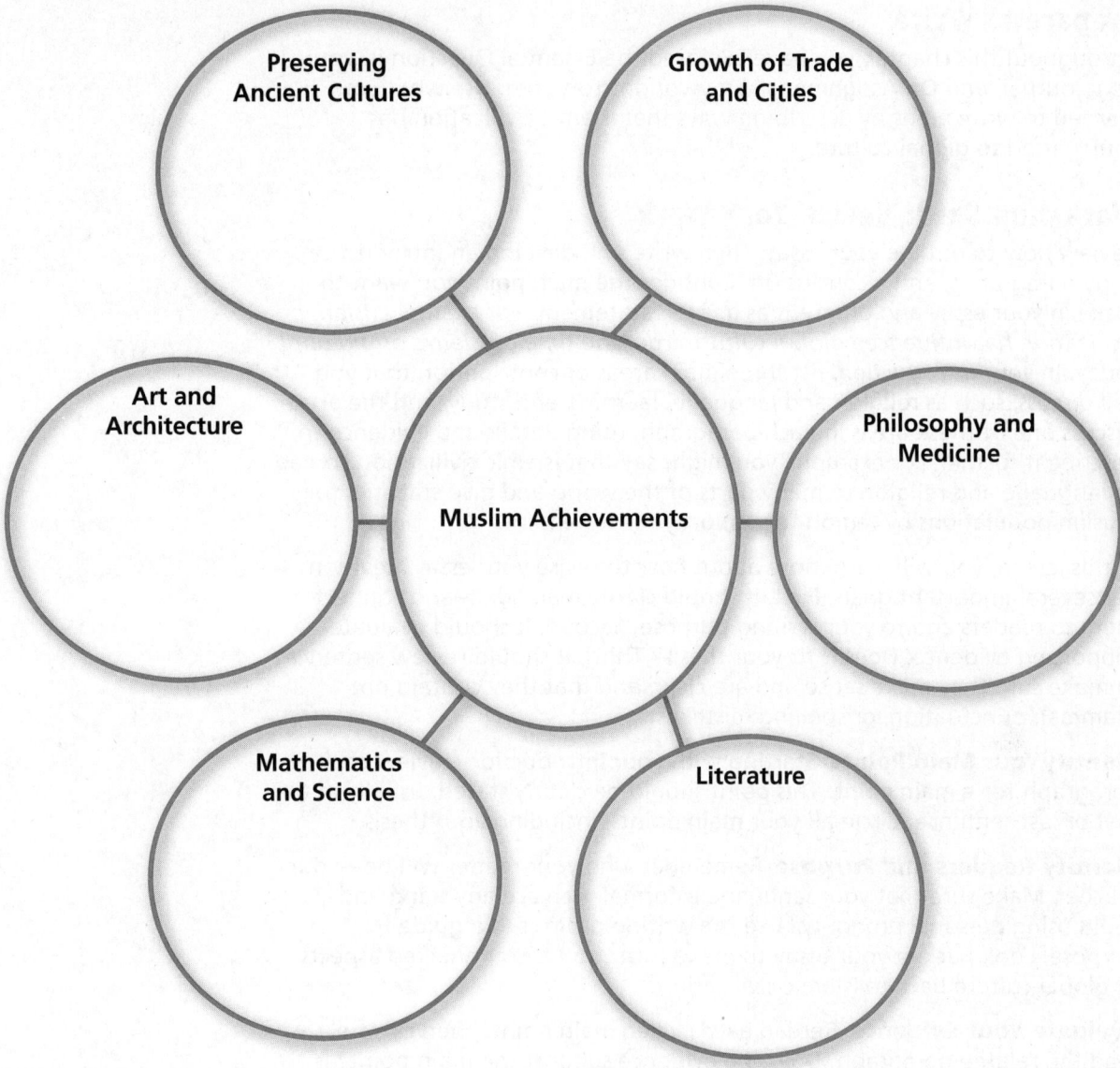

Preserving Ancient Cultures

Growth of Trade and Cities

Art and Architecture

Muslim Achievements

Philosophy and Medicine

Mathematics and Science

Literature

Essential Question

How did religion help increase literacy in Islamic civilization?

_____

_____

_____

Name _____ Class _____ Date _____

How are religion and culture connected?

Prepare to Write

Throughout this chapter, you have explored the Essential Question in your text, journal, and On Assignment at myworldhistory.com. Use what you learned to write an essay describing ways that Islamic civilization has contributed to global culture.

Workshop Skill: Revise Your Work

Review how to outline your essay. Then write and develop an introduction, body paragraphs, and a conclusion. Consider the main point you want to make in your essay and phrase it as a thesis statement. For example: *Islamic civilization has influenced global culture from the time of Islam's origin until today*. In your introduction, list three main areas of contribution that you will discuss, such as religion and language, learning and study, and the arts. Discuss one of these areas in each paragraph, using details and evidence to describe it further. For example, you might say that Islamic civilization spread its language and religion to many parts of the world and give statistics for Muslim populations by region to support your statement.

In this lesson, you will learn more about how to revise your essay. Revision has several important goals: First, it should clarify main ideas and connect them to readers and to your writing purpose. Second, it should evaluate supporting evidence: Does it fit your thesis? Third, it should review sentences to make sure they make sense and are clear, *and* that they contain no grammar, punctuation, or spelling mistakes.

Identify Your Main Points Starting with your introduction, review each paragraph for a main point. This point should be clearly stated, usually in the first or last sentence. Circle all your main points, including your thesis.

Identify Readers and Purpose Remember who your reader will be—your teacher. Make sure that your language is formal. Replace any slang and avoid using personal pronouns. Use the writing prompt as a guide to purpose. Look back at your essay to make sure you have connected aspects of global culture back to Islamic civilization.

Evaluate Your Evidence Reread each circled main point. Then carefully read the related paragraph. Does the evidence support the main point? Is the evidence organized in a logical manner? For example, you might want to list examples from history in chronological order. Also make sure the evidence supports your biggest main point, your thesis. You may need to reword your thesis slightly to fit the points you've made. Remaining sentences that don't support the thesis and main ideas should be cut.

Be Clear and Correct Now read your essay to yourself to see whether it makes sense. Rewrite confusing sentences or those that contain slang. Then use a computer spelling checker to find and correct any misspellings.

Here is a sample body paragraph with revisions. Notes in parentheses explain the big changes:

Islamic civilization has influenced language and religion in the global culture. For example, many people speak Arabic who otherwise would not. Others have learned to read Arabic so that they may study the Quran. In

(transition added to introduce new supporting evidence)

addition, a~~As~~ the civilization spread, it brought the Muslim faith to many new people and places. In fact, about 80 percent of Muslims today live outside the Arab community in which Islamic civilization began. These global communities have been shaped by Islamic values and religious practices, such

(not related to the main point)

as rules of the Sharia for how to conduct business. ~~The call of the muzzein also organizes ordinary peoples lives around prayer five times each day~~.

(The ritual of praying five times daily)   (makes the link to the essay thesis clear)

~~That's This ritual~~ is important to Muslims everywhere. The language in the market square and the faith people practice every day still directly reflects the influence of Islamic civilization.

Revise Your Essay

Now write a paragraph from your essay and revise it.

_____

_____

_____

_____

_____

_____

Draft Your Essay

Copy the revised paragraph back into your essay. Use it as a guide to revising the remaining paragraphs, checking each one for main ideas, supporting evidence, and grammar/punctuation.

Name _____ Class _____ Date _____

Places to Know!

Map Skills Use the maps in this unit to identify the Places to Know! on the outline map. Before the name of each place below, write the letter that shows its location on the map.

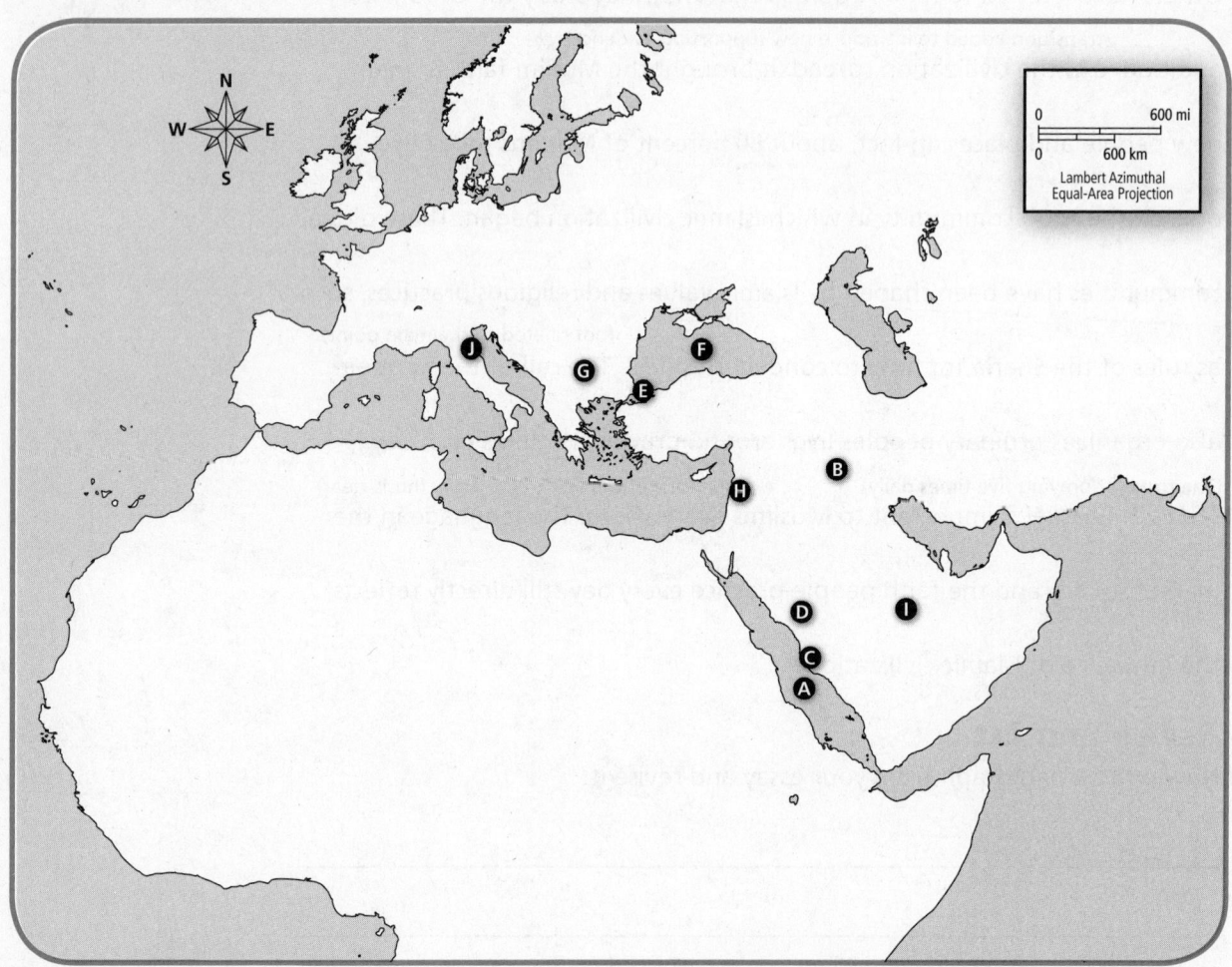

_____ Ravenna

_____ Mecca

_____ Constantinople

_____ Damascus

_____ Black Sea

_____ Medina

_____ Balkans

_____ Arabia

_____ Baghdad

_____ Red Sea

Name _____   Class _____   Date _____

Key Events

Timeline Use what you have read about the Byzantine empire and Islamic civilization to complete the timeline below. Draw a line from each event to its correct position on the timeline. Then write a brief description of each event.

A.D. 500

A.D. 527 _____
_____

A.D. 762 _____
_____

A.D. 600

A.D. 700

A.D. 529 _____
_____

A.D. 1054 _____
_____

A.D. 800

A.D. 900

A.D. 610 _____
_____

A.D. 1204 _____
_____

A.D. 1000

A.D. 1100

A.D. 1258 _____
_____

A.D. 1200

A.D. 630 _____
_____

A.D. 1453 _____
_____

A.D. 1300

Name _____ Class _____ Date _____

Essential Question

What are the consequences of trade?

Preview Before you begin this chapter, think about the Essential Question. Understanding how the Essential Question connects to your life will help you understand the chapter you are about to read.

Connect to Your Life

1 You probably eat many foods that are grown nearby, but some foods can grow only in other climates. They are obtained through international trade. Think of two food items that must be grown in other countries. Then complete the table below.

Trade Item	Where From?	Local Substitute?

2 How does trade affect you personally? Explain.

_____

_____

Connect to the Chapter

3 Skim this chapter's heads, subheads, and visuals to learn about trade in early African civilizations. Then complete the Venn diagram below. Predict the effects of trade on individuals, on nations, and on both individuals and nations.

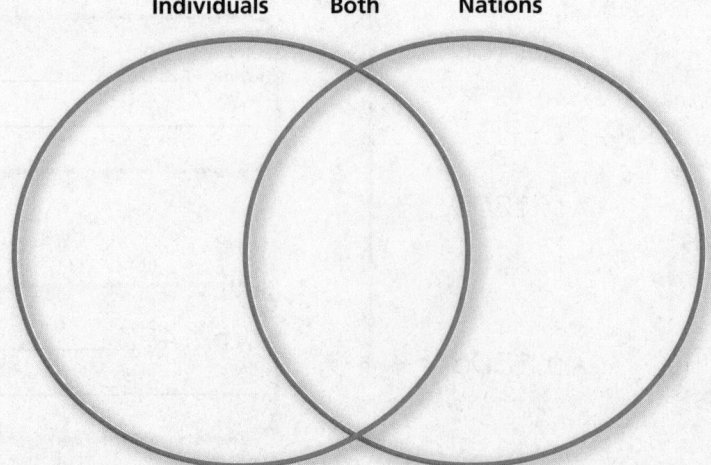

Individuals   Both   Nations

4 After you finish reading the chapter, look at this chart again. Circle your predictions that were correct.

Name _____ Class _____ Date _____

Connect to myStory: Mansa Musa: The Lion of Mali

1 Think about a trip you have taken in order to do something important, whether nearby in your community or somewhere far away. Were there distractions along your route? Did you stop because of them? How did you decide your priorities?

_____

_____

_____

2 Mansa Musa had many reasons to feel that he should not bow to the sultan. List them in the chart below. Then write what Mansa Musa did and explain why he did it.

Reasons Not to Bow to the Sultan	What Mansa Musa Did and Why

3 Think about the events from the story of Mansa Musa's trip. Then write two predictions about things you will learn about empires of ancient Africa.

_____

_____

_____

_____

Name _____ Class _____ Date _____

Word Wise

Use a Word Bank Choose one word from the word bank to fill in each blank. When you have finished, you will have a short summary of important ideas from the section.

Word Bank

labor specialization   natural resources
plateau   savanna
trans-Saharan

Africa has several landforms, including a flat, plate-like

_____ and the Sahara—a large desert. Bands of vegetation

also cross Africa. To the north there is a Mediterranean zone. Above and

below the equator is a grassland called the _____.

The rain forest grows along the equator. Trees, gold, salt, and other

_____ allowed empires to flourish throughout

Africa. Ghana became wealthy because it was along the routes

of the _____ trade in gold and salt.

As food became plentiful, not everyone had to be a farmer in

order to eat. Some people could do other jobs. This division of jobs

and skills is called _____.

Name _____ Class _____ Date _____

Take Notes

Summarize Use what you have learned about African geography and empires to fill in the word web below. Place the title of the section in the top bubble. Place the heads that are printed in red in the bubbles below the title. Then fill in the facts in each part of the section. Add more circles and connections as needed.

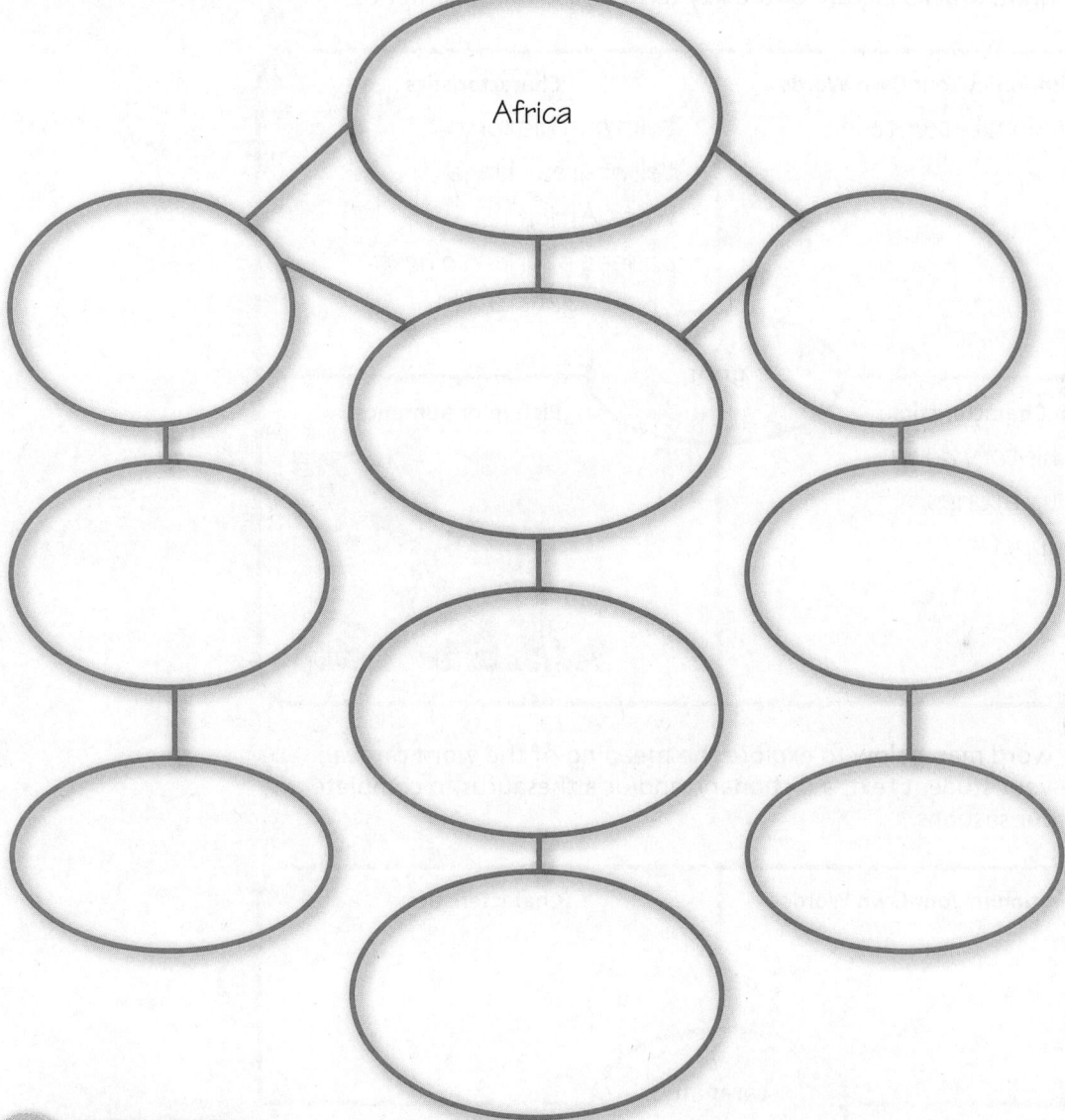

Africa

Essential Question
The Sisse clan became rulers of the Soninke. Explain whether this is an example of labor specialization.

_____

_____

_____

Name _____ Class _____ Date _____

Word Wise

Word Map Follow the model below to make a word map. The key term *griot* is in the center oval. Write the definition in your own words at the upper left. In the upper right, list Characteristics, which means words or phrases that relate to the term. At the lower left list Non-Characteristics, which means words and phrases that would *not* be associated with it. In the lower right, draw a picture of the key term *or* use it in a sentence.

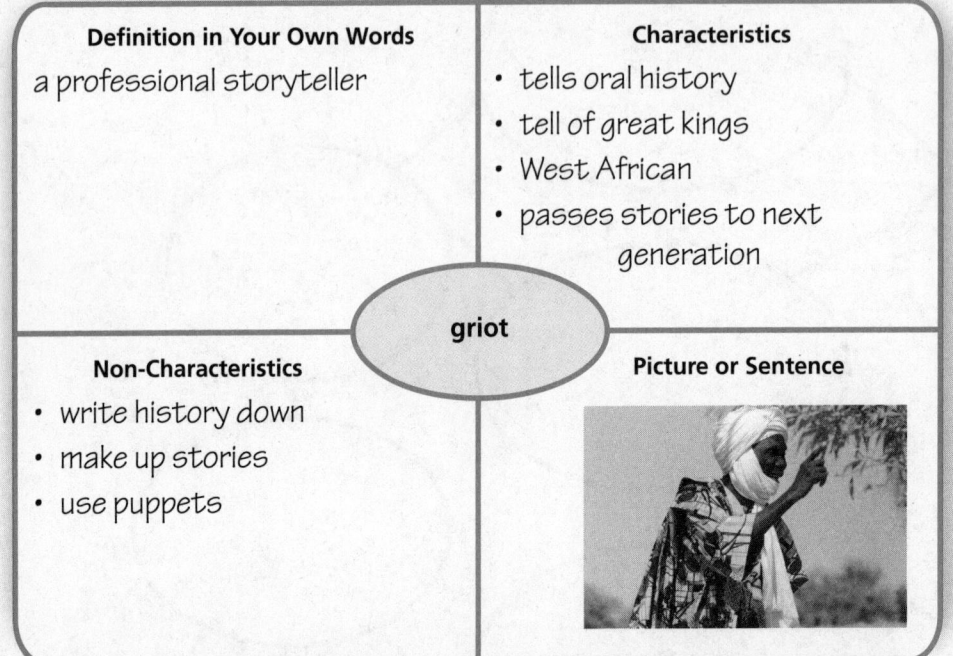

Definition in Your Own Words

a professional storyteller

Characteristics

- tells oral history
- tell of great kings
- West African
- passes stories to next generation

griot

Non-Characteristics

- write history down
- make up stories
- use puppets

Picture or Sentence

Now use the word map below to explore the meaning of the word *caravan*. You may use your student text, a dictionary, and/or a thesaurus to complete each of the four sections.

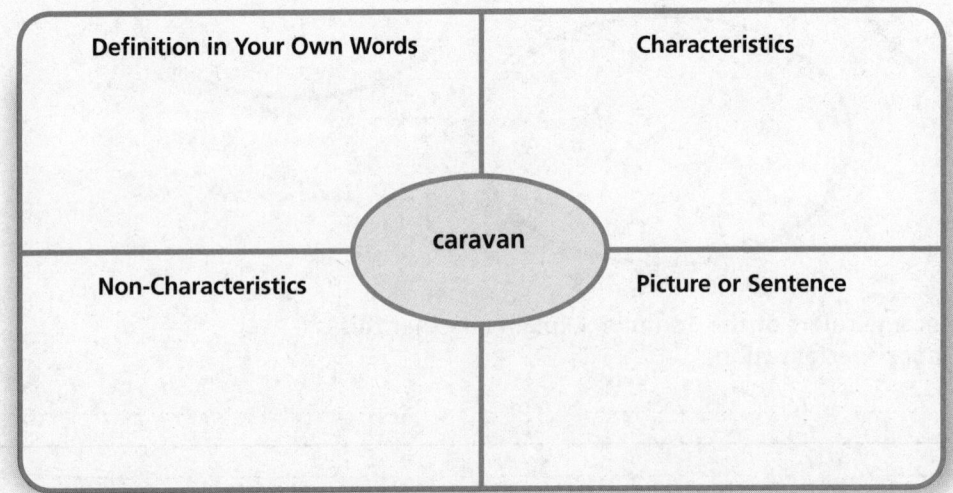

Definition in Your Own Words

Characteristics

caravan

Non-Characteristics

Picture or Sentence

Make a word map of your own on a separate piece of paper for key term: *scholarship.*

Name _____ Class _____ Date _____

Take Notes

Sequence Use what you have read about the rise of Mali and Songhai to complete the timeline. Identify the key event associated with each date on the timeline and give a brief description of the event and its importance.

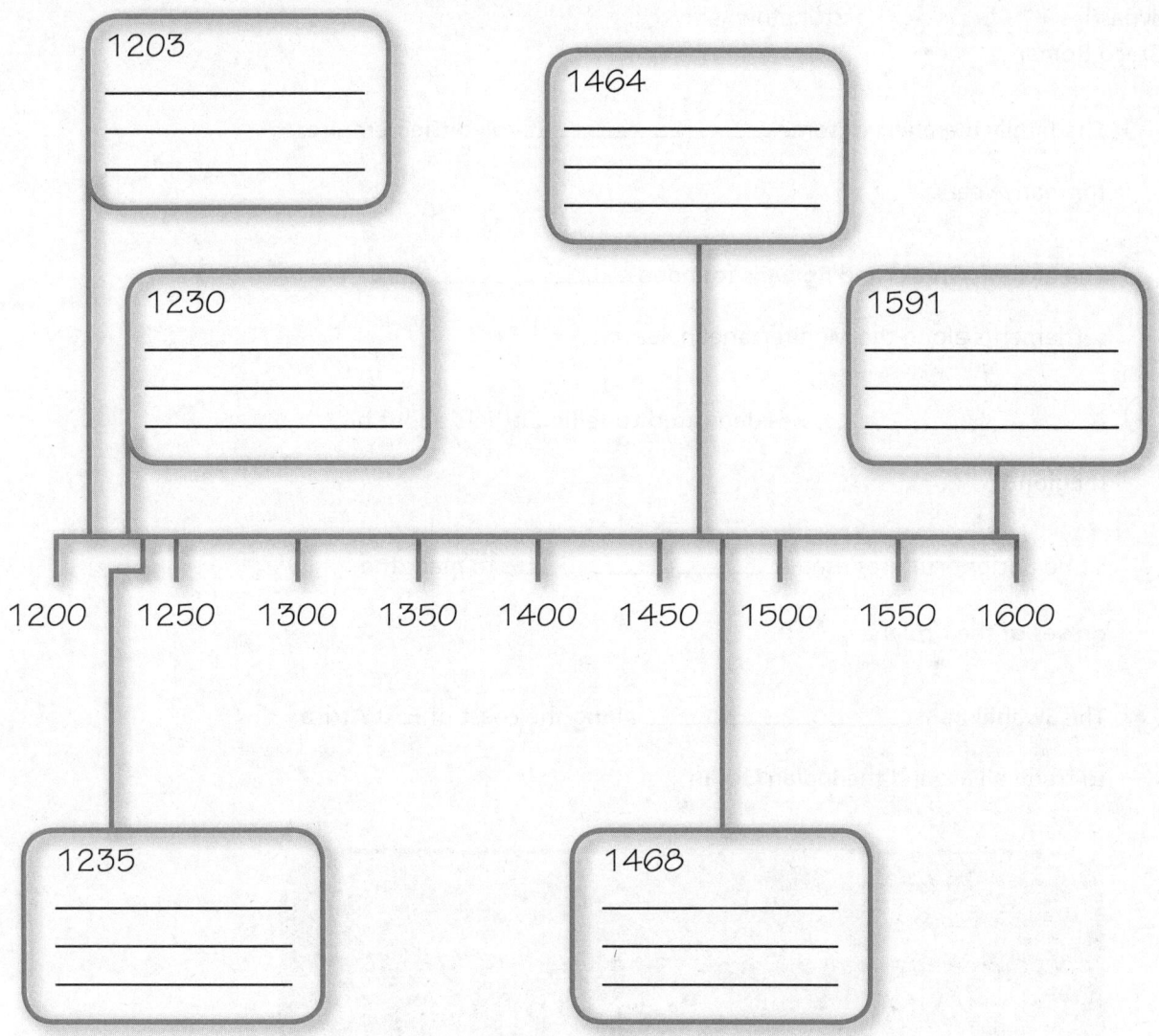

Essential Question

When Songhai became powerful, what do you think happened to the people of Ghana?

_____

_____

_____

Word Wise

Sentence Builder Complete the sentences using the information you learned in this section and the key terms below.

monk   stele
dynasties   stonetowns
Greco-Roman

① The family members of some _____ ruled their empires

for many years.

② The ancient Greeks and Romans founded _____

settlements along the Mediterranean Sea.

③ A _____ was dedicated to telling others about his

religion.

④ Some ancient cultures used a _____ to mark the

graves of their rulers.

⑤ The Swahili built _____ along the coast of East Africa

to trade all around the Indian Ocean.

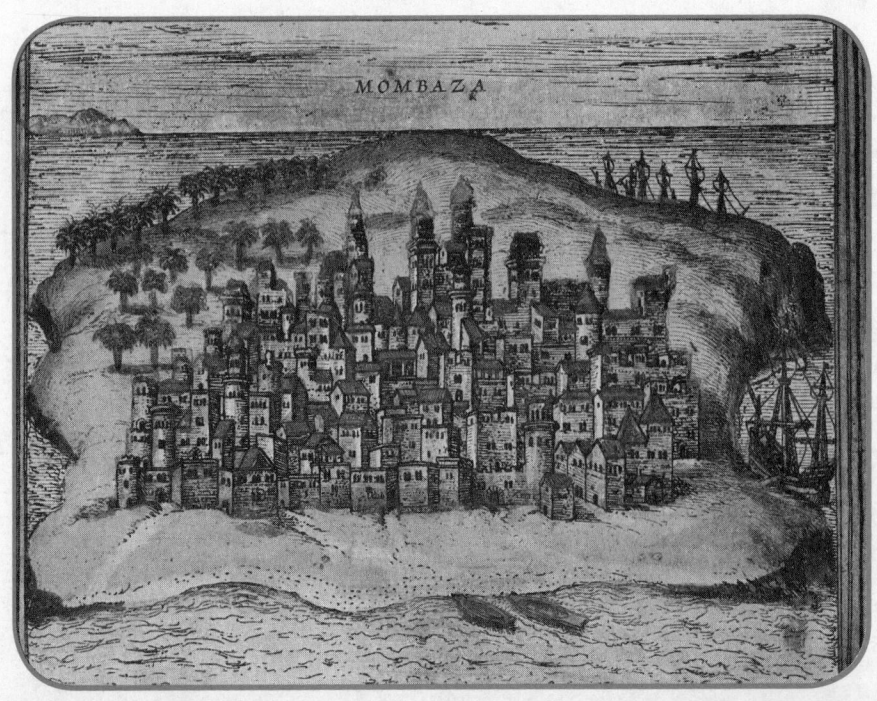

Name _____ Class _____ Date _____

Take Notes

Analyze Cause and Effect Use what you have read about civilizations in East Africa to complete the chart below. In the two boxes below that, write one fact from the paragraphs after the red heading. Below each fact, write one thing that happened as a result of it. The first chart has been filled out for you.

The Kingdoms of Kush and Axum

Fact 1: Kushite merchants traded heavily with Egypt, who wanted Kush's gold.

Result of Fact 1: Egypt took direct control of Kush.

Fact 2: Most trading along the Red Sea took place in Axum's port city of Adulis.

Result of Fact 2: Axum gained great wealth and power.

Christianity in East Africa

Fact 1:

Result of Fact 1:

Fact 2:

Result of Fact 2:

East African City States

Fact 1:

Result of Fact 1:

Fact 2:

Result of Fact 2:

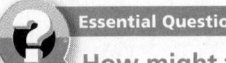 **Essential Question**

How might the lack of natural resources affect a region's ability to trade?

_____

_____

_____

205

Name _____ Class _____ Date _____

Word Wise

Crossword Puzzle The *Across* and *Down* clues are definitions of key terms from this section. Fill in the numbered *Across* boxes with the correct key terms. Then do the same with the *Down* clues.

Across	Down
3. What musical form uses more than one rhythm at a time?	1. Griots were very important in this form of communication.
6. Each person in early West Africa was born into one of these places in society.	2. You might use this type of brief saying to share a bit of wisdom.
7. Each _____ in West Africa has its own way of life and ways of doing things.	4. A person's cousins are all part of one of these.
	5. You might have this close connection with your extended family.

Name _____ Class _____ Date _____

Take Notes

Main Ideas and Details Use what you have read about the society and culture of ancient African empires to complete the chart below.

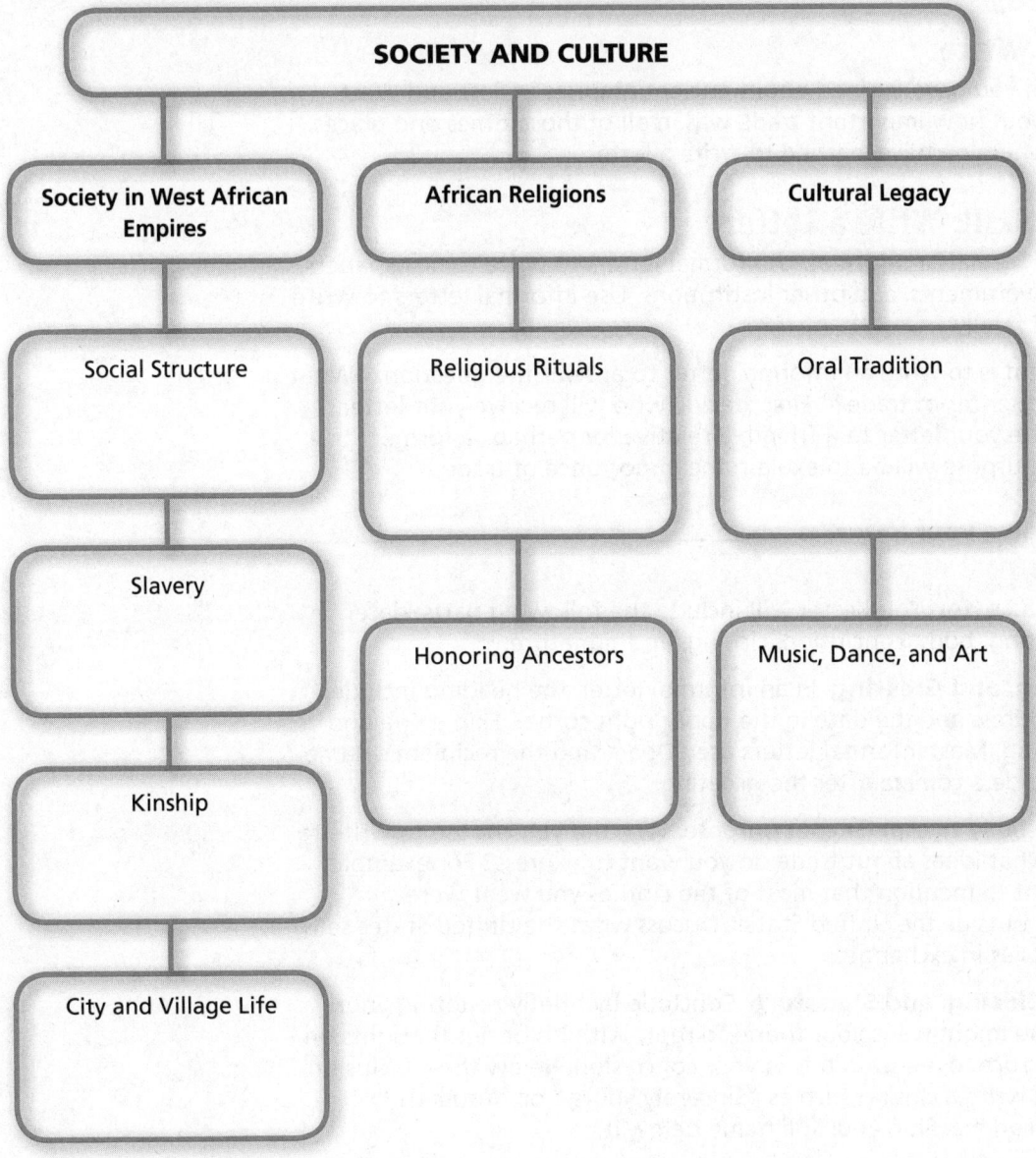

Essential Question

Are art and trade related? Explain.

_____

_____

_____

Name _____ Class _____ Date _____

What are the consequences of trade?

Prepare to Write

In this chapter, you have learned about ancient empires in East and West Africa, and about how important trade was in all of those times and places. You will use what you have learned to write a letter.

Workshop Skill: Write a Letter

Letters can be formal or informal. Use formal letters to write to newspapers, businesses, governments, and other institutions. Use informal letters to write to friends and family.

Your assignment is to write an informal letter to answer the question, "What are the consequences of trade?" First, decide who will receive your letter. You might write your letter to a friend, a relative, or perhaps a former teacher. Your purpose will be to explain the importance of trade.

Who will receive your letter? _____

The Parts of a Letter Your letter will include the following parts: date, heading, greeting, body, conclusion, closing, and signature.

Date, Heading, and Greeting In an informal letter, the heading includes your return address and the date in the upper right corner. Skip a line and add the greeting. Most informal letters use "Dear" and the recipient's name. Be sure to include a comma after the greeting.

Body Use the body to explain your purpose. Why did you choose to write to this person? What ideas about trade do you want to express? For example, you might want to mention that most of the clothes you wear were manufactured outside the United States. Discuss what the United States sells to other countries in exchange.

Conclusion, Closing, and Signature Conclude by briefly restating your main point. You might want your friend to reply with his or her thoughts on the matter. Be sure to mention this in your conclusion. Below the conclusion, skip a line and write a closing such as "Sincerely yours," or "Yours truly," followed by a comma. Sign your full name below it.

Draft Your Letter

Use the format below to write the first draft of your letter.

(your address and
date; do not include
your name) _____

_____

_____

Dear _____

Body _____

_____

_____

_____

_____

_____

_____

_____

_____

_____

_____

_____

_____

Conclusion _____

_____

_____

Closing _____

Your signature _____

Finalize Your Letter

Remember to follow the steps of the writing process to revise and edit your letter. Then neatly copy it onto a clean sheet of paper.

Name _____ Class _____ Date _____

Copyright © Pearson Education, Inc., or its affiliates. All Rights Reserved.

Essential Question

What are the consequences of technology?

Preview Before you begin this chapter, think about the Essential Question. Understanding how the Essential Question connects to your life will help you understand the chapter you are about to read.

Connect to Your Life

① Think of ways in which technology affects your life. Name the technology and then decide whether the effect is positive or negative.

Ways Technology Affects My Life		
Technology	Its Effect	Positive or Negative?

② Look at the table. Compare the effects of technology on your life. Are they always positive? Explain.

_____

_____

Connect to the Chapter

③ Preview the chapter by skimming the chapter's headings, photographs, and graphics. Look for references to technology. Use the information to identify one Chinese technological advance for each category. Then predict how that technology played a role in China's development.

	Technology	Prediction
Education		
Agriculture		
Navigation		
Military		

④ Read the chapter. Then review the predictions you listed in the chart. Which ones were incorrect? Explain why.

_____

_____

Name _____ Class _____ Date _____

Connect to myStory: Kublai Khan: How to Make an Impression

1. Marco Polo saw many remarkable things at Kublai Khan's court. If you had been there with Marco Polo, what would have impressed you the most? Explain.

_____

_____

_____

2. Which three technologies impressed Marco Polo at Kublai Khan's court?

Technology: _____

Technology: _____

Technology: _____

3. How do you think the use of paper money affected China? What did it replace as a means of exchange? What did it do for trade? Write at least two predictions.

_____

_____

_____

_____

Word Wise

Vocabulary Quiz Show Some quiz shows ask a question and expect the contestant to give the answer. In other shows, the contestant is given an answer and must supply the question. If the blank is in the Question column, write the question that would result in the answer in the Answer column. If the question is supplied, write the answer.

QUESTION	ANSWER
1 What do you call a method of promotion based on skills and talent?	**1** _____
2 _____	**2** porcelain
3 What system uses currency rather than bartering?	**3** _____
4 _____	**4** urbanization
5 What were civil servants in China called?	**5** _____
6 _____	**6** bureaucracy

Name _____ Class _____ Date _____

Take Notes

Identify Main Ideas and Details Use what you have read about the Tang and Song dynasties to complete the concept web. Fill in the web with examples of technologies that were invented or improved during these dynasties.

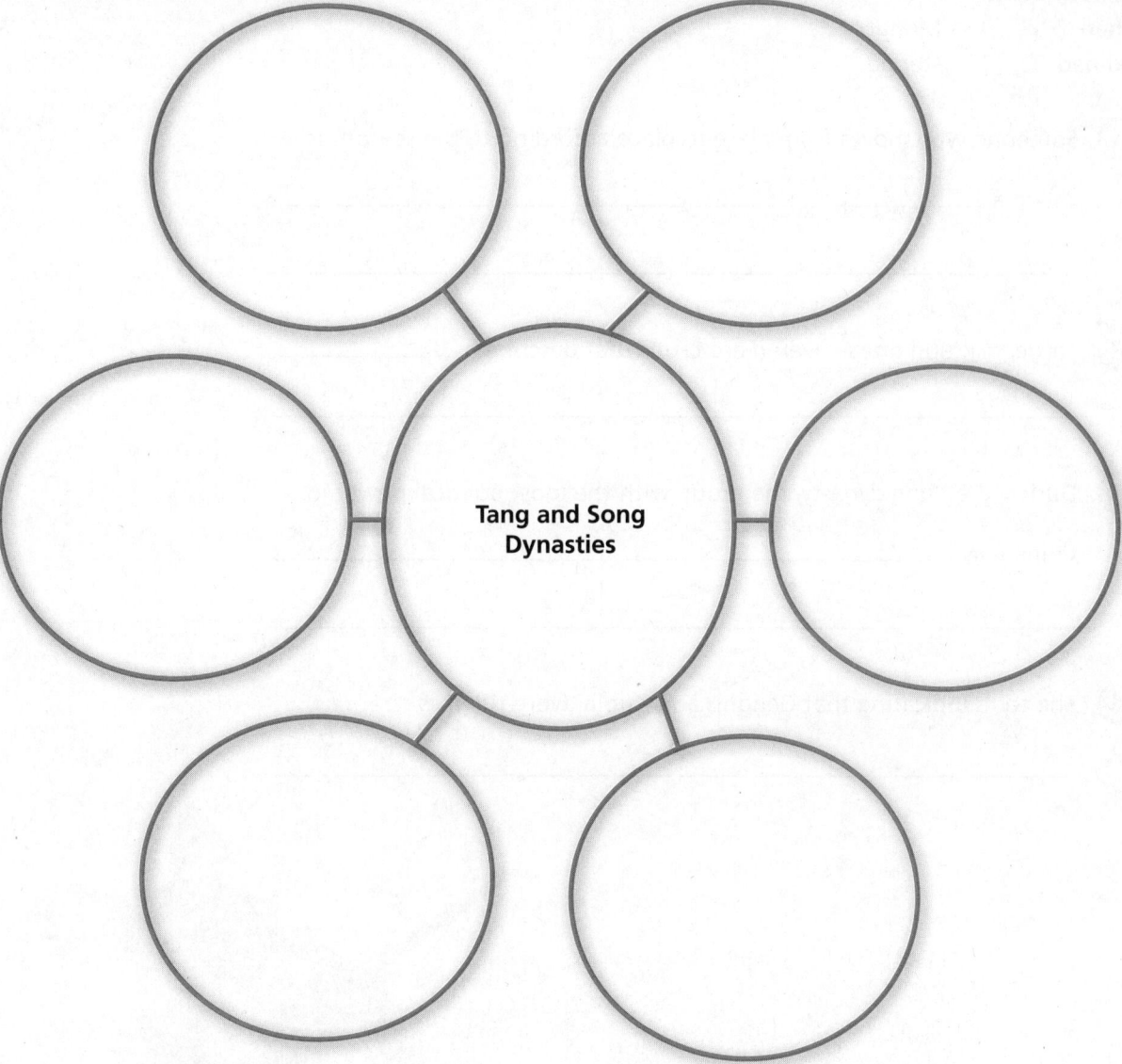

Tang and Song Dynasties

Essential Question

How did new technologies lead to prosperity in China?

_____

_____

_____

Name _____ Class _____ Date _____

Word Wise

Sentence Builder Complete the sentences using the information you learned in this section.

Word Bank
khan   Mongol
nomad   steppe

(1) Someone who moves from place to place according to the seasons is

called a _____

_____.

(2) *Large*, *dry*, and *grass-covered* are terms that describe a _____

_____.

(3) During the Yuan dynasty, the group with the most political power in

China was _____

_____.

(4) The term indicating that Genghis and Kublai were rulers is

_____.

Name _____ Class _____ Date _____

Take Notes

Sequence Use what you have read about the Mongol empire to complete the timeline below. In each box, describe the event that took place in that year. Then, briefly explain why it was important.

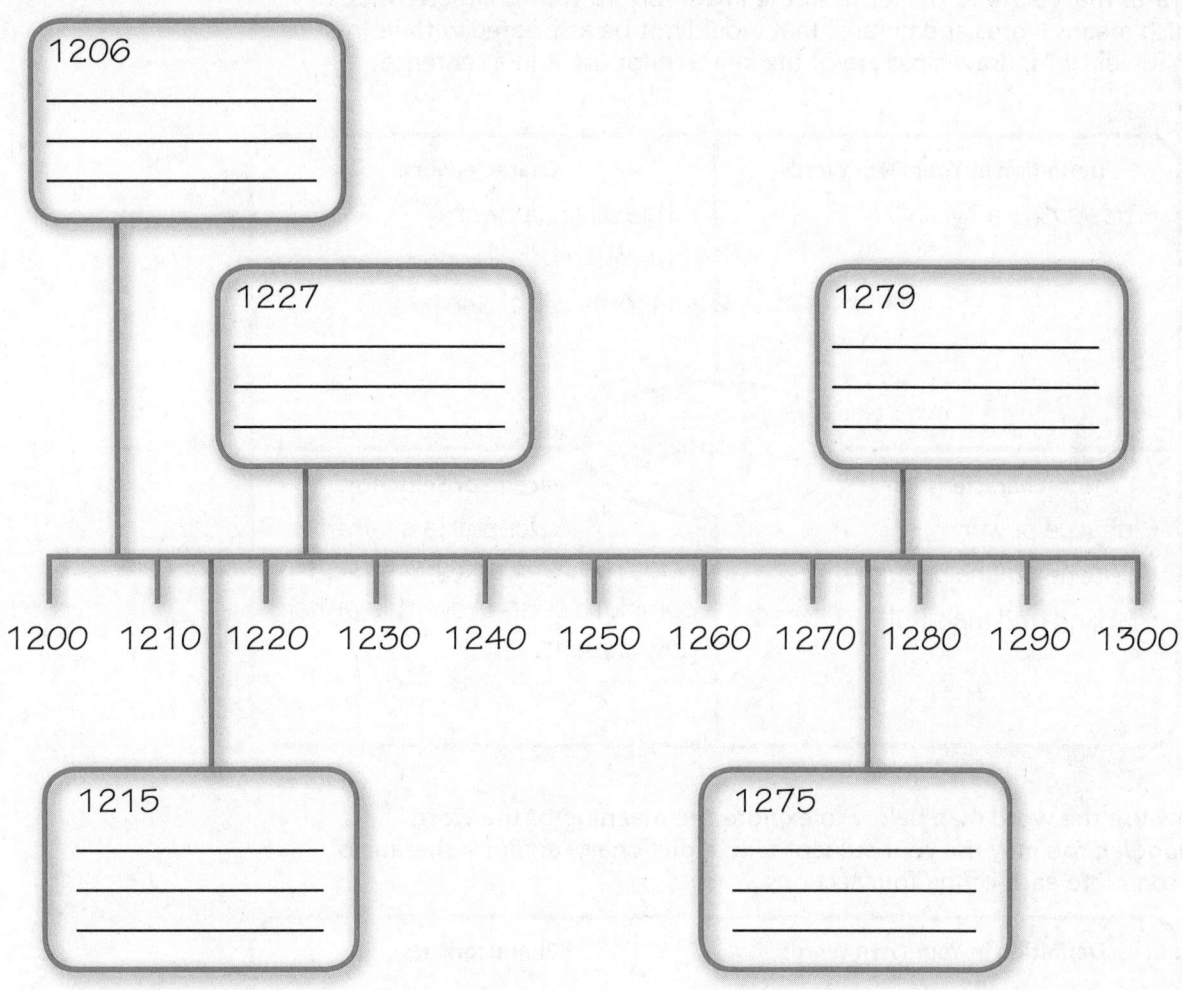

1206 _____

1227 _____

1279 _____

1215 _____

1275 _____

1200 1210 1220 1230 1240 1250 1260 1270 1280 1290 1300

Essential Question

How did military technology help the Mongols?

_____

_____

_____

Name _____ Class _____ Date _____

Word Wise

Word Map Follow the model below to make a word map. The key term *despot* is in the center oval. Write the definition in your own words at the upper left. In the upper right, list Characteristics, which means words or phrases that relate to the term. At the lower left list Non-Characteristics, which means words and phrases that would not be associated with it. In the lower right, draw a picture of the key term or use it in a sentence.

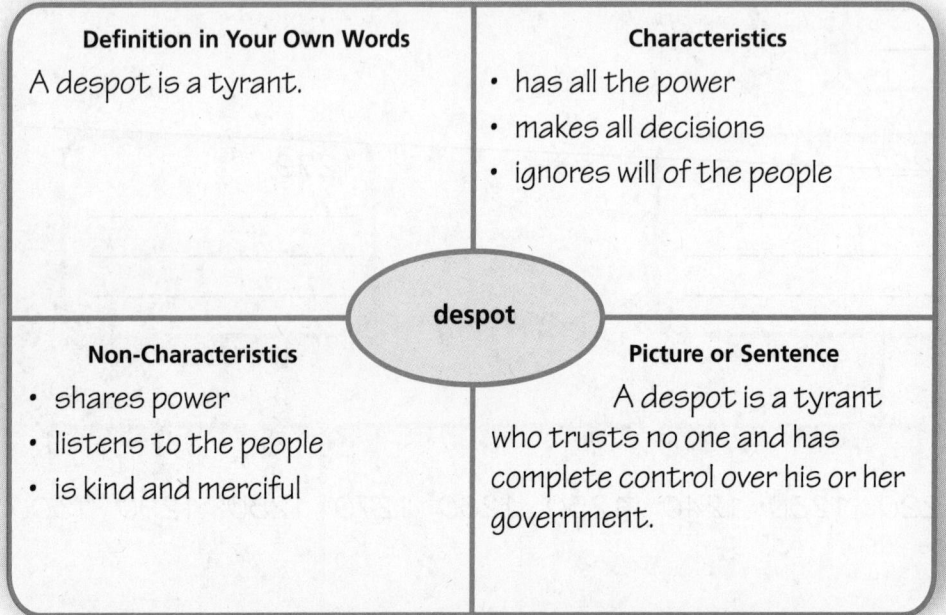

Definition in Your Own Words

A *despot* is a tyrant.

Characteristics

- has all the power
- makes all decisions
- ignores will of the people

despot

Non-Characteristics

- shares power
- listens to the people
- is kind and merciful

Picture or Sentence

A *despot* is a tyrant who trusts no one and has complete control over his or her government.

Now use the word map below to explore the meaning of the word *smuggler*. You may use your student text, a dictionary, and/or a thesaurus to complete each of the four sections.

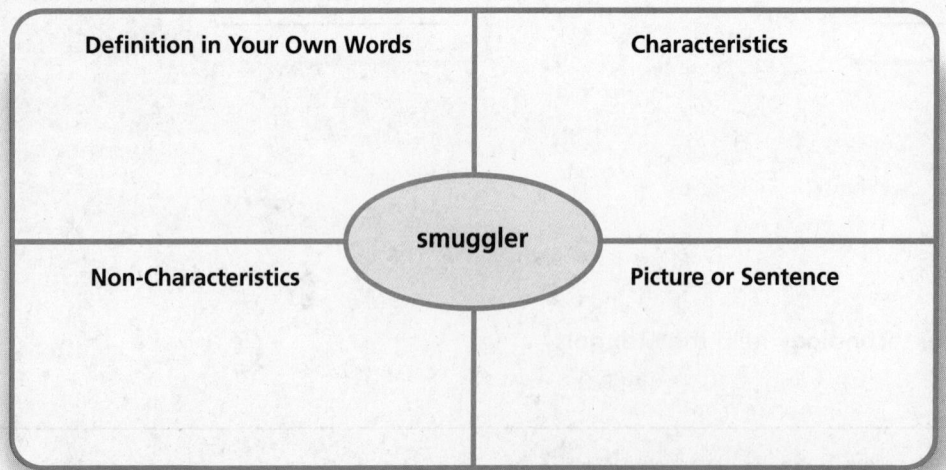

Definition in Your Own Words

Characteristics

smuggler

Non-Characteristics

Picture or Sentence

Make a word map of your own on a separate piece of paper for this word: *tribute.*

Name _____ Class _____ Date _____

Take Notes

Summarize Use the table below to summarize important aspects of the Ming dynasty. In the box on the left, list ways in which the Ming strengthened the government. In the box on the right, list features of Ming foreign policy.

Ming Dynasty	
Government Strengthened by	**Foreign Policy Features**

Essential Question

How did technology allow China to expand the tribute system?

_____

_____

Word Wise

Words In Context For each question below, write an answer that shows your understanding of the boldfaced key term.

(1) What steps does **block printing** involve?

_____

_____

_____

(2) What advantage did the **compass** provide?

_____

_____

_____

(3) What does **Daoism** teach?

_____

_____

_____

(4) What are the basic values of **Confucianism**?

_____

_____

_____

(5) Why was **Buddhism** appealing to the Chinese during troubled times?

_____

_____

_____

Name _____ Class _____ Date _____

Take Notes

Identify Main Ideas and Details Use the chart below to provide as many examples as you can of Chinese technology in each category.

Agriculture	Shipping	Manufacturing	Printing

Essential Question

How did Chinese technology affect the rest of the world?

_____

_____

_____

What are the consequences of technology?

Prepare to Write

In this chapter, you have explored the Essential Question in your text, journal, and On Assignment at myworldhistory.com. Use what you've learned to write an essay about the consequences of technology in China. Write about two or three important technologies. Describe how they affected Chinese people or Chinese culture. You may also describe how they affected other regions of the world.

Workshop Skill: Understand the Four Types of Essays

Before you begin, decide what type of essay you want to write. There are four essay types: narrative, expository, research, and persuasive. Read a description of each type of essay below.

Narrative Essay This essay is most like a story. It has characters, a setting, and a plot.

- Characters are the people that the story is about. The setting is the time and place in which the story happens.
- A plot is the sequence of events that take place. Plots include conflict and lead up to a climax, which is the turning point of the story.

Expository Essay This essay has a main idea supported by evidence and examples.

- An introductory paragraph opens with a thesis sentence that states the main idea.
- The introduction is followed by body paragraphs. Each body paragraph discusses a point that supports the main idea. Evidence and examples are used to show that the supporting points are true.
- The conclusion sums up the essay by restating the thesis and supporting points.

Research Essay This essay has the same structure as an expository essay. However, it uses a different type of evidence to prove supporting points.

- Evidence and examples should come from a wide range of reliable sources.
- Writers use quotations, footnotes, and a bibliography to show where they found evidence.

Persuasive Essay This essay is written when the author wants to persuade readers to adopt an opinion or to take some action.

- The introduction tells why the topic is important. The thesis statement explains what the writer wants readers to think or do.
- In the body paragraphs, the writer uses strong arguments and evidence to prove the supporting points.
- The conclusion reviews the main points and urges the reader to accept the opinion or take the action mentioned.

Identify Essay Types

Read the descriptions in the table below. In the column on the right, identify the essay described as narrative, expository, research, or persuasive.

Essay Description	Type
1. This essay shows technology in China led to more trade.	_____
2. This essay uses evidence from scientific articles to explain where the first emperor of China was buried.	_____
3. This essay argues that the design of Chinese ships was the most important Chinese technology.	_____
4. This essay tells about the many adventures of Marco Polo in China.	_____

Plan Your Essay

Decide on the type of essay you will write.

Type of essay: _____

Your essay will contain an introduction, three body paragraphs, and a conclusion.

Now express the main point you want to make about Chinese technology as a thesis statement. For example, "China achieved great success in some areas and little success in others."

Write your thesis statement:

_____

In your introduction, you will support your thesis with three ideas. Each idea will be a topic sentence for one of your body paragraphs. Remember that a topic sentence clearly states the main idea of the paragraph.

First Body Paragraph Topic Sentence

_____

Second Body Paragraph Topic Sentence

_____

Third Body Paragraph Topic Sentence

_____

Draft Your Essay

Write your essay on your own paper. Use the topic sentences you wrote to begin each body paragraph. Include supporting details and a concluding sentence in each body paragraph. Use the concluding paragraph to sum up your ideas or the information you presented.

Name _____ Class _____ Date _____

What distinguishes one culture from another?

Preview Before you begin this chapter, think about the Essential Question. Understanding how the Essential Question connects to your life will help you understand the chapter you are about to read.

Connect to Your Life

(1) Culture affects you in many ways. Your life is different from the lives of people in other countries and other times. Think of some ways that the culture of the United States affects you. List at least one way in each column.

How Culture Affects Me			
Traditions	• Food	• Entertainment	• Education

(2) Look at the table. Which cultural aspect affects you the most? Which would be the hardest to do without? Explain.

_____

_____

_____

Connect to the Chapter

(3) Preview the chapter by skimming the chapter's heads, photographs, and graphics. In the table below, list at least one cultural aspect in each category.

Feudal Japan	Cultural Aspect
Government	
Traditions	
Entertainment	
Religion	

(4) Read the chapter. Then return to this page and circle the predictions that were correct.

Name _____ Class _____ Date _____

Connect to myStory: Murasaki Shikibu: Life Behind the Screen

① Think of something that you and your friends do because it is expected or required.

_____

_____

Now think of an activity or interest that sets you or a friend apart, such as being a good singer or being good at a sport.

_____

_____

② Murasaki was expected to behave in certain ways at court. There were things that she was expected to do. There also were things that she was not supposed to do. List three of each kind of behavior on the lines below.

Expected Behavior

a. _____

b. _____

c. _____

Forbidden Behavior

a. _____

b. _____

c. _____

③ Based on your knowledge of life at the Heian court, what prediction would you make about the nature of culture in Japan before modern times?

_____

_____

_____

_____

Word Wise

Vocabulary Quiz Show Some quiz shows ask a question and expect the contestant to give the answer. In other shows, the contestant is given an answer and must supply the question. If the blank is in the Question column, write the question that would result in the answer in the Answer column. If the question is supplied, write the answer.

QUESTION	ANSWER
① What is an area that is part of a continent?	① _____
② _____	② archipelago
③ What is the name for a group of people with a common ancestor?	③ _____
④ _____	④ regent
⑤ What is a holy being that represents a spirit of nature, a sacred place, an ancestor, or a clan?	⑤ _____

Name _____ Class _____ Date _____

Take Notes

Sequence Use what you have read about the rise of Japan to complete the timeline below. In each box, write the event that occurred on that date.

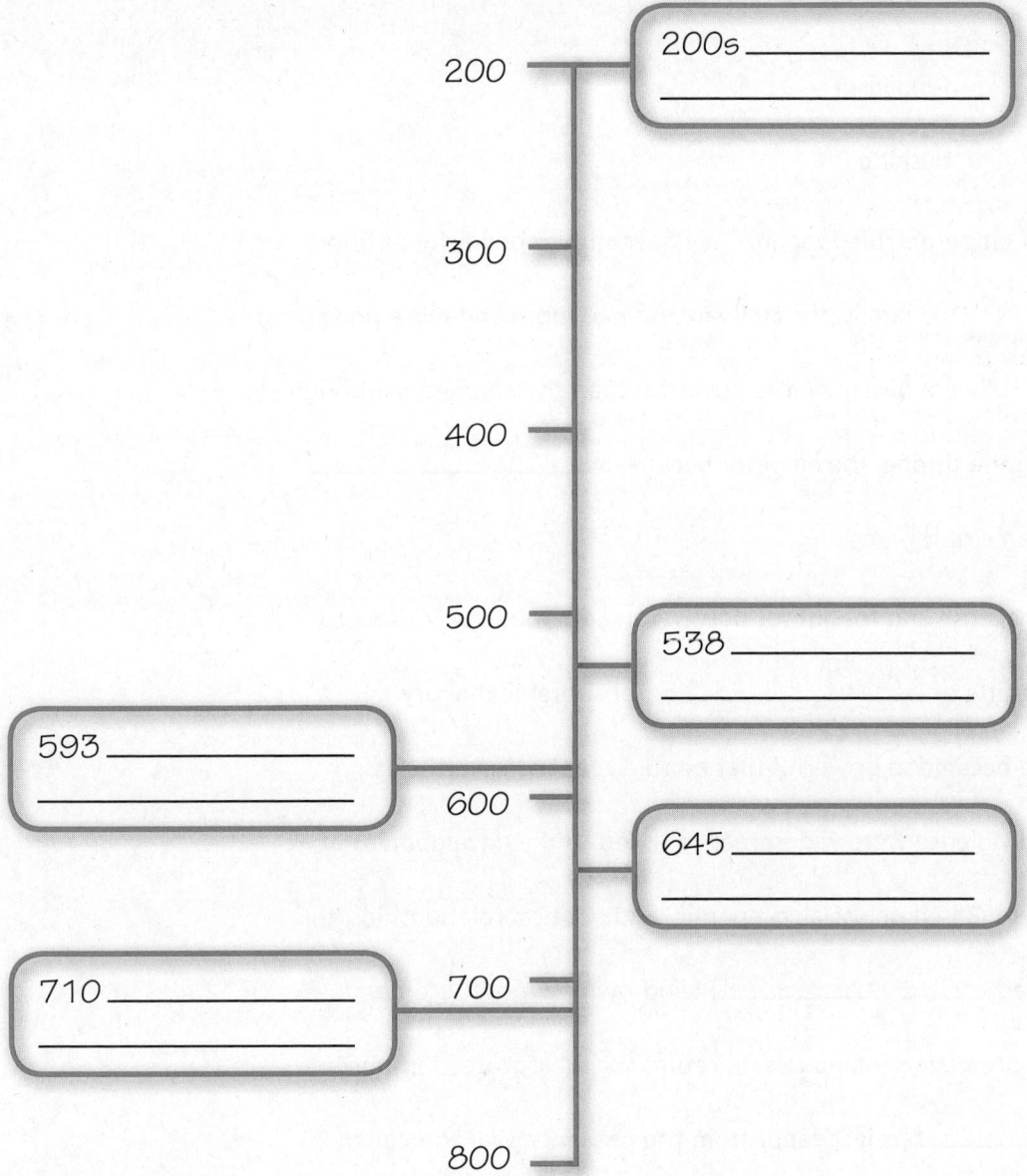

200

200s _____
_____

300

400

500

538 _____
_____

593 _____
_____

600

645 _____
_____

710 _____
_____

700

800

Essential Question

What aspects of Chinese government and culture did the Japanese adopt?

_____

_____

Word Wise

Use a Word Bank Choose one word from the word bank to fill in each blank. When you have finished, you will have a short summary of important ideas from the section.

Word Bank

figurehead	feudalism
shogun	samurai
daimyo	bushido

A series of emperors ruled Japan. They gave nobles powerful positions within their courts. One family, the Fujiwara, gained more and more power. Eventually, the Fujiwara became more powerful than the emperor. Although he remained on the throne, the emperor became a _____ who ruled in name only.

Other clans arose and fought for power. A member of the Minamoto clan gained the title of _____, or supreme military commander. He became so powerful that he ruled Japan. Nevertheless, lawlessness and violence were widespread. This led to the development of a new social system. Based on social, economic, and political relationships, this system was called _____. Land-owning lords became responsible for protecting the people. In return for their protection, the _____ received labor from the peasants. Warriors called _____ also served the lords. These warriors followed the code of _____. Each warrior took great care with his personal appearance and practiced extreme loyalty to his lord.

Name _____ Class _____ Date _____

Take Notes

Analyze Cause and Effect Use what you have read about the development
of feudalism in Japan to fill in the chart below. In the left box, write the
causes of feudalism. In the right box, indicate how Japan changed under
feudalism.

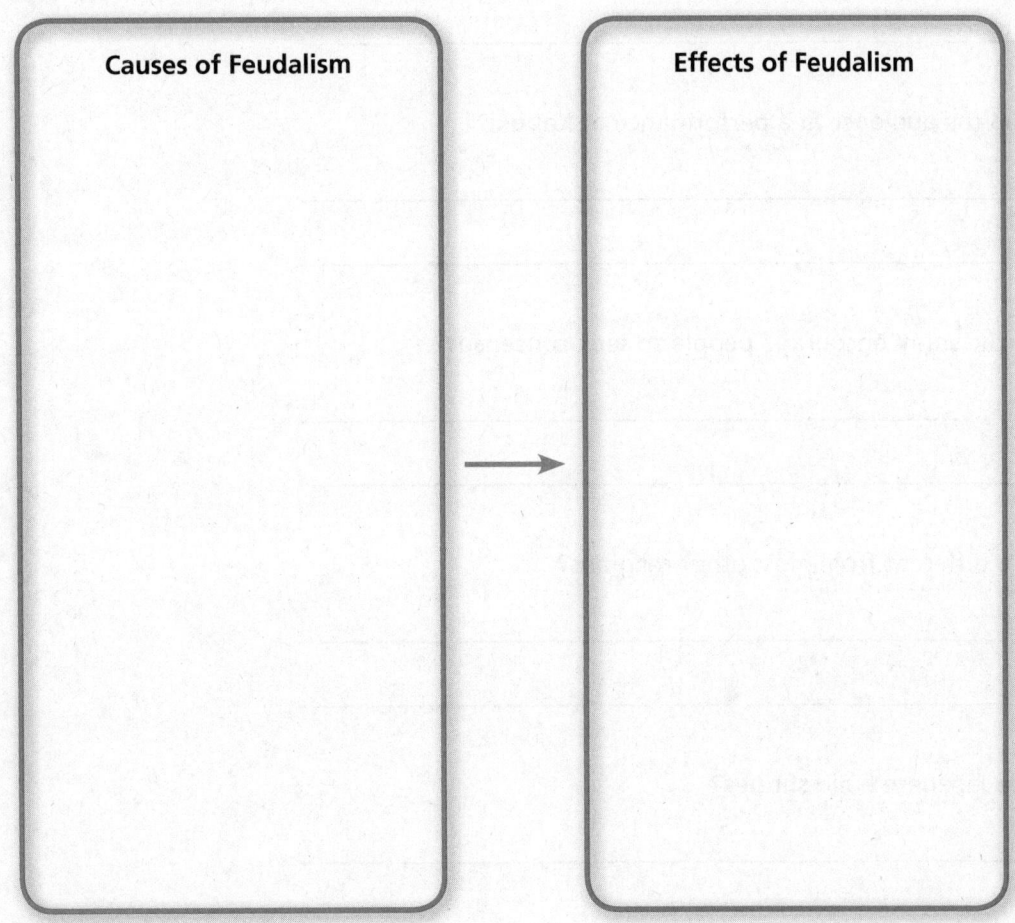

Causes of Feudalism

Effects of Feudalism

Essential Question

How did the role of the Japanese emperor differ from the role of the
Chinese emperor?

_____

_____

_____

Word Wise

Words in Context For each question below, write an answer that shows your understanding of the boldfaced key term.

(1) Which classes were most likely to enjoy **Noh**?

_____

_____

(2) Who made up the audience at a performance of **Kabuki**?

_____

_____

(3) Why did Confucianism encourage people to seek **consensus**?

_____

_____

(4) How is **Shinto** different from most other religions?

_____

_____

(5) Where do the Japanese build **shrines**?

_____

_____

(6) What is the purpose of a **mantra**?

_____

_____

Name _____ Class _____ Date _____

Take Notes

Identify Main Ideas and Details You have read about the development of Japan's unique culture. Aspects of Japanese culture appear in the table below. Complete the table by adding details that were uniquely Japanese in each category.

Japanese Culture	
The Arts	**Religion**

Essential Question

In what ways did Japanese artists and writers develop Japanese culture?

_____

_____

_____

What distinguishes one culture from another?

Prepare to Write

Throughout this chapter, you have explored the Essential Question in your text, journal, and by going On Assignment at myworldhistory.com. Use what you've learned to write an essay explaining what distinguished the culture of Japan before Modern Times from that of other cultures.

Workshop Skill: Use the Writing Process

In this lesson you will explore the four steps of the writing process—prewriting, drafting, revising, and presenting. Each step involves aspects of writing that you already may have studied.

Prewrite Prewriting is anything you do before you start to write. Prewriting activities may include gathering information, taking notes, brainstorming, and outlining.

- **Gathering information** may include research, interviewing, and reviewing what you already know.
- **Taking notes** will provide a record of the information gathered.
- **Brainstorming** is a way to collect your own ideas about a subject. Use the web to brainstorm ideas for your essay. First, write your topic in the center of the web. Then write one idea in each of the outer bubbles. As you brainstorm, add as many bubbles to your web as you need.

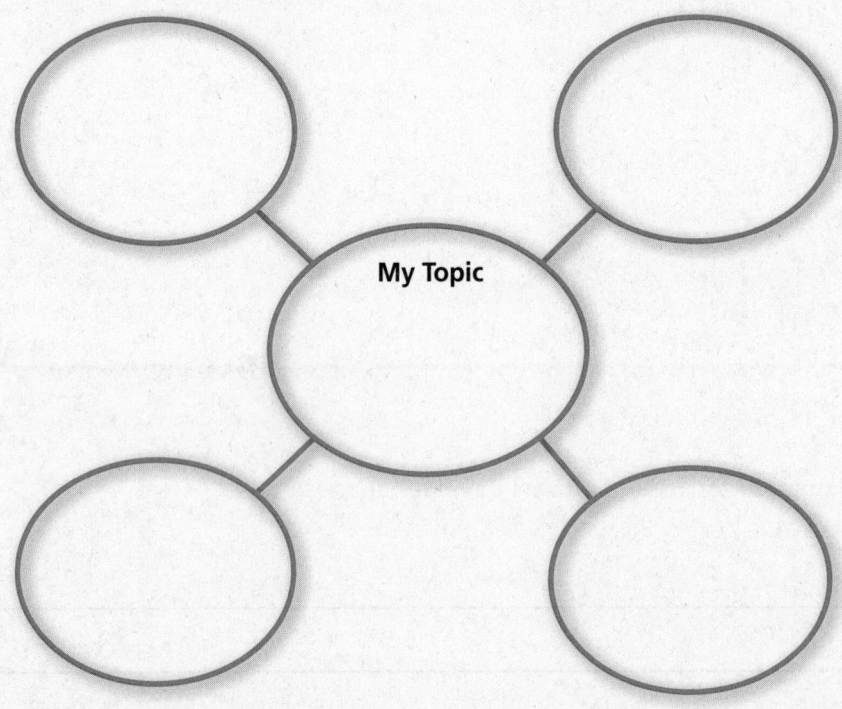

Once you have finished brainstorming, evaluate your ideas. Decide which to use as main points in your essay.

- **Outlining** On a separate sheet of paper, outline your essay, using your ideas and notes. Before you begin, you may want to review the structure of the five-paragraph essay. Outline each part: introduction, three body paragraphs, and conclusion.

Draft Your Essay Now put your notes and ideas into sentences and paragraphs. Use your outline as a basic framework. Don't worry too much about spelling or grammar. Instead, concentrate on explaining your ideas as clearly and completely as possible. Remember to include a thesis statement in your introduction and a topic sentence in each body paragraph.

Revise Revising offers you the opportunity to improve your essay. The key is to put yourself in the reader's place. As you read over your essay, think about whether the reader will be able to understand your ideas. Use the checklist below as a guide.

_____ Are there terms that readers might not know?

_____ Is each sentence clear?

_____ Are there supporting details or arguments for each main point?

_____ Does the organization make sense?

_____ Are grammar and spelling correct?

Make any changes or corrections that will improve your essay.

Present Write the final version of your essay on your own paper. Include your name, the date, and a title. Use a double-spaced format.

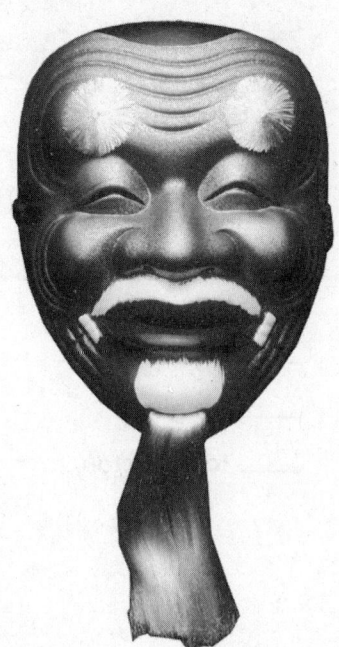

Places to Know!

Map Skills Use the maps in this unit to identify the Places to Know! on the outline map. Before the name of each place below, write the letter that shows its location on the map.

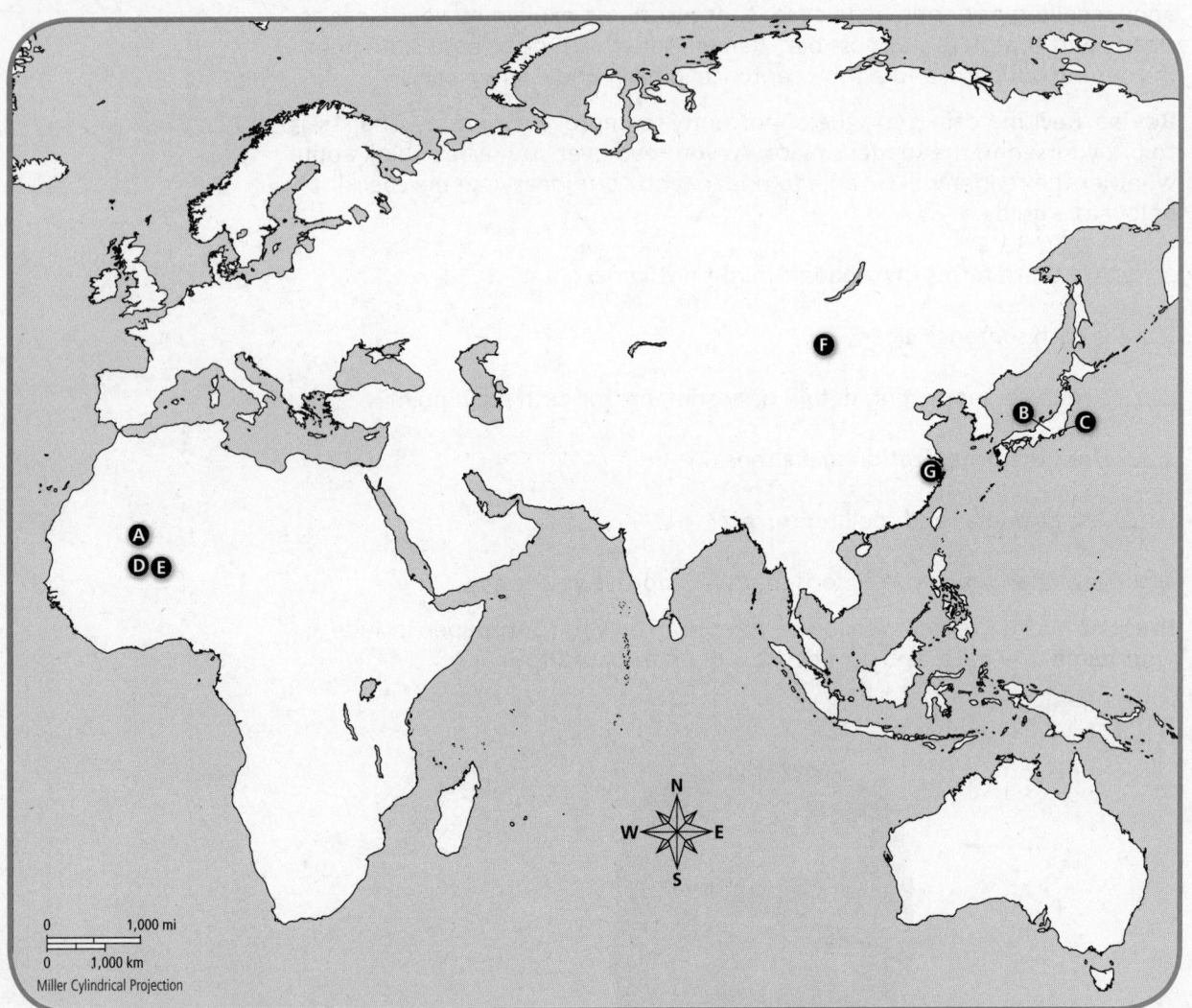

_____ Edo (Tokyo)   _____ Mount Fuji

_____ Gao   _____ Songhai

_____ Hangzhou   _____ Tombouctou

_____ Mongolia

Name _____ Class _____ Date _____

Key Events

Timeline Use what you have read about African and Asian civilizations to complete the timeline below. Draw a line from each event to its correct position on the timeline. Then write a brief description of each event.

500 B.C.

350 B.C. _____
_____

250 B.C. _____
_____

250 B.C.

A.D. 1

A.D. 538 _____
_____

A.D. 618 _____
_____

A.D. 250

A.D. 500

A.D. 960 _____
_____

A.D. 1279 _____
_____

A.D. 750

A.D. 1000

A.D. 1312 _____
_____

A.D. 1464 _____
_____

A.D. 1250

A.D. 1500

Name _____ Class _____ Date _____

? Essential Question

What distinguishes one culture from another?

Preview Before you begin this chapter, think about the Essential Question. Understanding how the Essential Question connects to your life will help you understand the chapter you are about to read.

Connect to Your Life

① There are many aspects of your life that are part of your culture, but that might not be part of another culture. In the table below, write examples of how each aspect of culture affects your life.

How Culture Affects Me			
Music	• School	• Sports	• Other

② Write one or two sentences explaining how one of the subjects in the chart creates part of your culture and how it might be different in another culture.

_____

_____

Connect to the Chapter

③ Preview the chapter. Skim the headings, photos, and graphics. In the table below, predict how their culture affected the lives of the Maya people.

	Effect on Daily Life
Government	
Astronomy	
Sports	
Mathematics	

④ After you read the chapter, return to the chart and circle the predictions that were correct.

Name _____ Class _____ Date _____

Connect to myStory: Moctezuma Ilhuicamina: He Frowned Like a Lord, He Pierces the Sky Like an Arrow

(1) Imagine that you had been one of Moctezuma's subjects. Which of his qualities would make you proud to serve him? Which qualities would you dislike? Explain your answers.

_____

_____

_____

(2) Moctezuma wanted to preserve and strengthen his people. To do this, he needed prisoners, so he conquered nearby people. In the table below, on the left side, write Moctezuma's actions. On the right side, write Moctezuma's reasons for doing what he did.

Moctezuma's Actions	Reasons for His Actions

(3) Think about the events from the story of Moctezuma. Then write two predictions about things you will learn about the Aztec empire.

_____

_____

_____

Word Wise

Use a Word Bank Choose one word from the word bank to fill in each blank. When you have finished, you will have a short summary of important ideas from the section.

Word Bank

drought

observatory

obsidian

hieroglyphic

quetzal

slash-and-burn agriculture

Several civilizations grew in Mesoamerica between about 1200 B.C. and

A.D. 1500. Farmers of the Olmec did not use artificial fertilizers to improve

their soils. Instead, they used a method called _____. Using

this method, they cut down trees and other plants on an area to be farmed.

They then burned the plants and used the ashes as fertilizer.

_____, a type of natural glass that volcanoes produce, was

an important trade item for Maya merchants. They traded it for feathers

from a tropical bird called the _____. The Maya also

had many achievements in architecture, including creating a(n)

_____ to study the stars and planets. Between A.D 800 and

1000, many of the Maya cities fell into ruin. One reason may have been

prolonged periods of _____, when little rain fell. One way

we know about the Maya rulers is through carved stone pillars that tell

about their deeds. The information is carved in _____, a

system of writing in which a symbol stands for a word.

Name _____ Class _____ Date _____

Take Notes

Sequence Use what you have learned about Mesoamerican civilizations to complete the timeline. Identify the key event associated with each date on the timeline and give a brief description of the event and its importance.

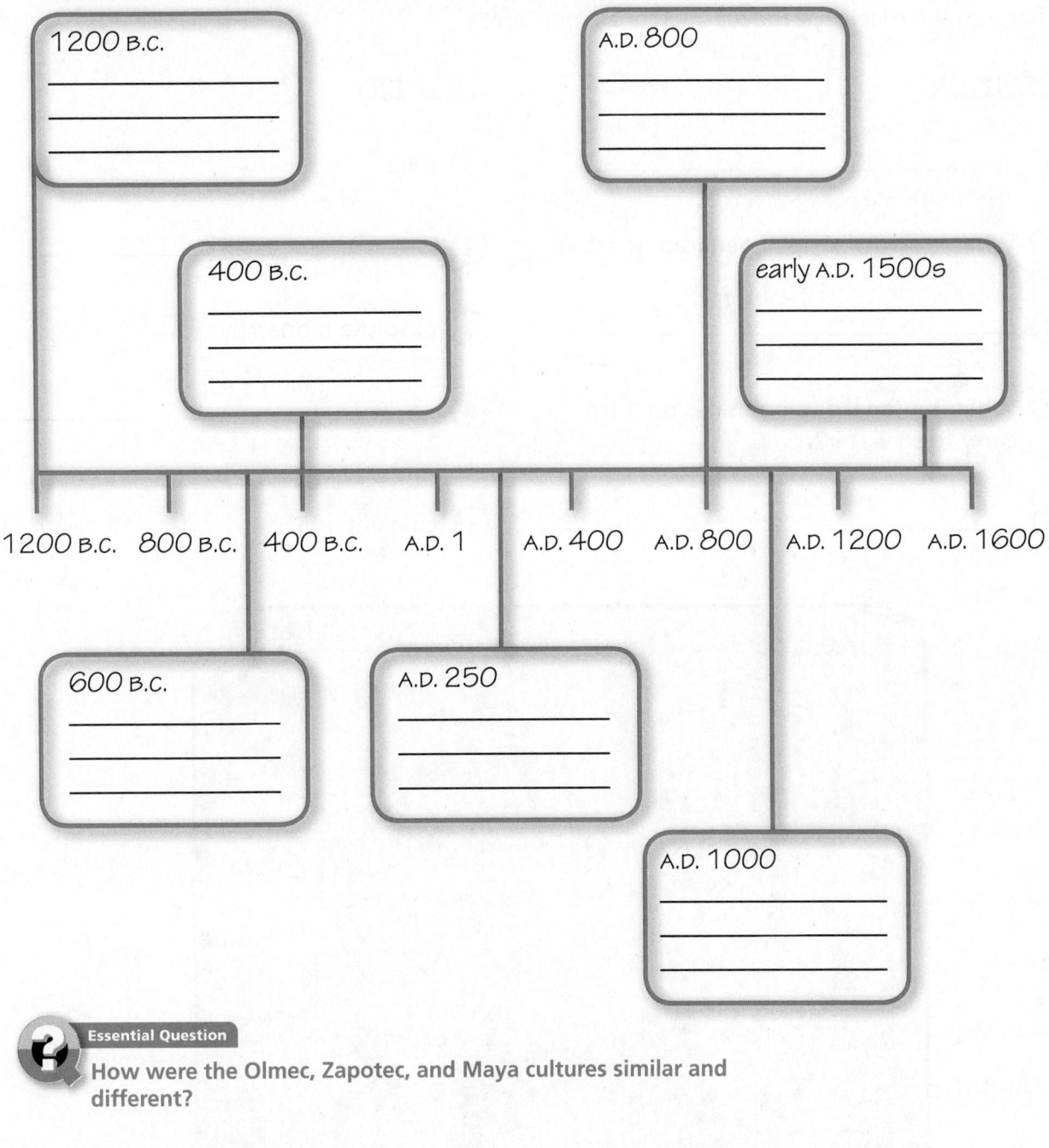

1200 B.C.
_____
_____
_____

A.D. 800
_____
_____
_____

400 B.C.
_____
_____
_____

early A.D. 1500s
_____
_____
_____
_____

1200 B.C.   800 B.C.   400 B.C.   A.D. 1   A.D. 400   A.D. 800   A.D. 1200   A.D. 1600

600 B.C.
_____
_____
_____

A.D. 250
_____
_____
_____

A.D. 1000
_____
_____
_____

Essential Question

How were the Olmec, Zapotec, and Maya cultures similar and different?

_____

_____

_____

237

Name _____ Class _____ Date _____

Word Wise

Vocabulary Quiz Show Some quiz shows ask a question and expect the contestant to give the answer. In other shows, the contestant is given an answer and must supply the question. If the blank is in the Question column, write the question that would result in the answer in the Answer column. If the answer is supplied, write the appropriate question.

QUESTION

(1) _____

(2) What is a bowl-shaped geographic area?

(3) _____

(4) What is a canal or pipe that is built to carry fresh water?

(5) _____

ANSWER

(1) dike

(2) _____

(3) absolute monarchy

(4) _____

(5) chinampa

Name _____ Class _____ Date _____

Take Notes

Summarize Use what you have read about the Aztecs to complete the table below. For each topic, give details and then write a one-sentence summary.

Land	Government	Society	Achievements

_____

_____

_____

_____

Essential Question

How was Aztec civilization similar to and different from Maya civilization?

_____

_____

_____

Essential Question | Writer's Workshop

What distinguishes one culture from another?

Prepare to Write

Throughout this chapter, you have explored the essential Question in your text, journal, and On Assignment at myworldhistory.com. Use what you've learned to write an essay on the topic of what causes cultures to be similar to or different from other cultures.

Workshop Skill: Outline an Essay

A five-paragraph essay has an introductory paragraph that hooks the reader, states a thesis, and introduces three supporting ideas. Each of the three body paragraphs develops one supporting idea. The final paragraph summarizes the supporting ideas and restates the thesis.

Identify the Main Idea Remember that a main idea is not the same thing as the topic. The topic of your essay is how cultures are alike or different. Your main Idea will be your *opinion* about the topic. Express your main idea in the form of a thesis statement.

Write a Thesis Statement _____

_____

Choose Supporting Points Choose three supporting points to prove your statement. For example, if you think that the Maya had the most advanced culture, one point might be the fact that they developed a calendar.

_____

_____

Outline the Introductory Paragraph

Outline your introductory paragraph here:

Hook _____

_____

Thesis Statement _____

_____

Sentence Summarizing the Supporting Ideas _____

_____

Outline Body Paragraphs

Each paragraph needs a topic sentence that states the main idea. Include evidence to support the main idea. End the paragraph with a concluding sentence that tells how the information supports your thesis statement.

Body Paragraph 1
Topic Sentence

_____

_____

Supporting Detail

_____

_____

Supporting Detail

_____

_____

Concluding Sentence

_____

_____

Follow this format to write two more body paragraphs.

Outline Your Conclusion

In the conclusion, you review your thesis, summarize your supporting points, explain how those points proved your statement, and end by telling the reader why this topic matters.

Paragraph 5: Conclusion

Restate the Thesis _____

Summary of Supporting Points _____

What the Supporting Points Prove _____

Why the Topic Matters _____

Draft Your Essay

Write your essay on your own paper. When you have finished, proofread it with a partner.

Name _____ Class _____ Date _____

Essential Question

How much does geography affect people's lives?

Preview Before you begin this chapter, think about the Essential Question. Understanding how the Essential Question connects to your life will help you understand the chapter you are about to read.

Connect to Your Life

① Think of the climate and physical features in your community. Describe them below.

Climate: _____

Landscape/Waterways: _____

Resources: _____

② Now consider how these geographic features affect you and others in your community. Fill in the table below with your ideas. List both positive and negative effects.

Local Geographic Features	Positive Effects of Geographic Features	Negative Effects of Geographic Features
Climate		
Landscape/Waterways		
Resources		

Connect to the Chapter

③ Preview the chapter. Skim the headings, photos, and graphics. In the table below, predict how geography affected civilizations of early North and South America.

Geographic Features	Effect on Incas	Effect on Early North American Peoples
Climate		
Landscape/Waterways		
Resources		

④ After reading the chapter, return to this page. Circle your predictions that were correct.

Connect to myStory: The Incan Ice Maiden: Frozen for Five Hundred Years

1 Name two ways that you and others can help your neighborhood or region.

_____

_____

_____

2 How did Juanita help her people?

_____

_____

3 Why did the Incas believe that her help was necessary?

_____

_____

4 Where was she discovered?

_____

_____

5 Why is the discovery of Juanita important?

_____

_____

6 How do you think the Andes affected life in the Incan empire? Write at least two predictions.

_____

_____

_____

Name _____ Class _____ Date _____

Word Wise

Vocabulary Quiz Show Some quiz shows ask a question and expect the contestant to give the answer. In other shows, the contestant is given an answer and must supply the question. If the blank is in the Question column, write the question that would result in the answer in the Answer column. If the answer is supplied, write the appropriate question.

QUESTION	ANSWER
① What social ranking system did the Incas use?	① _____
② _____	② They increased farmland.
③ What mountain range was home to the Incas?	③ _____
④ _____	④ a tool used to keep records
⑤ What was a group of related families called?	⑤ _____
⑥ _____	⑥ providing labor to pay taxes

Name _____ Class _____ Date _____

Take Notes

Summarize Use the chart below to summarize features of the Incan empire. Write at least two characteristics or achievements in each category.

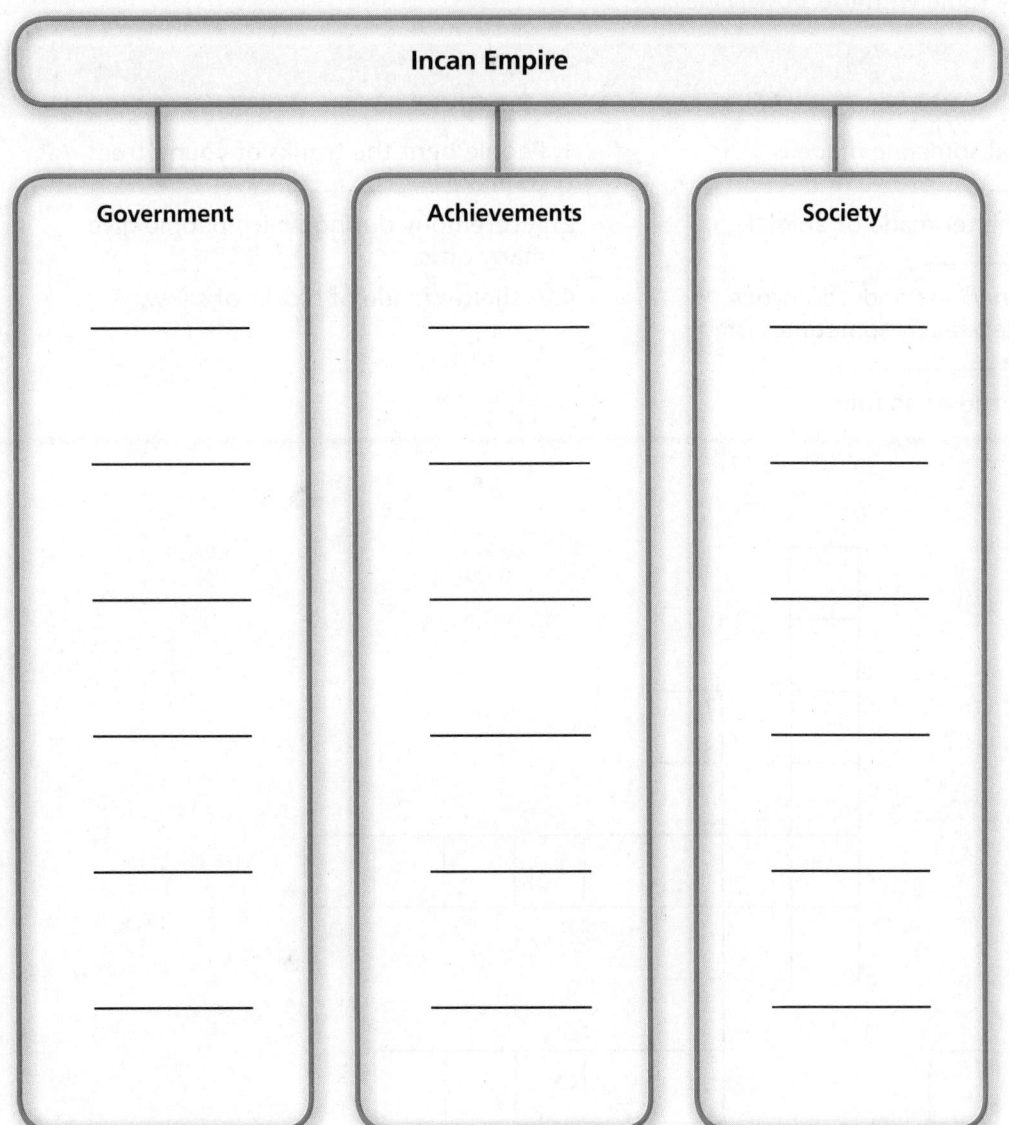

Incan Empire

Government	Achievements	Society
_____	_____	_____
_____	_____	_____
_____	_____	_____
_____	_____	_____
_____	_____	_____
_____	_____	_____

Essential Question

In what ways were the Incas shaped by their environment?

_____

_____

_____

Word Wise

Crossword Puzzle The *Across* and *Down* clues are definitions of key terms from this section. Fill in the numbered *Across* boxes with the correct key terms. Then do the same with the *Down* clues.

Across	Down
3. An object that someone made is called an _____.	1. People bent the trunks of young trees to make a _____.
5. A portable shelter made of animal hide is a _____.	2. A ceremony during which people give many gifts.
6. In the Eastern Woodlands, branches of an extended family sometimes lived together in a _____.	4. A shelter made of blocks of snow.
7. A period of little or no rain.	

Name _____ Class _____ Date _____

Take Notes

Compare and Contrast Use what you have read about early North American cultures to complete the table below. For each region, name the type or types of homes people lived in and the materials used.

Northeastern Woodlands	Southeastern Woodlands	Great Plains	North and Northwest

Essential Question

Choose one Native American culture region. How did geography affect the housing available there?

_____

_____

_____

How much does geography affect people's lives?

Prepare to Write

Throughout this chapter, you have explored the Essential Question in your text, journal, and On Assignment at myworldhistory.com. Use what you've learned to write an essay discussing the effects of geography on the early peoples of North and South America. Think about how people living in various regions adapted to their environment. Include the effects of climate, landforms, and available resources on the way they lived.

Workshop Skill: Write an Introduction and Thesis Statement

In this lesson, you will learn or review how to write an introduction and a thesis statement.

First, decide on the kind of essay you will write. Review the four types of essay: narrative, persuasive, expository, and research. Choose the one that you think will be best for answering the Essential Question. Write your choice here.

_____

The Introduction

The introduction is the first paragraph in a five-paragraph essay. It tells the reader what the essay is about and why the topic is important. To create a successful essay, the writer must use the following elements to build the introduction.

The Hook The introduction begins with a hook, which aims to catch the reader's attention. It may be in the form of a question or a statement, and may be one sentence or more, as long as it is brief. For example, if you were writing an essay about Juanita, the Ice Maiden, you might use the following hook: *Would you be willing to die for the good of others? Juanita was a young woman who answered, "Yes."*

Write your hook:

_____

The Thesis Statement The thesis states the main idea of your essay and includes a summary of three points that support your main idea. In the essay you are about to write, the thesis statement will answer the question, *How much does geography affect people's lives?* The statement must be clear and specific.

Example *Geography has a major effect on people's lives in the areas of*

_____, _____, and _____.

If you feel that your sentence is too long, state your supporting points in a separate sentence.

Example *Geography has a major effect on people's lives. Geography*

determines _____, _____,

and _____.

Write your thesis statement:

_____

Supporting Points Expand each supporting point into a sentence.

Supporting point _____

Supporting point _____

Supporting point _____

Write Your Introduction

_____

_____

_____

_____

_____

_____

_____

Review and Revise Read over your introduction and ask yourself these questions. Does your introduction begin with a hook? Does your thesis statement clearly express the main idea of your essay? Is your thesis statement specific? Have you included three points that support your main idea? If you answered "no" to any question, revise your introduction. After drafting your essay, answer the questions again. You may find that your ideas changed as you wrote.

Draft Your Essay

Write your essay on another sheet of paper, beginning with the introduction you have just written. When you have completed your essay, proofread it with a partner.

Name _____ Class _____ Date _____

Places to Know!

Map Skills Use the maps in this unit to identify the Places to Know! on the outline map. Before the name of each place below, write the letter that shows its location on the map.

_____ Cuzco   _____ Yucatán Peninsula

_____ Andes   _____ Caribbean Sea

_____ Gulf of Mexico   _____ Amazon River

Key Events

Timeline Use what you have read about civilizations of the Americas to complete the timeline below. Draw a line from each event to its correct position on the timeline. Then write a brief description of each event.

1500 B.C.

1200 B.C. _____
_____

1000 B.C.

A.D. 1438 _____
_____

A.D. 250 _____
_____

500 B.C.

A.D. 1

A.D. 1521 _____
_____

A.D. 1150 _____
_____

A.D. 500

A.D. 1533 _____
_____

A.D. 1200 _____
_____

A.D. 1000

A.D. 1911 _____
_____

A.D. 1500

A.D. 1325 _____
_____

A.D. 2000

Name _____ Class _____ Date _____

Copyright © Pearson Education, Inc., or its affiliates. All Rights Reserved.

Essential Question

What is power? Who should have it?

Preview Before you begin this chapter, think about the Essential Question. Understanding how the Essential Question connects to your life will help you understand the chapter you are about to read.

Connect to Your Life

(1) Think of the levels of power you can observe in public life. For example, your town might have many officials with different levels of power. List five people who have power in your community.

a. _____

b. _____

c. _____

d. _____

e. _____

(2) Place the letter next to the person or group above on the line below to show where each falls on the power scale below, from little power to great power.

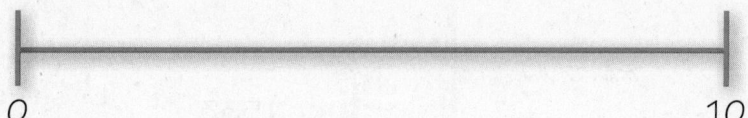

0   10

Little Power _____ **Great Power**

Connect to the Chapter

(3) Skim the chapter text, subheads, and visuals and look for information about the division of power in medieval Europe. In the table below, predict how power was divided in Europe during the Middle Ages.

Division of Power in Medieval Europe				
Who holds power?	Charlemagne and Franks	Vikings	Magyars	Muslims
Where?				
When?				

(4) After reading the chapter, return to this page. Circle your predictions that were correct.

252

Name _____ Class _____ Date _____

Connect to myStory: Charlemagne and Leo: The Sword and the Crown

1. Think about how Charlemagne helped protect Leo from his enemies. Suppose someone you know needed protection from bullies. Would you help him or her? What would you do? Explain your answer.

_____

_____

2. Think about the power struggle between Charlemagne and Leo. Why did Leo ask for Charlemagne's help? Why did Charlemagne agree to help him?

_____

_____

3. Using clues from the story about Charlemagne and Leo, predict how power struggles affected life in medieval Europe. Write your predictions in the chart below.

Power in Medieval Europe
Church
Government
Nobility
Society

Word Wise

Vocabulary Quiz Show Some quiz shows ask a question and expect the contestant to give the answer. In other shows the contestant is given an answer and must supply the question. If the blank is in the Question column, write the question that would result in the answer in the Answer column. If the question is supplied, write the answer.

QUESTION

① What is the term for the period from A.D. 500 to 1500?

② _____

③ What is the term for the physical features of Earth's surface?

④ _____

ANSWER

① _____

② medieval

③ _____

④ clergy

Name _____ Class _____ Date _____

Take Notes

Sequence Reread the text under each red heading in your textbook. Take notes about information under each heading to complete the concept web below.

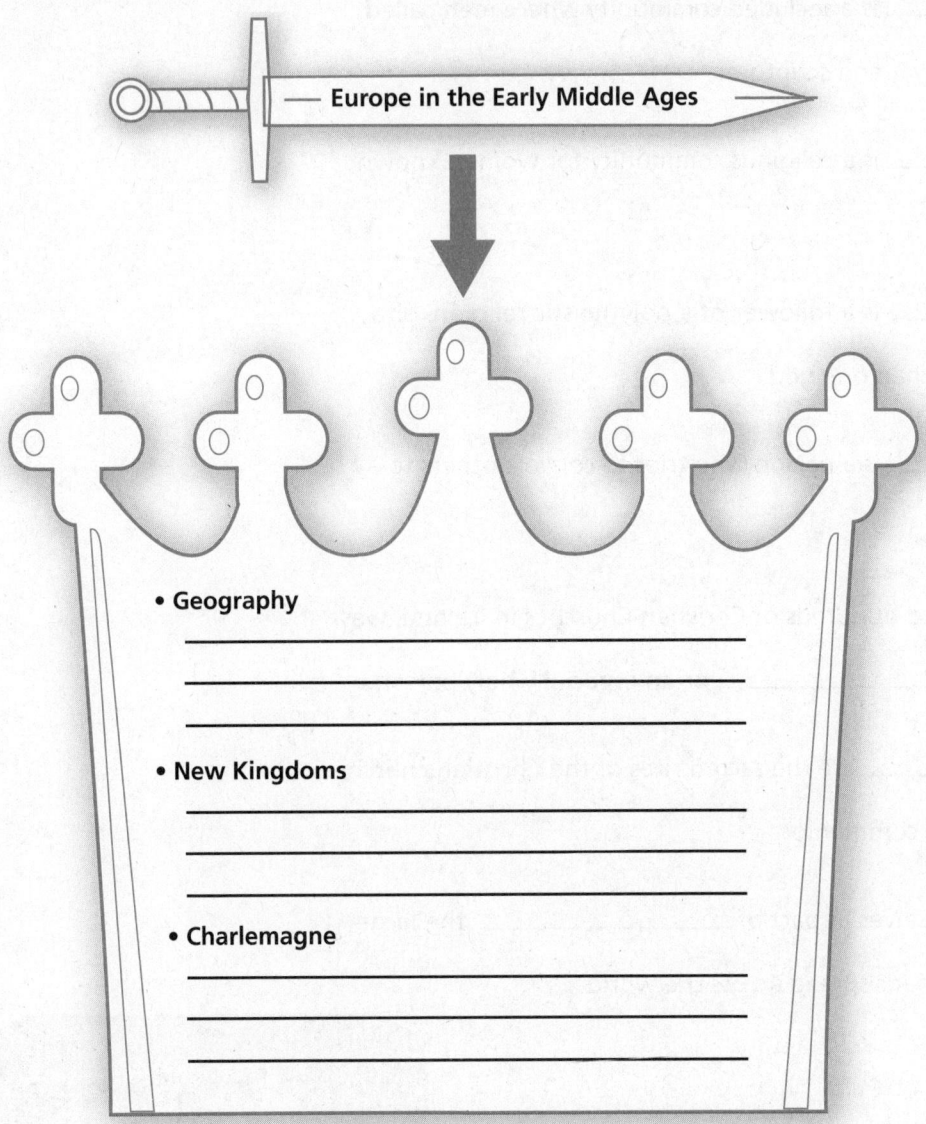

• **Geography**

_____
_____
_____

• **New Kingdoms**

_____
_____
_____

• **Charlemagne**

_____
_____
_____

Essential Question

How did different groups and individuals take power in early medieval Europe?

_____
_____
_____

Name _____ Class _____ Date _____

Word Wise

Sentence Builder Complete the sentences using the information you learned in this section.

① A _____ is a secluded community where men called monks focus on prayer and scripture.

② A _____ is a religious community for women known as nuns.

③ A _____ is a follower of a polytheistic religion, or a religion with more than one god.

④ A _____ is a person who tries to convert others to a particular religion.

⑤ Patrick, who founded hundreds of Christian Churches in Ireland, was recognized as a _____, or an especially holy person.

⑥ The _____ are the sacred rites of the Christian church, such as baptism and communion.

⑦ Christians saw themselves as part of _____, the large community of Christians spread across the world.

Name _____ Class _____ Date _____

Take Notes

Summarize The column headings in the table below match the headings in your textbook. Reread each section. Summarize information under each column's subheadings to complete the chart below. Remember that a summary is one or two sentences that give an overview of information, not specific details.

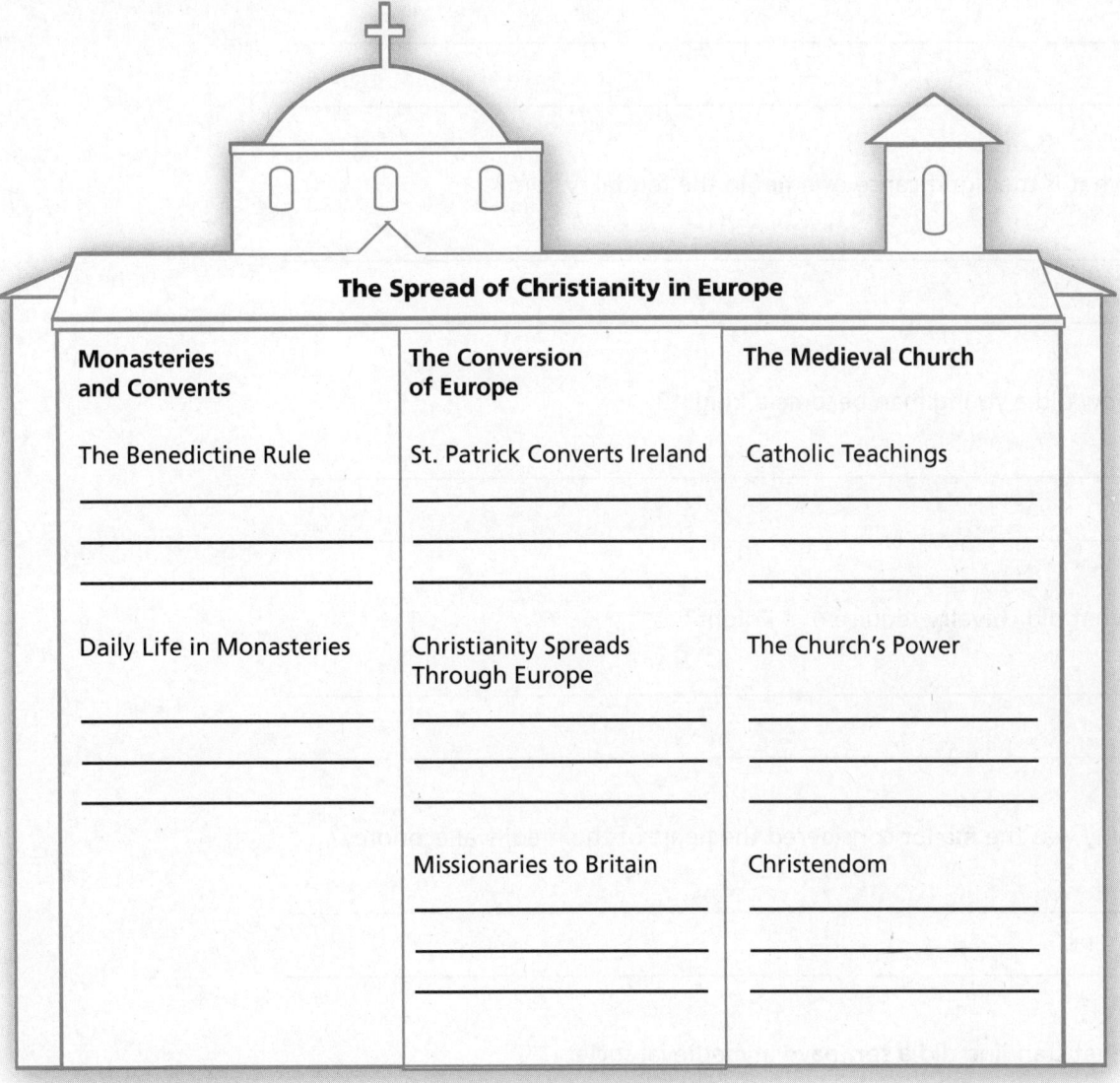

The Spread of Christianity in Europe

Monasteries and Convents	The Conversion of Europe	The Medieval Church
The Benedictine Rule	St. Patrick Converts Ireland	Catholic Teachings
_____	_____	_____
_____	_____	_____
_____	_____	_____
Daily Life in Monasteries	Christianity Spreads Through Europe	The Church's Power
_____	_____	_____
_____	_____	_____
_____	_____	_____
	Missionaries to Britain	Christendom
	_____	_____
	_____	_____
	_____	_____

Essential Question

Describe the power of the Catholic Church in medieval Europe.

_____

_____

_____

Word Wise

Words in Context For each question below, write an answer that shows your understanding of the boldfaced key term.

(1) In exchange for land, what did a **vassal** pledge to a more powerful lord?

_____

_____

(2) What is the significance of a **fief** in the feudal system?

_____

_____

(3) How did a young man become a **knight**?

_____

_____

(4) What did **chivalry** require of a knight?

_____

_____

(5) Why was the **manor** considered the heart of the medieval economy?

_____

_____

(6) What standing did a **serf** have in medieval society?

_____

_____

Name _____ Class _____ Date _____

Take Notes

Identify Main Ideas and Details Use what you have read about the development of European feudalism to fill in the key ideas from this section of the chapter in the table below.

A Violent Time	A Feudal Society	The Medieval Manor
Key Ideas	**Key Ideas**	**Key Ideas**
•	•	•
•	•	•
•	•	•

Essential Question

How did feudalism and the manor system affect the lives of people in medieval Europe?

_____

_____

_____

Essential Question Writer's Workshop

What is power? Who should have it?

Copyright © Pearson Education, Inc., or its affiliates. All Rights Reserved.

Prepare to Write

Throughout this chapter, you have explored the Essential Question in your text, journal, and On Assignment at myWorldHistory.com. Use your notes and what you've learned to write an essay describing how power struggles affected Europe in the Middle Ages.

Workshop Skill: Write Body Paragraphs

Review how to write an outline for your essay. Think about the main point you want to make in your essay. Your essay will contain five paragraphs: an introduction, three body paragraphs, and a concluding paragraph. In this lesson, you will learn how to write the body paragraphs.

Write a Topic Sentence Each of your body paragraphs should begin with a topic sentence. A topic sentence should clearly state the main idea of the body paragraph. It should also connect the idea to your essay's thesis. Skim through the chapter and take notes about how power played a part in medieval Europe. For example, Pope Leo III stengthened the Church's power when he crowned Charlemagne emperor.

Use Supporting Details Each of your topic sentences should be supported by facts and details. These details should provide the proof that your statement is true. For example, by crowning Charlemagne, Pope Leo III established the idea that only the pope had the power to name an emperor. This statement supports the idea that the act of crowning Charlemagne strengthened the Church's power.

Write a Concluding Sentence Each paragraph should end with one or two concluding sentences. The conclusion should relate back to the topic sentence and sum up the supporting details.

Here is a sample body paragraph:

Topic sentence *The relationship between King Charlemagne and Pope Leo III shows how the Church's growing power caused conflict during the Middle Ages.*

Supporting detail *Charlemagne helped protect Pope Leo III from enemies in Rome; in return, Leo crowned Charlemagne emperor.*

_____

_____

Supporting detail *By crowning Charlemagne, Pope Leo III established the idea that only the pope had the power to name an emperor.*

_____

_____

Supporting detail *Leo's action angered the Byzantine empire and the Eastern Orthodox Church.*

_____

Supporting detail *This conflict led to a split between the eastern and western Christian worlds.*

_____

Concluding sentence(s) *As a result of Pope Leo's power to crown Charlemagne emperor, the Church's power grew. Though this increased the Church's power, the conflict led to a split in the Church during the Middle Ages.*

Write a Body Paragraph

Now write one of your own concluding paragraph for your essay.

Topic Sentence _____

_____

Supporting detail _____

_____

Supporting detail _____

_____

Supporting detail _____

_____

Supporting detail _____

_____

Concluding sentence(s) _____

_____

Draft Your Essay

Review and revise your body paragraph to be sure your thoughts are clearly presented. Use it in your complete essay (written on another sheet of paper). Make sure each of your body paragraphs has a topic sentence, supporting details, and a concluding sentence. Then write your essay and proofread it with a writing partner.

Name _____ Class _____ Date _____

Essential Question

How should we handle conflict?

Preview Before you begin this chapter, think about the Essential Question. Understanding how the Essential Question connects to your life will help you understand the chapter you are about to read.

Connect to Your Life

(1) What do you think are the most common causes of conflict? _____

_____

(2) Complete the chart below with examples of how you think conflicts should be solved.

Conflict	Best Way to Solve Conflict
Someone pushes you out of the way to be first in line.	
Two people want to be captain of the team.	
Someone has been spreading lies about your best friend.	

Connect to the Chapter

(3) Skim this chapter's text, subheads, and visuals and look for information about conflicts in medieval Europe. In the table below, use the information to make predictions about the reasons for those conflicts.

Conflicting Sides	Sources of Conflict
Popes and Kings	
Kings and Nobles	
Crusaders and Muslims	
Christians and Moors	

(4) After reading the chapter, return to this page. Change any predictions that were incorrect.

262

Name _____ Class _____ Date _____

Connect to myStory: Henry II's Murderous Words

(1) Think of a person in your life or in American history who has faced conflict to uphold a principle. How did that person solve the conflict?

_____

_____

(2) What do you think is the best way to "fight" for something you believe in?

_____

_____

(3) In the myStory, what was the conflict between the Church and monarchy in England?

_____

_____

(4) In the myStory, why was Henry II so angry?

_____

_____

(5) What was the result of Henry II's outburst?

_____

_____

(6) Who do you think should hold the most power in a country: a government leader or a religious leader? Why?

_____

_____

Name _____ Class _____ Date _____

Word Wise

Words In Context For each question below, write an answer that shows your understanding of the boldfaced key term.

(1) Why was Henry IV probably stunned by Pope Gregory's claim of authority over **secular** leaders?

_____

_____

_____

(2) What did Henry IV do after he was **excommunicated** by Pope Gregory?

_____

_____

_____

(3) Why did people make a **pilgrimage** to Canterbury?

_____

_____

_____

Take Notes

Compare and Contrast Use what you have read about popes and rulers in Section 1 to fill in the diagram below.

Holy Roman Empire

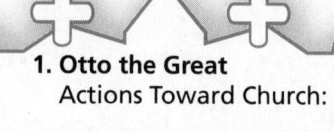

1. Otto the Great
Actions Toward Church:

_____
_____
_____

2. Henry IV
Actions Toward Church:

_____
_____
_____

4. Outcome:

_____
_____
_____

3. Pope Gregory VII
Actions Toward King:

_____
_____
_____

England

5. Henry II
Actions Toward Church:

_____
_____
_____

7. Outcome:

_____
_____
_____

6. Thomas Becket
Actions Toward King:

_____
_____
_____

Strong Kingdoms Emerge in 1100s

8. Philip II Augustus
Accomplishments:

_____
_____
_____

9. England's Monarchy
Accomplishments:

_____
_____
_____

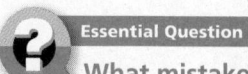 **Essential Question**

What mistakes did Henry II make in his conflict with the Church?

_____

Word Wise

Vocabulary Quiz Show Some quiz shows ask a question and expect the contestant to give the answer. In other shows, the contestant is given an answer and must supply the question. If the blank is in the Question column, write the question that would result in the answer in the Answer column. If the question is supplied, write the answer.

QUESTION	ANSWER
(1) _____	(1) Magna Carta
(2) _____	(2) common law
(3) What phrase refers to a court order to bring an arrested person before a judge or court?	(3) _____
(4) What term means "court order"?	(4) _____
(5) _____	(5) parliament

Take Notes

Identify Main Ideas and Details The column headings below match the topics in Section 2 of your textbook. Under each column heading, write the main idea of the topic and details that support it.

Kings, Nobles, and the Magna Carta

The Norman Conquest	Norman England	Limits on Royal Power
Main Idea:	**Main Idea:**	**Main Idea:**
_____	_____	_____
_____	_____	_____
_____	_____	_____
_____	_____	_____
_____	_____	_____
Details	**Details**	**Details**
• _____	• _____	• _____
_____	_____	_____
• _____	_____	_____
_____	• _____	• _____
• _____	_____	_____
_____	• _____	• _____
• _____	_____	_____
_____	• _____	• _____
• _____	_____	_____
_____	• _____	• _____
• _____	_____	_____
_____	• _____	• _____

Essential Question

How did the barons resolve their conflict with King John?

_____

_____

_____

Word Wise

Word Map Follow the model below to make a word map. The key term *Crusades* is in the center oval. Write the definition in your own words at the upper left. In the upper right, list Characteristics, which means words or phrases that relate to the term. At the lower left, list Non-Characteristics, which means words and phrases that would *not* be associated with it. In the lower right, draw a picture of the key term *or* use it in a sentence.

Definition in Your Own Words	Characteristics
a series of military campaigns to establish Christian control over the Holy Land	• proposed by Pope Urban II • Slogan was "God wills it!" • Jerusalem remained in Muslim hands.

Crusades

Non-Characteristics	Picture or Sentence
• well organized • always successful • Crusaders always respected Muslims.	The Crusades failed to achieve their goals, but they did have lasting effects in Europe.

Now use the model above to explore the meaning of the word *heresy*. Use your student text and a dictionary or thesaurus to complete each of the four sections to understand the meaning of this word.

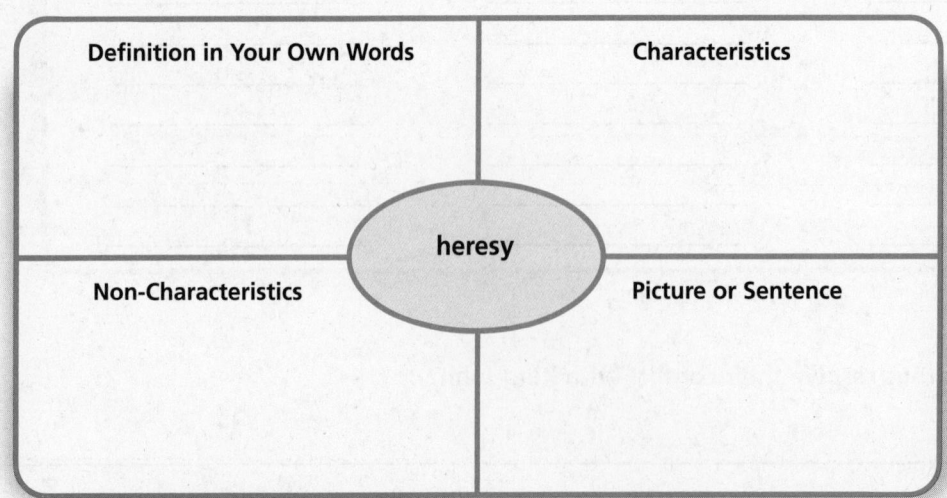

Definition in Your Own Words	Characteristics

heresy

Non-Characteristics	Picture or Sentence

Make a word map of your own on a separate piece of paper for the following word: *Inquisition.*

Name _____ Class _____ Date _____

Take Notes

Sequence Use what you have read in this section to add details to the timeline below.

Religious Crusades

1071 • 1. _____
            _____

1095 • 2. _____
            _____

1099 • 3. _____
            _____

1144 • 4. _____
            _____

     • The Second Crusade fails.

1187 • 5. _____
            _____

     • Saladin and Richard the Lionheart sign a truce that ends the Third Crusade.

1204 • 6. _____
            _____

     • The Children's Crusade fails miserably.

1290 • 7. _____
            _____

1291 • 8. _____
            _____

1307 • 9. _____
            _____

Essential Question

Why did the conflicts known as the Crusades fail to achieve their goal?

_____

_____

_____

Word Wise

In context For each question below, write an answer that shows your understanding of the boldfaced key term.

1 What kind of culture developed in the **Iberian Peninsula** during the 700s?

_____

_____

_____

2 Who were the **Moors**?

_____

_____

_____

3 What happened during the **Reconquista**?

_____

_____

_____

Name _____ Class _____ Date _____

Take Notes

Summarize Use what you have read in Section 4 to summarize key ideas about the topics in the table below.

Spain Under Muslim Rule	
Moorish Culture	
A Multicultural Society	
The Reconquista	
Military Campaigns	
Uniting the Kingdoms	
Religious Persecutions	

? Essential Question

Why did religious intolerance lead to conflict in Spain?

_____

_____

_____

Essential Question | Writer's Workshop

How should we handle conflict?

Prepare to Write

Throughout this chapter, you have explored the Essential Question in your text, journal, and On Assignment at myworldhistory.com. Use what you have learned in this chapter to write an outline about conflict in medieval Europe. Consider the conflicts between kings and popes, kings and barons, crusaders and Muslims, and Catholics and non-Christians in Muslim Spain.

Workshop Skill: Write a Conclusion

Remember that drafting an essay requires writing a thesis statement, an introduction, at least three body paragraphs, and a conclusion. The conclusion wraps up your essay and brings everything together.

Before Writing Your Conclusion Before you write your conclusion, reread your essay. Think about the thesis as well as the main ideas and details that support it.

What Makes a Strong Conclusion? A strong conclusion should tie together the different strands of your essay. It should give your reader the feeling that everything adds up and makes sense.

Follow These Steps When you're ready to write your conclusion, do so in a logical, organized way. Follow steps on a checklist like the one below. As you complete each step, check it off your list.

_____ Write a topic sentence to remind the reader of the main idea of the essay.

_____ Summarize the most important ideas.

_____ Restate your thesis in a way that is different from your introduction.

_____ Write a concluding sentence.

Writing a strong conclusion requires thought and effort. Remember, it is the last impression that your essay makes on your readers.

Sample Conclusions Here are some sample sentences that could be used to form a cohesive conclusion.

- Sample topic sentence: *Kings and popes fought for power during the Middle Ages.*

- Summary of an important idea: *Popes believed they had authority over both Church and secular leaders.*

272

- Sample of thesis restatement: *At a time when religion influenced every part of daily life, the Church had as much if not more power than kings.*

- Sample of concluding sentence: *Kings may have wielded their power through armies, but popes used their power of excommunication.*

Write Your Conclusion

Now write your own concluding paragraph for your essay.

Topic Sentence

_____

_____

Summary of an important idea

_____

_____

Summary of another important idea

_____

_____

Summary of a final important idea

_____

_____

Restatement of thesis

_____

_____

Concluding sentence

_____

_____

Draft Your Essay

Use the concluding paragraph above in your completed essay. Write your essay on another sheet of paper.

Name _____ Class _____ Date _____

How are religion and culture connected?

Preview Before you begin this chapter, think about the Essential Question. Understanding how the Essential Question connects to your life will help you understand the chapter you are about to read.

Connect to Your Life

① What religions are you aware of in your local community?

_____

② In the table below, give examples of elements of your local culture. Then note whether and how religion influences these elements.

Elements of Local Culture	Description or Example	Influence of Religion
Clothing		
Trade		
Celebrations		

Connect to the Chapter

③ Preview the chapter. Skim the headings, photos, and graphics. In the table below, predict how religion influenced Europe during the Middle Ages.

Elements of Medieval Culture	Description or Example	Influence of Religion
Farms		
Towns		
Architecture		

④ After you have read the chapter, return to this page. Circle the predictions that were correct.

Name _____ Class _____ Date _____

Connect to myStory: Joan of Arc: Voices of Victory

① What was occurring in Europe at the time of this myStory?

_____

_____

② Would you have followed Joan of Arc? Why or why not?

_____

_____

③ What characteristics do you think best describe Joan of Arc? Write these characteristics in the diagram below.

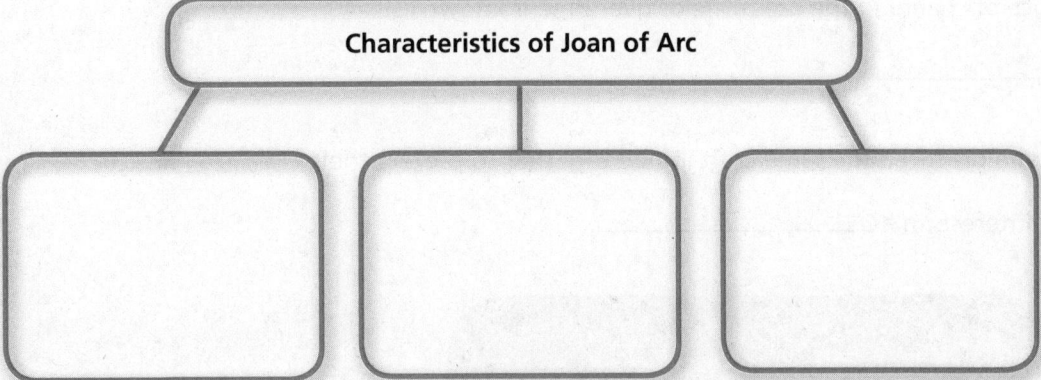

Characteristics of Joan of Arc

④ In the table below, list three ways that Joan of Arc helped the French.

Actions of Joan of Arc
a.
b.
c.

⑤ Why were the people accepting of Joan's belief that she heard voices of saints?

_____

_____

Name _____ Class _____ Date _____

Word Wise

Sentence Builder Finish the sentences below with a key term from this section. You may have to change the form of the words to complete the sentences.

Word Bank

crop rotation   fallow
three-field system   guild

① Farmers planted spring crops, winter crops, and no crops in the

_____.

② To allow the soil to recover some of its natural fertility, farmers every

year left one field _____.

③ The practice of changing the use of fields over time is known

as _____.

④ Workers who practiced the same craft joined together to protect their

economic interests in a _____.

Name _____ Class _____ Date _____

Take Notes

Compare and Contrast In the diagram below, describe and compare the changes made in life on farms, trade, and life in towns during the Middle Ages.

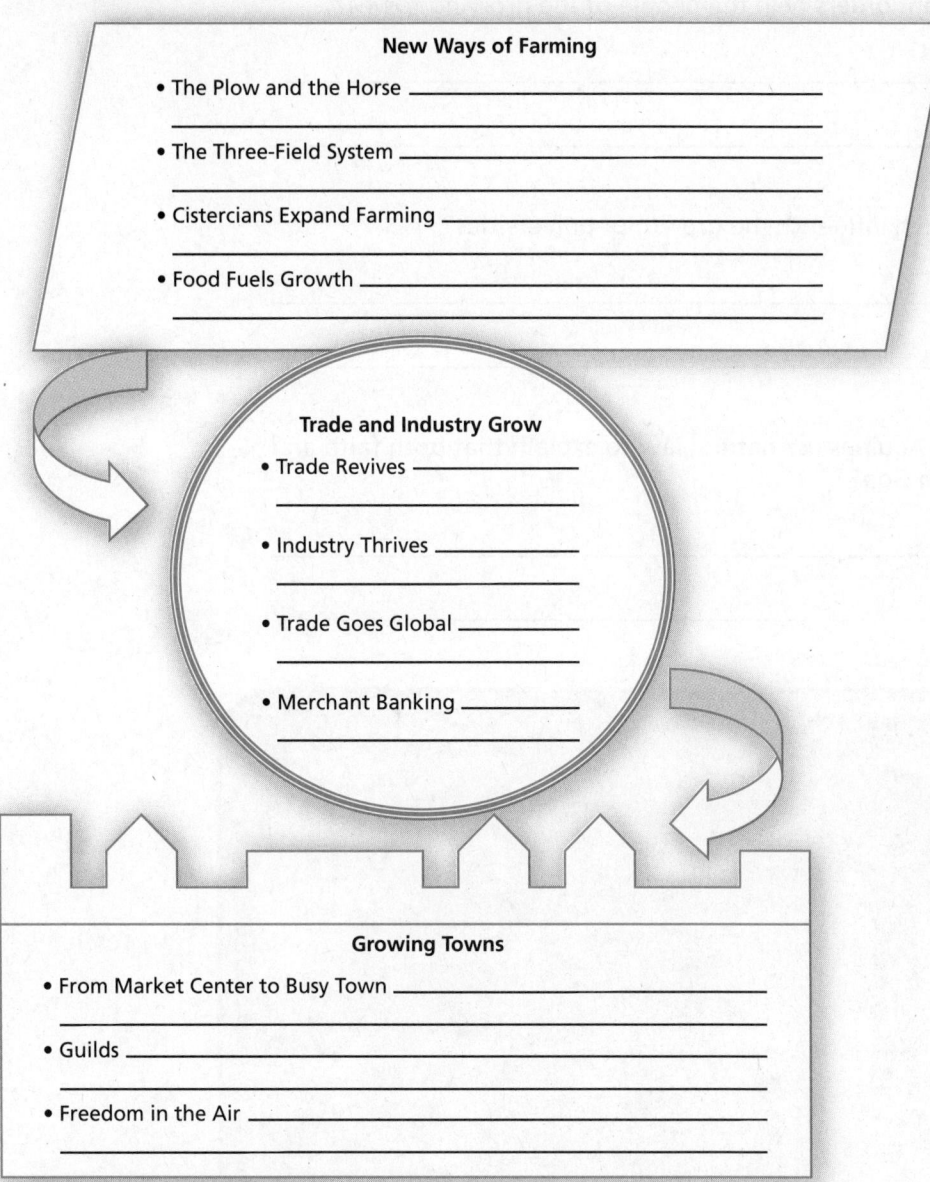

New Ways of Farming

- The Plow and the Horse _____
  _____
- The Three-Field System _____
  _____
- Cistercians Expand Farming _____
  _____
- Food Fuels Growth _____
  _____

Trade and Industry Grow

- Trade Revives _____
  _____
- Industry Thrives _____
  _____
- Trade Goes Global _____
  _____
- Merchant Banking _____
  _____

Growing Towns

- From Market Center to Busy Town _____
  _____
- Guilds _____
  _____
- Freedom in the Air _____
  _____

Essential Question

What effects did increasing wealth in towns have on church building?

_____

_____

_____

Word Wise

Words In Context For each question below, write an answer that shows your understanding of the boldfaced key term.

1 How did **mendicant orders** help the people of the growing towns?

_____

_____

2 How did the Church influence the growth of **universities**?

_____

_____

3 How did Thomas Aquinas use **natural law** to explain that both faith and reason come from God?

_____

_____

Name _____ Class _____ Date _____

Take Notes

Summarize Use Section 2 to summarize information about religion during the Middle Ages in the diagram below.

Forms of Devotion	Medieval Religion and Culture	The Growth of Learning
Religious Orders _____ _____ _____	Revival of Drama _____ _____ _____	Medieval Universities _____ _____ _____
St. Francis and St. Clare _____ _____ _____	New Architecture _____ _____ _____	Thomas Aquinas _____ _____ _____
	The Church Shapes Chivalry _____ _____ _____	An Age of Confidence _____ _____ _____

Essential Question

In what ways did religion affect culture in the Middle Ages?

_____

_____

Name _____ Class _____ Date _____

Word Wise

Vocabulary Quiz Show Some quiz shows ask a question and expect the contestant to give the answer. In other shows, the contestant is given an answer and must supply the question. If the blank is in the Question column, write the question that would result in the answer in the Answer column. If the question is supplied, write the answer.

QUESTION

① _____

② What name was later given to the epidemic known as the Great Dying?

③ _____

④ After manor lords limited the surviving serfs' wages and movements, what event occurred?

ANSWER

① Hundred Years' War

② _____

③ bubonic plague

④ _____

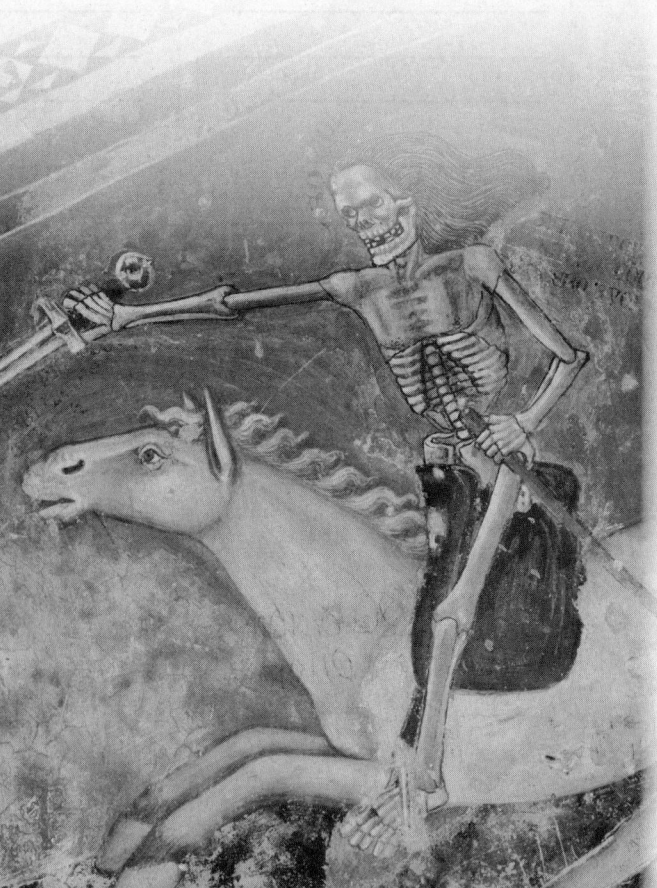

280

Name _____ Class _____ Date _____

Take Notes

Analyze Cause and Effect For each cause listed below, describe the effect(s).

Causes	Effects

From 1315 to 1317, rain fell throughout much of Europe. → 1.

The English invented the longbow. → 2.

Joan of Arc claims to hear voices from heaven that tell her to lead the French army. → 3.

People infected with the plague ride merchant ships from the East to ports throughout Europe. → 4.

People do not know what the plague is or how it spreads. → 5.

The Black Death kills about one third of all Europeans. → 6.

→ 7.

→ 8.

 Essential Question

Why might the Black Death have shaken people's confidence in the Church?

_____

_____

_____

Name _____ Class _____ Date _____

Essential Question   Writer's Workshop

How are religion and culture connected?

Prepare to Write

Throughout this chapter, you have explored the Essential Question in your text, journal, and On Assignment at myworldhistory.com. Use what you have learned in this chapter to write an essay about how religion and culture were connected in medieval Europe. Consider the following: how Cistercian monks helped crop and sheep farming; how the Crusades influenced trade and banking; how towns with relics attracted pilgrims; how mendicant orders influenced townspeople; and how the Church influenced education, drama, art, sculpture, architecture, and chivalry.

Workshop Skill: Revise Your Work

Review how to outline your essay, and then write and develop an introduction, body paragraphs, and a conclusion. Consider the main point you want to make in your essay and phrase it as a thesis statement. For example: *The Catholic Church influenced every part of life during the Middle Ages.* In your introduction, list three influences of the Church. In each body paragraph, develop one of these influences using details and evidence to support it.

In this lesson, you will learn more about how to revise your essay. Revision has several important goals: First, you should clarify main ideas and connect them to both the readers and your writing purpose. Second, you should evaluate each piece of evidence to ensure that it fits your thesis. Third, you should review sentences to make sure that they make sense and contain no grammar, punctuation, or spelling errors.

Identify Your Main Points

_____ Starting with your introduction, check that each paragraph has a main point.

_____ This point should be clearly stated and is usually the first or last sentence.

_____ Circle all your main points, including your thesis.

Think About Your Readers and Purpose

_____ Remember who your reader will be—your teacher.

_____ Make sure that your language is formal. Replace any slang, and do not use personal pronouns.

_____ Use the writing prompt to guide your purpose.

_____ Look back at your essay to make sure you have connected the causes and effects.

Evaluate Your Evidence

_____ Reread each circled main point. Carefully read the rest of the paragraph.

_____ Does the evidence support the main point?

_____ Is the evidence organized in a logical or chronological manner?

_____ Make sure the evidence supports your thesis.

_____ Reword your thesis slightly, if necessary, to fit the points you've made. Sentences that don't support the thesis and main ideas should be eliminated.

Be Clear and Correct

_____ Read your essay aloud. Never skip this step! Hearing your sentences will help you notice when they don't flow or if they don't make sense.

_____ Ask yourself what you meant to say and use that restatement to rewrite confusing sentences.

_____ Reread silently or use a computer grammar and spelling checker to find and correct any errors.

Revise Your Essay

Now look critically at one paragraph from your essay and make revisions to improve it. Write your corrected paragraph below.

_____

_____

_____

_____

_____

_____

_____

_____

_____

Draft Your Essay

Copy the revised paragraph into your essay. Use it as a guide in revising the remaining paragraphs. Make sure to check each paragraph for a main idea, supporting evidence, and appropriate spelling, grammar, and punctuation.

Places to Know!

Map Skills Use the maps in this unit to identify the Places to Know! on the outline map. Before the name of each place below, write the letter that shows its location on the map.

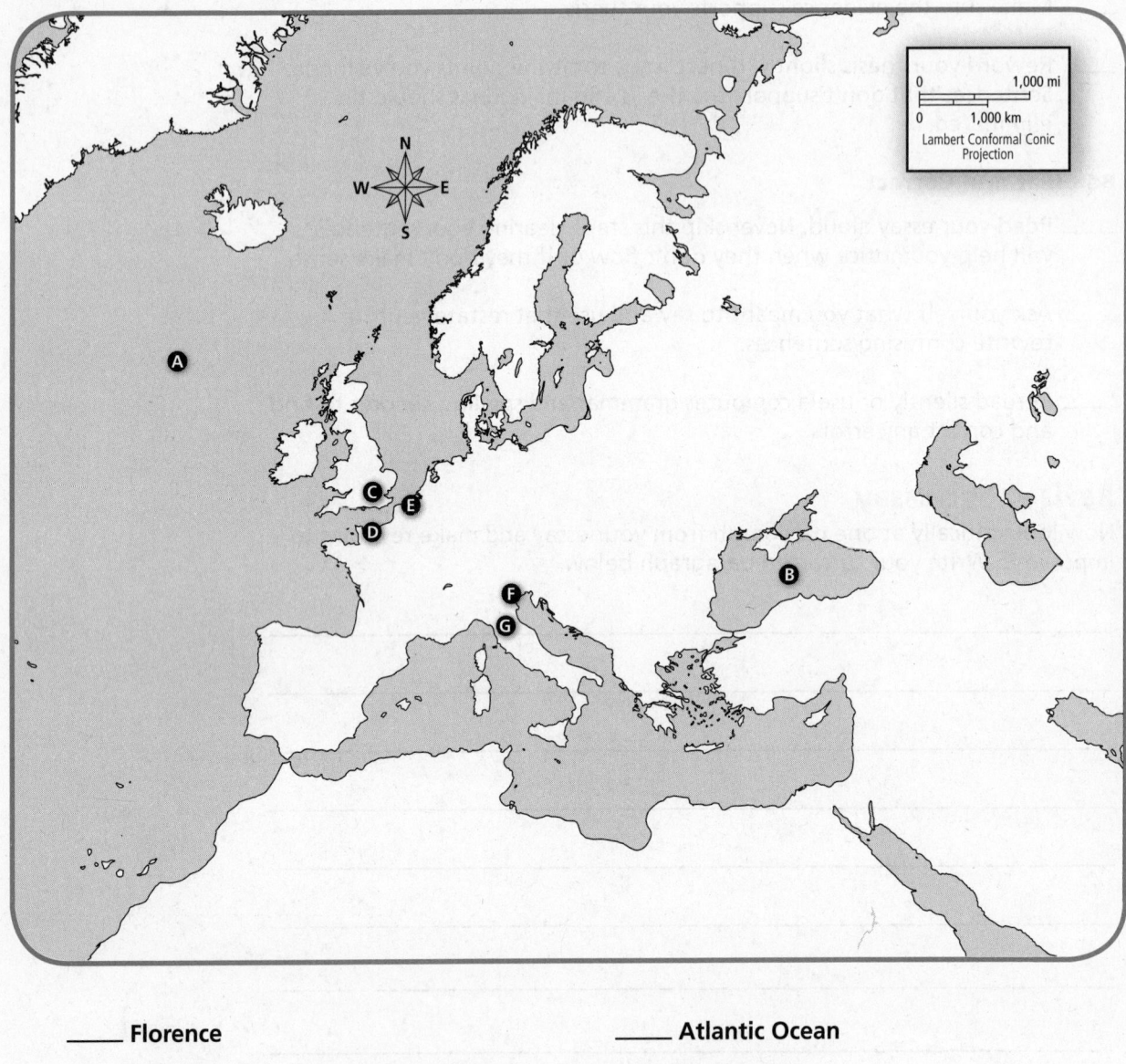

_____ Florence

_____ London

_____ Black Sea

_____ Venice

_____ Atlantic Ocean

_____ Normandy

_____ Flanders

Key Events

Timeline Use what you have read about Europe in the Middle Ages to complete the timeline below. Draw a line from each event to its correct position on the timeline. Then write a brief description of each event.

529 _____
_____

732 _____
_____

800 _____
_____

1066 _____
_____

1096 _____
_____

1337 _____
_____

1215 _____
_____

1347 _____
_____

500

700

900

1100

1300

1500

Name _____ Class _____ Date _____

Essential Question

What distinguishes one culture from another?

Preview Before you begin this chapter, think about the Essential Question. Understanding how the Essential Question connects to your life will help you understand the chapter you are about to read.

Connect to Your Life

(1) Think about your culture—the things that make your daily life different from life in other countries or other centuries. What is the main way culture affects your life? Explain your answer.

_____

_____

_____

(2) Record your ideas about how culture affects you in the areas below.

How Culture Affects Me			
Government/Laws	Technology	Traditions	Other

Connect to the Chapter

(3) Preview the chapter. Skim the headings, photos, and graphics. In the table below, make predictions about which kinds of cultural changes occurred during the Renaissance.

	Cultural Change
Government	
Language	
Science and Technology	
Art	

(4) Read the chapter. Then return to this page and circle the predictions you made that were correct.

Name _____ Class _____ Date _____

Connect to myStory: "So Many Things Unknown"

① Leonardo da Vinci said, "Obstacles cannot crush me. He who is fixed to a star does not change his mind." Do you agree with Leonardo? How could such a belief affect your life?

_____

_____

_____

② Leonardo da Vinci was a brilliant man who worked in many fields. Record details of his interests and accomplishments in the web below.

Leonardo's Interests and Accomplishments

③ Artists and scholars like Leonardo had to depend on wealthy and powerful people for support. What were some problems of this way of life?

_____

_____

_____

Word Wise

Make a Word Map Follow the model below to make a word map. The Key Term *mercantile* is in the center oval. Write the definition in your own words at the upper left. In the upper right, list Characteristics, which mean words or phrases that relate to the term. At the lower left, list Non-Characteristics, which means words and phrases that would not be associated with it. In the lower right, draw a picture of the Key Term or use it in a sentence.

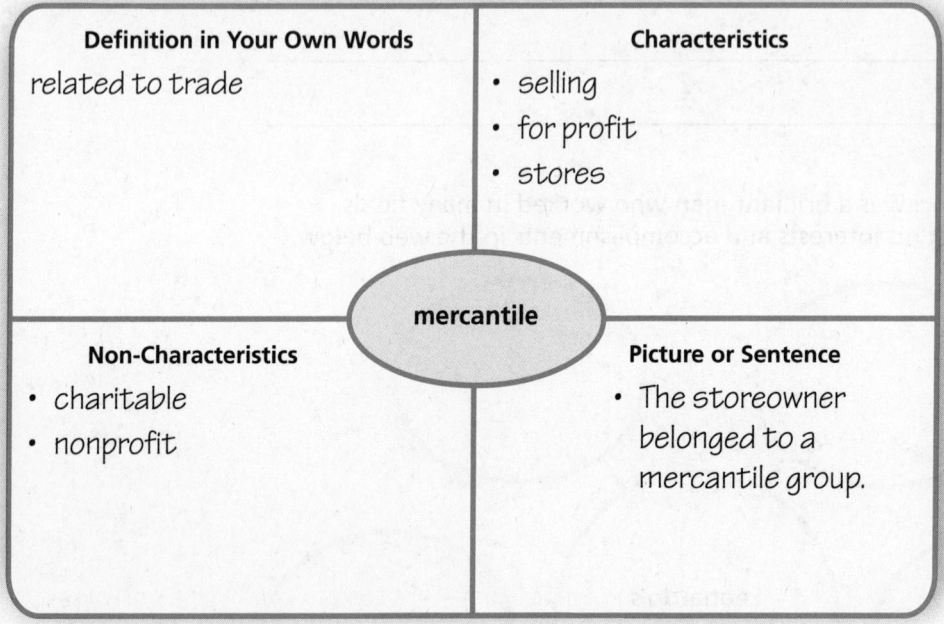

Definition in Your Own Words
related to trade

Characteristics
- selling
- for profit
- stores

mercantile

Non-Characteristics
- charitable
- nonprofit

Picture or Sentence
- The storeowner belonged to a mercantile group.

Now use the word map below to explore the meaning of the word *Renaissance*. You may use your student text, a dictionary, and/or thesaurus to complete each of the four sections.

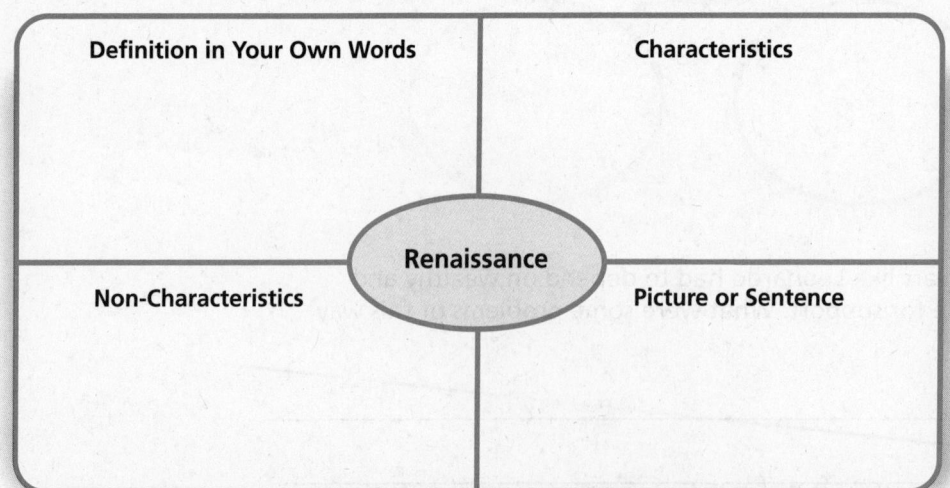

Definition in Your Own Words

Characteristics

Renaissance

Non-Characteristics

Picture or Sentence

Make a word map of your own on a separate piece of paper for this Key Term: *patron*.

Name _____ Class _____ Date _____

Take Notes

Cause and Effect Use what you have read about the origins of the
Renaissance to complete the cause-and-effect charts below.

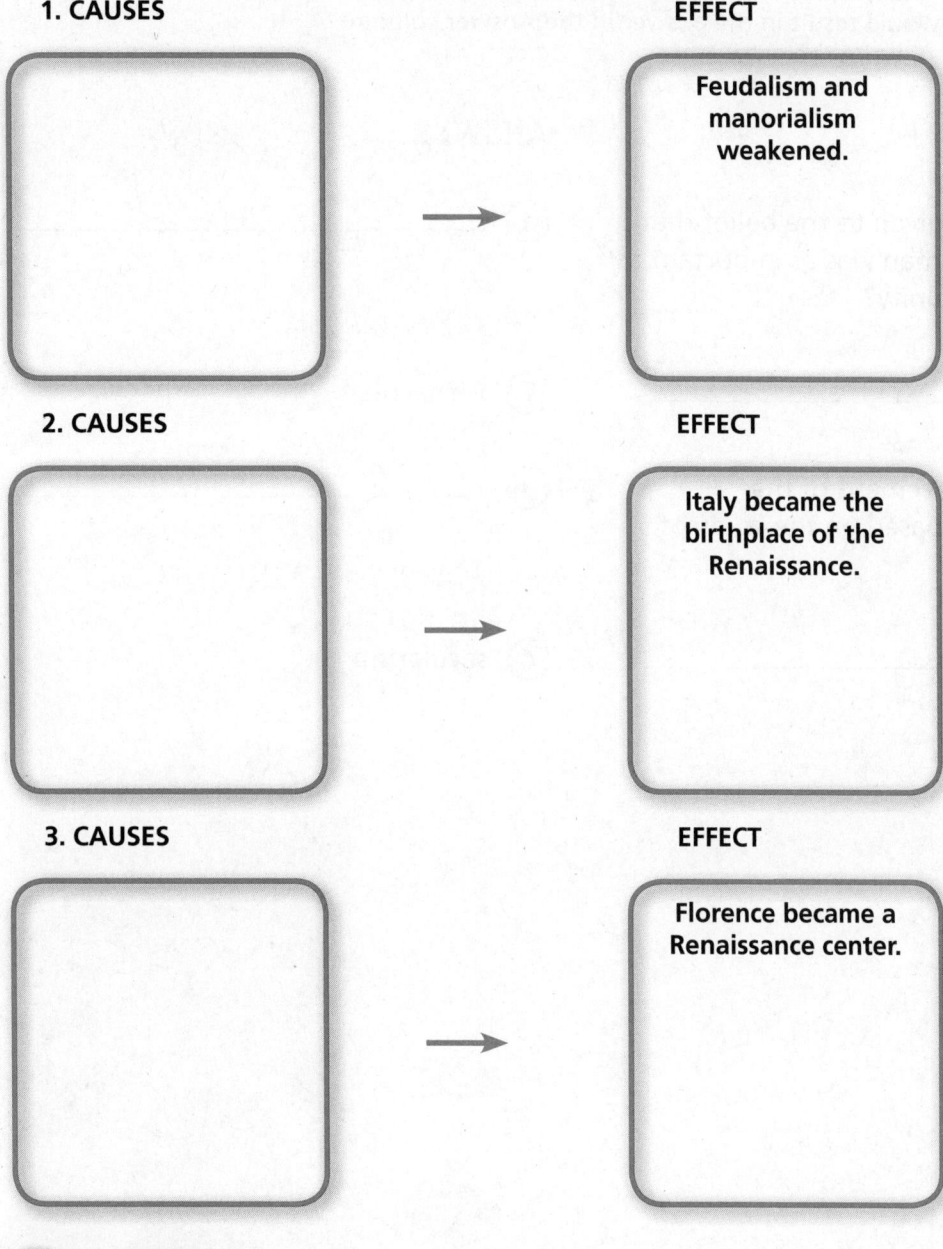

1. CAUSES

EFFECT

Feudalism and
manorialism
weakened.

2. CAUSES

EFFECT

Italy became the
birthplace of the
Renaissance.

3. CAUSES

EFFECT

Florence became a
Renaissance center.

Essential Question

How was the culture of Italian cities different from rural culture?
How were the cultures of Venice and Florence different?

_____

_____

_____

Word Wise

Vocabulary Quiz Show Some quiz shows ask a question and expect the contestant to give the answer. In other shows, the contestant is given an answer and must supply the question. If the blank is in the Question column, write the question that would result in the answer in the Answer column. If the question is supplied, write the answer.

QUESTION

1. What name was given to the belief that each separate human was as important as the whole community?

2. _____

3. What cultural movement of the Renaissance was based on the study of classical works?

4. _____

ANSWER

1. _____

2. vernacular

3. _____

4. secularism

Name _____ Class _____ Date _____

Take Notes

Compare and Contrast Use what you have read about the Middle Ages and Renaissance to record similarities and differences between the two periods on the Venn diagram below.

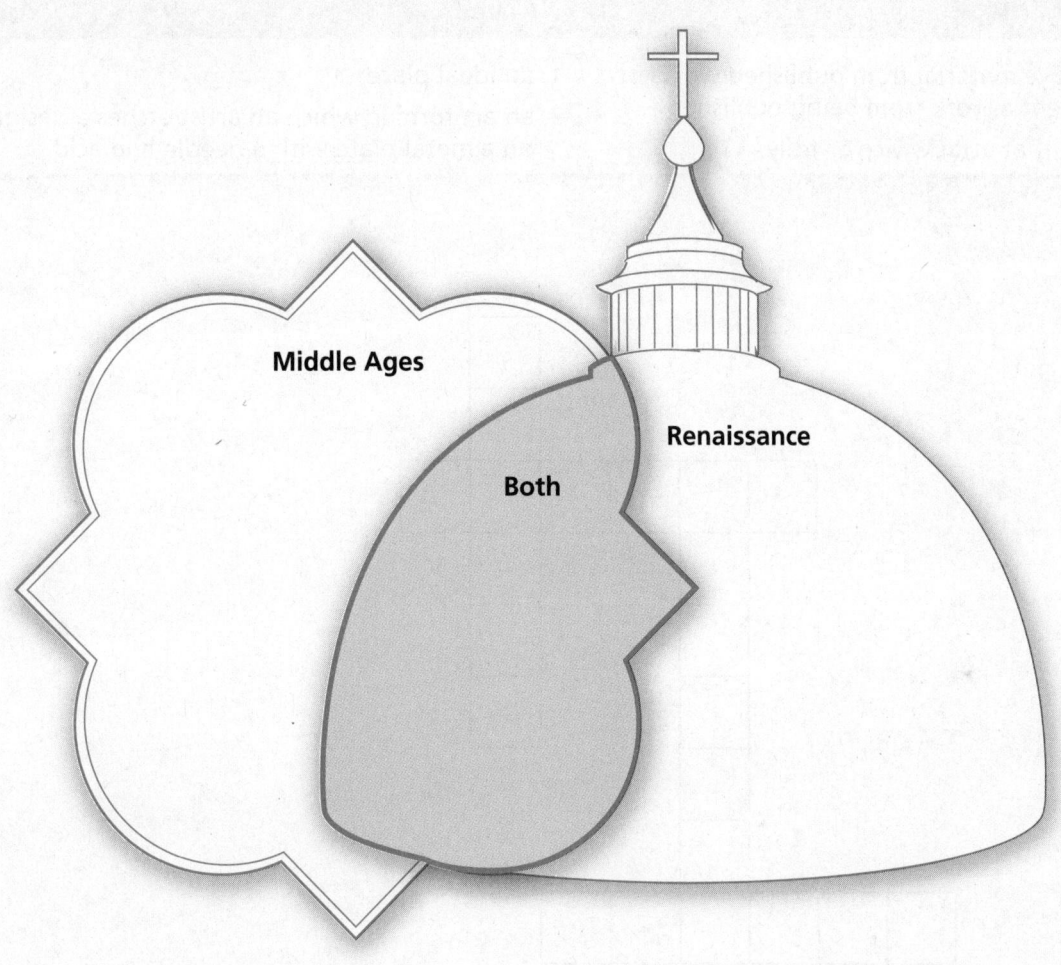

Middle Ages

Both

Renaissance

Essential Question

How did humanism differ from medieval education? How was Renaissance art different from medieval art?

_____

_____

_____

Word Wise

Crossword Puzzle The *Across* and *Down* clues are definitions of key terms from this section. Fill in the numbered *Across* boxes with the correct key terms. Then do the same with the *Down* clues.

Across	Down
2. to remove material from published works or to prevent a work from being published	1. an ideal place
4. writing that attacks vice or folly	3. an art form in which an artist etches a design on a metal plate with a needle and acid

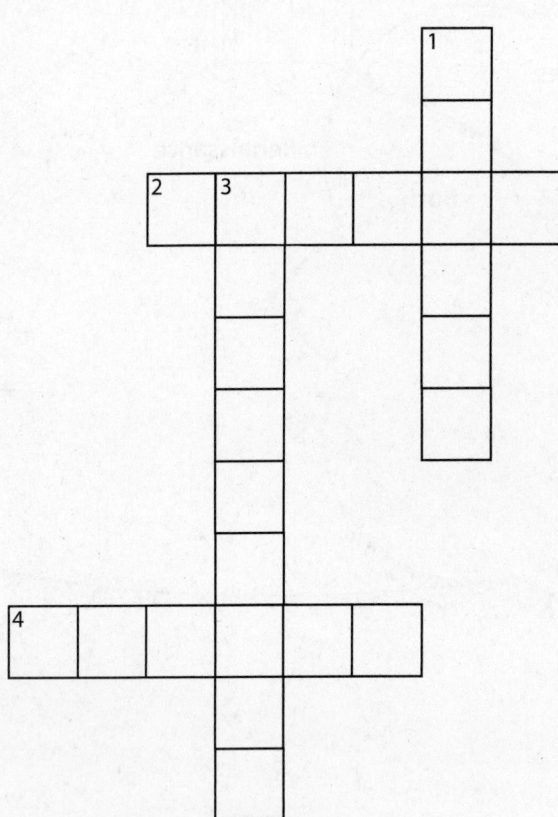

Name _____ Class _____ Date _____

Take Notes

Identify Main Ideas and Details Use what you have read about the
Renaissance to add details to the chart below.

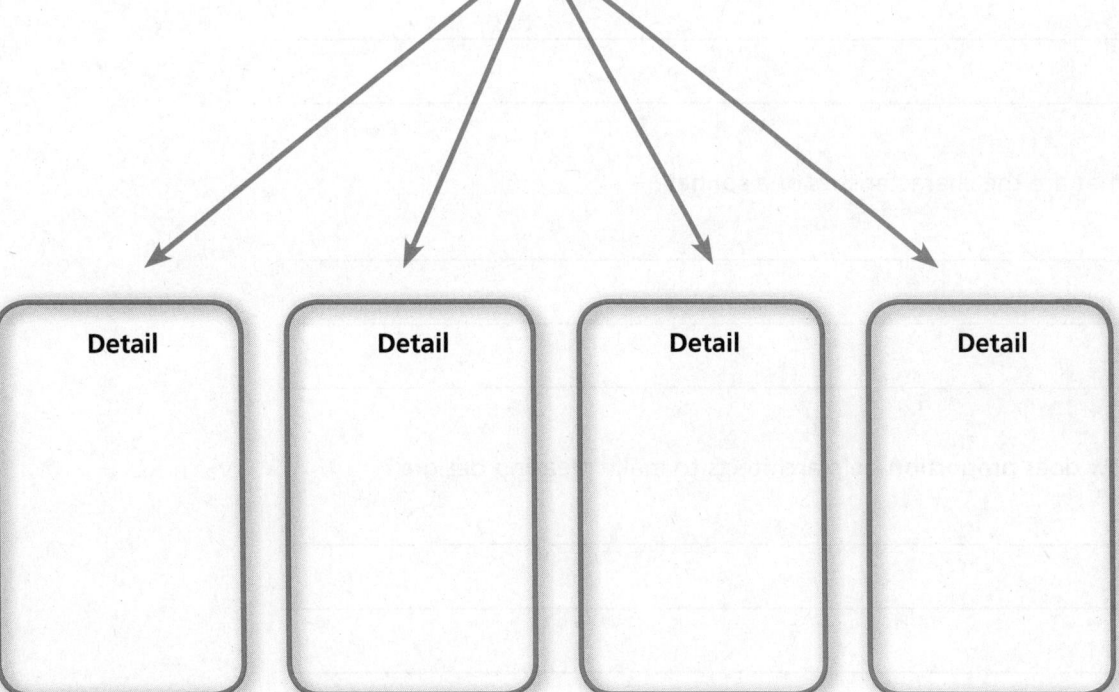

Main Idea

Renaissance ideas spread.

Detail

Detail

Detail

Detail

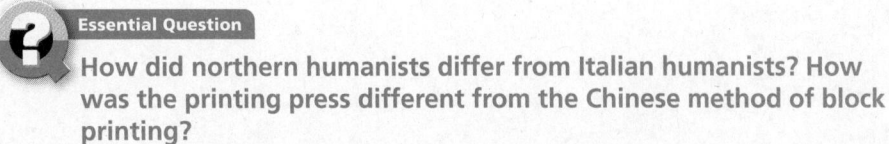

Essential Question

How did northern humanists differ from Italian humanists? How
was the printing press different from the Chinese method of block
printing?

_____

_____

_____

Name _____ Class _____ Date _____

Word Wise

Words in Context For each question below, write an answer that shows your understanding of the boldfaced Key Term.

1. What kind of story does a **picaresque** novel tell?

   _____

   _____

   _____

2. What does **linear perspective** allow artists to do?

   _____

   _____

   _____

3. What are the characteristics of a **sonnet**?

   _____

   _____

   _____

4. How does **proportion** help architects to make pleasing designs?

   _____

   _____

   _____

Name _____ Class _____ Date _____

Take Notes

Summarize Use what you have read about the Renaissance to summarize the main achievements in architecture, art, and literature in the table below.

Renaissance Architecture	Renaissance Art	Renaissance Literature

Essential Question
How did Miguel de Cervantes draw on medieval culture to write his novel? How did the ideal of the Renaissance man differ from medieval ideals?

_____

_____

_____

Essential Question Writer's Workshop

What distinguishes one culture from another?

Prepare to Write

Throughout this chapter, you have explored the Essential Question in your text, journal, and by going On Assignment at myworldhistory.com. Use what you have learned to write an e-mail letter to a European department of tourism. Tell the official at the agency that you are preparing for a trip and want to know how the culture of his or her country differs from American culture.

Workshop Skill: Write a Letter

Review what you have already learned about writing letters, including appropriate greetings and conclusions and what the body of a letter includes. Then think about how a letter written as an e-mail will differ from a letter sent through the U.S. mail.

In this lesson, you will learn how to write a letter via e-mail. First, think about how to write a concise, clear subject line. You will then learn how to change what you already know about writing letters to fit the format of an e-mail. You will also consider how to use formatting to strengthen your e-mailed letter.

Make the Subject Clear Unlike formal letters, there is no need for an address heading before the greeting in an e-mail. However, the subject line of your e-mail must be clear and concise. Many people will not open e-mails from people they do not know. Therefore, your subject line needs to explain the purpose of your letter in such a way that the recipient will consider it safe to open.

For instance, if you are writing to a customer service department about a problem with something you purchased, a good subject line would be *Product complaint.*

Write a clear, concise subject line for your e-mail to the Department of Tourism:

_____

Get Your Point Across Quickly Like its subject line, an e-mail letter needs to be as concise as possible. Most people have more difficulty processing information in a long e-mail than in reading a long hard-copy letter. Keep your e-mail short enough that the reader scrolls as little as possible.

Plan Your Paragraphs Suppose that your e-mail to the European tourism official is three paragraphs, as described below. Record the main points you want to get across in each paragraph.

Paragraph 1: Briefly introduce yourself and your travel plans.	_____ _____
Paragraph 2: Describe the kind of information you would like the official to give you about European culture. Explain how this information will help you plan your trip.	_____ _____ _____ _____ _____
Paragraph 3: Provide your contact information and the dates of your trip. Thank the official for his or her time.	_____ _____ _____ _____

Take Advantage of Technology Think about how to use your e-mail program's features to your advantage. For example, a spell-checker is helpful. You may wish to use formatting features like boldfacing and italics to make text stand out. Don't overuse these features. Avoid emoticons and casual abbreviations. Also, do not write words in solid capitals, as many people consider that rude in an e-mail.

Now draft the second paragraph of your e-mail using your notes above. Circle instances where you would use features of your e-mail program, such as the spell-checker or formatting features.

_____

_____

_____

Be Ready for a Quick Reply Conclude your e-mail with appropriate thanks, complete contact information (such as your street address and phone number), and your full name. There is no need to include your e-mail address since the recipient will probably just hit the reply button. The speed of e-mail means that you might receive a reply faster than you expected. Be prepared to write a quick reply thanking him or her for the response.

Write Your E-mail Letter

Now use the information you jotted down above to create a complete e-mail on a computer. Be sure your e-mail includes a clear subject line, a concise body, neat formatting, and a proper conclusion. E-mail it to a classmate "official" for feedback.

Name _____ Class _____ Date _____

Essential Question

How should we handle conflict?

Before you begin this chapter, think about the Essential Question. Understanding how the Essential Question connects to your life will help you understand the chapter you are about to read.

Connect to Your Life

(1) Think about conflicts that you have seen on the news or in your daily life. Where is conflict most likely to arise? What causes conflict? Why does tension sometimes turn into fighting?

_____

_____

(2) Record examples of conflict that you have observed in the following table.

	Type of Conflict	Source of Conflict
Neighborhood		
Public Places (Stores, Highways, and so on)		
Between Friends		

Connect to the Chapter

(3) Before you read the chapter, flip through every page and note the red headings, maps, and other pictures. In the table below, make predictions about what kinds of conflict occurred during the Reformation.

	Who Was Involved	Source of Conflict
Conflicts Within the Catholic Church		
Conflicts Between Different Groups of Christians		

(4) After reading the chapter, return to this page. Change any predictions that were incorrect.

_____

_____

Name _____ Class _____ Date _____

Connect to myStory: "Kidnapped!"

1 Why did the masked horsemen kidnap Martin Luther?

_____

_____

_____

2 In the table below, record what Martin Luther did during his time in Wartburg and the effect of his actions.

Luther's Actions While at Wartburg	The Effect of Those Actions

3 How did Luther handle conflict? What might he have done differently?

_____

_____

_____

Word Wise

Sentence Builder Complete the sentences using the information you learned in this section.

① People who believe in **predestination** think that _____

_____

② Geneva was considered a **theocracy** under John Calvin because _____

_____

③ Luther objected to the sale of **indulgences** because _____

_____

④ During the **Reformation**, Martin Luther and John Calvin _____

_____

⑤ By asking Martin Luther to **recant**, church leaders wanted him to _____

_____

⑥ The spread of Luther's ideas increased the number of **sects** in Europe,

which means _____.

Name _____ Class _____ Date _____

Take Notes

Analyze Cause and Effect Use what you have read about the Reformation to complete the cause-and-effect chart below.

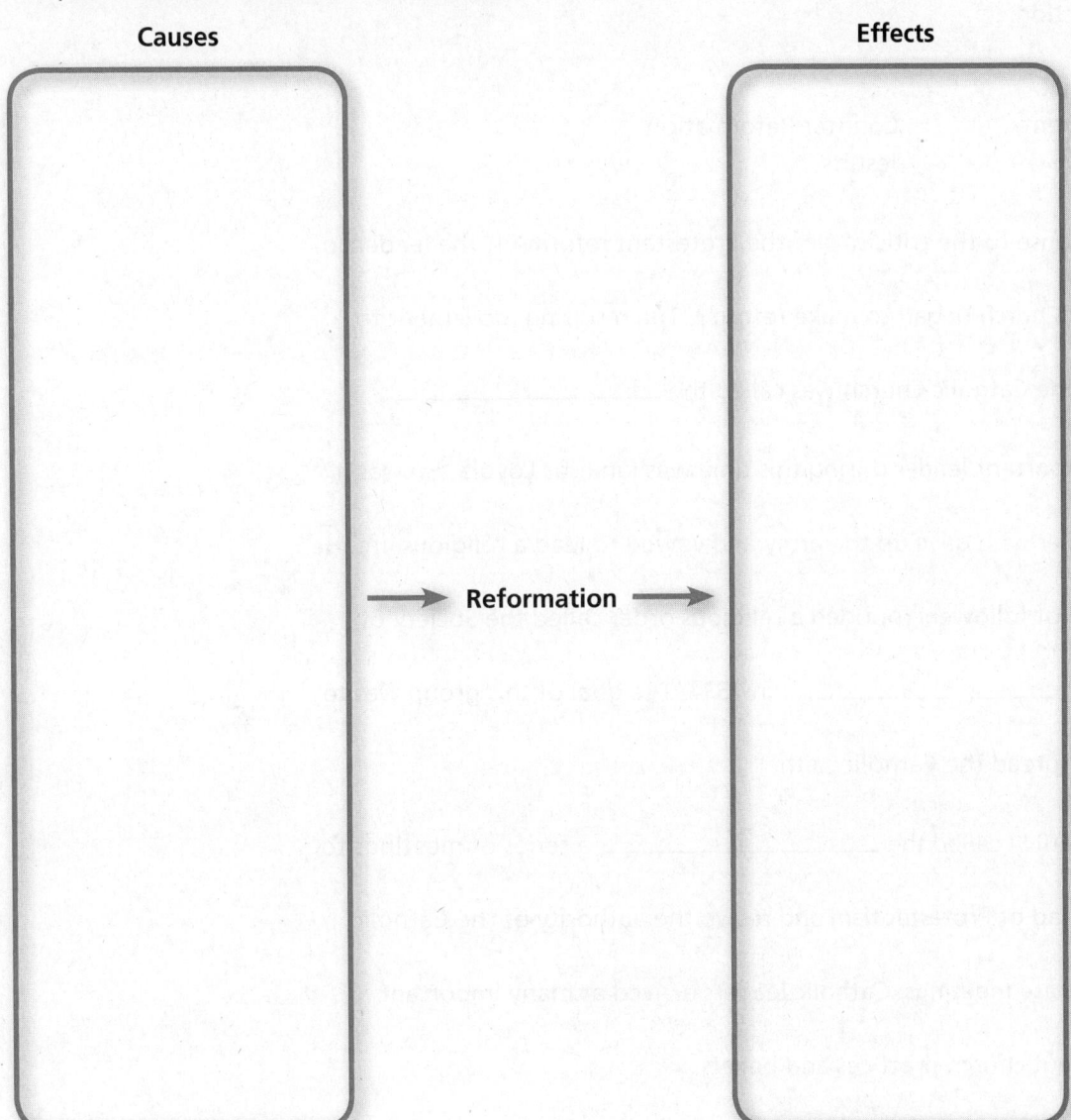

Causes

Effects

→ **Reformation** →

? Essential Question

How did Luther express his conflict with the Church? How did the Church respond to Luther's actions?

_____

_____

_____

Word Wise

Word Bank Choose one word from the word bank to fill in each blank. When you have finished, you will have a short summary of important ideas from the section.

Word Bank

Council of Trent	Counter-Reformation
ghetto	Jesuits

In response to the criticisms of the Protestant reformers, the leaders of

the Catholic Church began to make reforms. The resulting movement to

strengthen the Catholic Church was called the _____.

One important leader during this time was Ignatius Loyola. He was a

Spanish soldier who gave up the army and vowed to lead a religious life. He

and a group of followers founded a religious order called the Society of

Jesus, or the _____, in 1534. The goal of this group was to

defend and spread the Catholic faith.

Pope Paul III called the _____, a series of meetings to

stop the spread of Protestantism and revive the authority of the Catholic

Church. At these meetings, Catholic leaders arrived at many important

decisions about church practices and beliefs.

The Church enforced those decisions through the Inquisition, a court

that tried people suspected of heresy. During this period, religious

intolerance spread, and conflicts occurred between Catholics and

Protestants. In addition, Jews suffered discrimination. For example, in Venice,

Jews were forced to live in the _____, a separate, walled

neighborhood.

Name _____ Class _____ Date _____

Take Notes

Summarize Use what you have read about the Counter-Reformation to record the decisions made by the Council of Trent on the chart below.

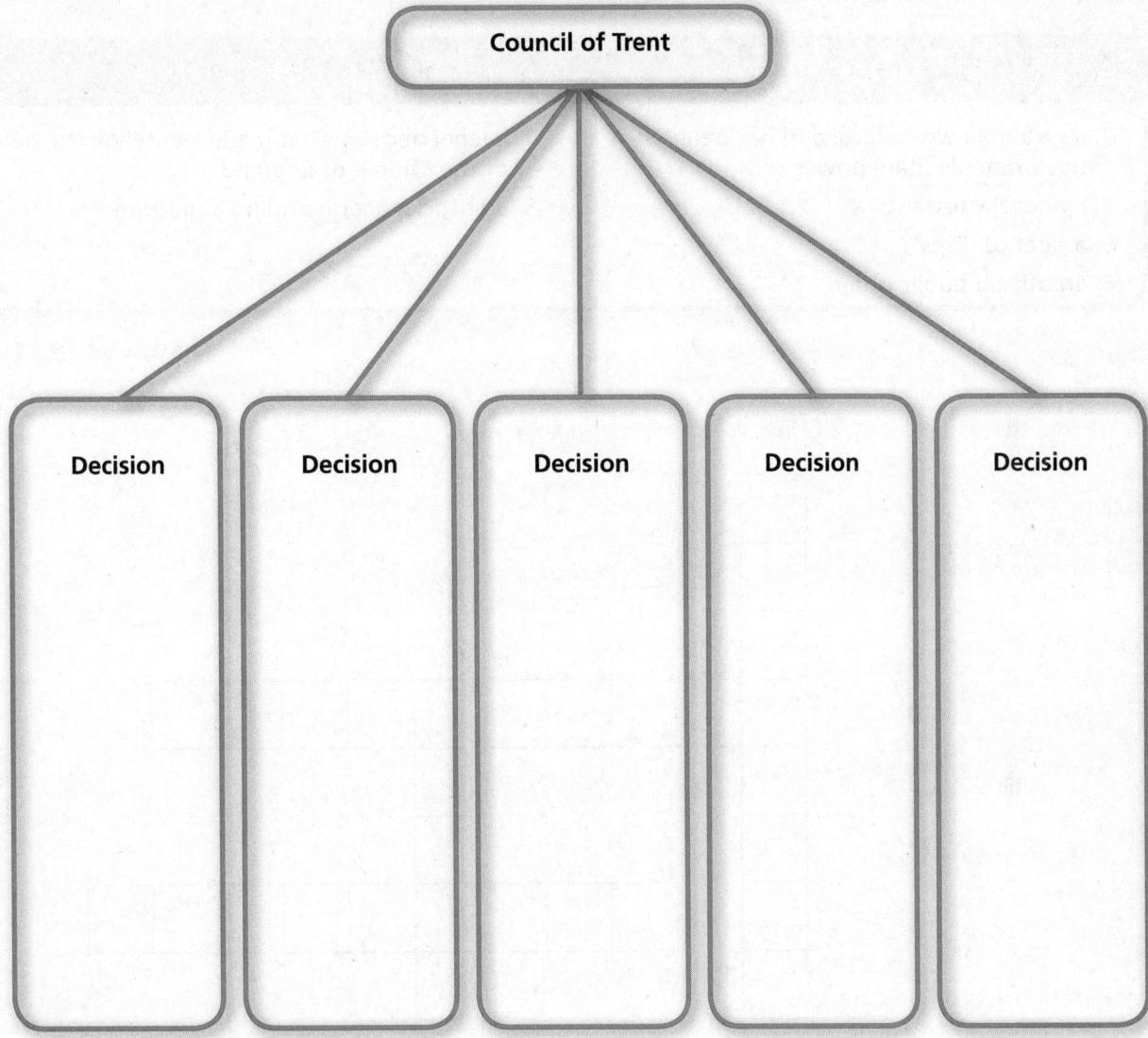

Essential Question

How did the Council of Trent attempt to stop the loss of church members to Protestantism? Did the Council's actions tend to decrease or increase conflict?

_____

_____

_____

Word Wise

Crossword Puzzle The *Across* and *Down* clues are definitions of key terms from this section. Fill in the numbered *Across* boxes with the correct key terms. Then do the same with the *Down* clues.

Across	Down
2. a system in which local and national governments share power	1. a legal decision that made Henry VIII the head of the Church of England
4. French Protestants	3. an official action ending a marriage
5. a fleet of ships	
6. an official public order	

Name _____ Class _____ Date _____

Take Notes

Sequence Use what you have read about the Reformation to add details about religious conflicts to the timeline below.

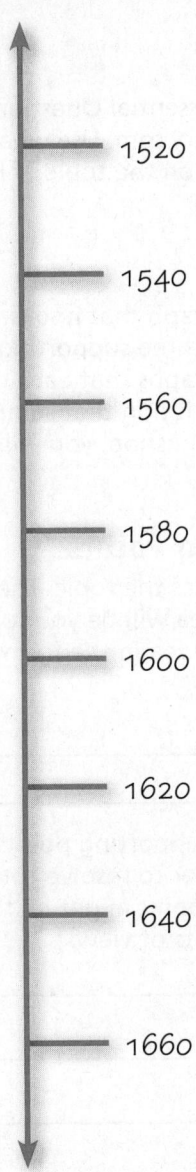

— 1520

— 1540

— 1560

— 1580

— 1600

— 1620

— 1640

— 1660

Essential Question

How did Henry of Navarre end civil war in France? How was the Thirty Years' War resolved?

_____

_____

_____

Name _____ Class _____ Date _____

Prepare to Write

Throughout this chapter, you have explored the Essential Question in your text, journal, and On Assignment at myworldhistory.com. Use what you have learned to outline and draft an explanatory essay on the topic of how to handle conflict.

Workshop Skill: Outline An Essay

A five-paragraph essay has an introductory paragraph that hooks the reader's attention, states a thesis, and introduces three supporting ideas. The introduction is followed by three body paragraphs that each develop one supporting idea. The final paragraph is a conclusion that summarizes the supporting ideas and restates the thesis. In this workshop, you will learn how to outline an essay using this structure.

Identify the Main Idea and Supporting Points

Remember that a main idea is not the same thing as the topic. The topic of your essay is how to handle conflict. Your main idea will be your opinion about the best way to do that. Express your main idea in the form of a thesis statement.

My Thesis Statement _____

_____

Choose Supporting Points Then choose three supporting points to prove your statement. For example, if you think it is better to resolve conflict by negotiating rather than fighting, one supporting point might be that negotiation allows both sides to express their points of view.

1. _____

2. _____

3. _____

Outline the Essay

Use the format below to outline your essay. Because this is an outline, you may record your ideas using words and phrases rather than complete sentences.

I. Introductory Paragraph

Hook _____

Thesis Statement _____

_____

Three Supporting Ideas _____

_____

II. Body Paragraph A
Topic sentence _____

Supporting Detail _____

Supporting Detail _____

Tie to Thesis _____

III. Body Paragraph B
Topic Sentence _____

Supporting Detail _____

Supporting Detail _____

Tie to Thesis _____

IV. Body Paragraph C
Topic Sentence _____

Supporting Detail _____

Supporting Detail _____

Tie to Thesis _____

V. Conclusion
Restate the Thesis _____

_____

Restate the Supporting Points _____

_____

_____

What the Supporting Points Prove _____

_____

Why the Topic Matters _____

_____

Draft Your Essay

Congratulations. You have outlined a five-paragraph essay. Remember to use the steps of the writing process to draft, revise, and edit the essay.

Name _____ Class _____ Date _____

Copyright © Pearson Education, Inc., or its affiliates. All Rights Reserved.

Essential Question

What are the consequences of trade?

Preview Before you begin this chapter, think about the Essential Question. Understanding how the Essential Question connects to your life will help you understand the chapter you are about to read.

Connect to Your Life

(1) Think about a time when you traded with someone else. You might have traded sports cards, food, games, chores, or something else. What did you give up and gain in that trade?

What You Traded Away	What You Received in Return

(2) Did you think the trade was fair? What "rules" did you follow to try to make the trade fair? Did either of you get the better deal? Explain.

_____

_____

Connect to the Chapter

(3) Preview the chapter. Note the trade that took place between European nations and their colonies in the Americas. How might the consequences of that trade be different for the two regions? Record your predictions on the Venn diagram below.

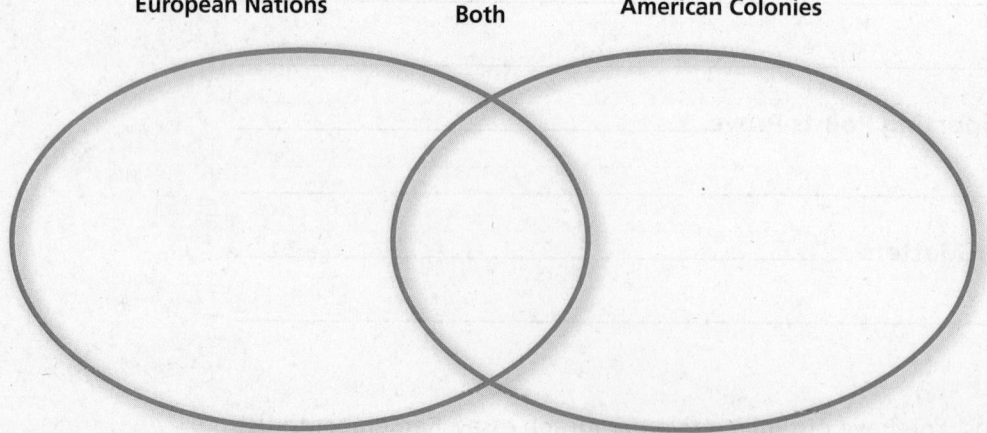

European Nations   Both   American Colonies

(4) Read the chapter. When you have finished, return to the predictions you have made. Circle the predictions that were correct.

Connect to myStory: Journey into Dark Waters

(1) Why was Columbus's journal so important to him? Explain by using details from the story.

_____

_____

_____

(2) What was a long sea voyage like for ordinary sailors? Record details on the table below.

What Did Sailors Fear?	What Was Life Aboard Ship Like?

(3) What was Columbus's reason for undertaking this voyage? How did it relate to trade?

_____

_____

_____

(4) How did Columbus try to keep his men calm during the voyage?

_____

_____

Word Wise

Make a Word Map Follow the model below to make a word map. The Key Term *missionary* is in the center oval. Write the definition in your own words at the upper left. In the upper right, list Characteristics, which means words or phrases that relate to the term. At the lower left, list Non-Characteristics, which means words and phrases that would not be associated with it. In the lower right, draw a picture of the Key Term or use it in a sentence.

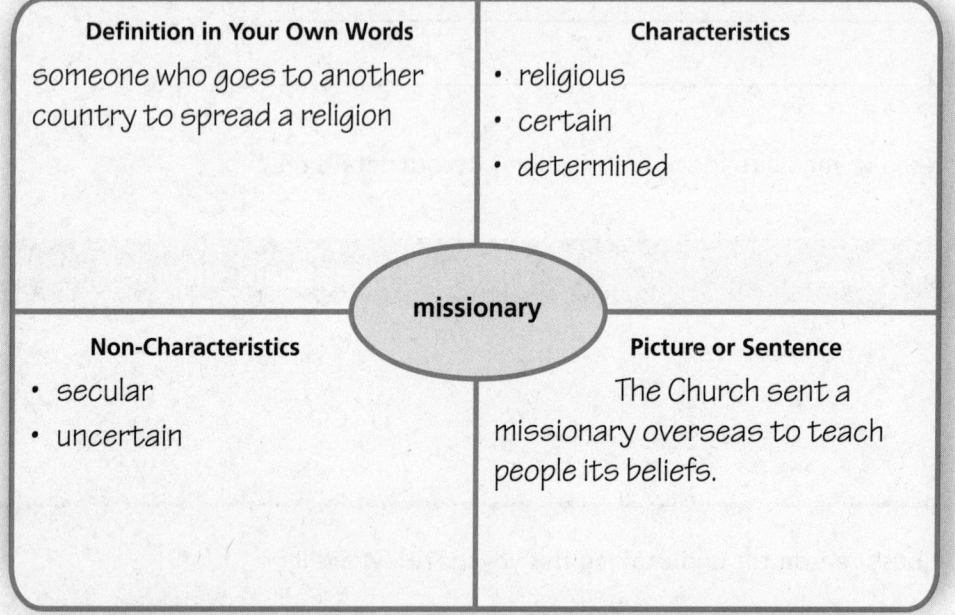

Definition in Your Own Words
someone who goes to another country to spread a religion

Characteristics
- religious
- certain
- determined

missionary

Non-Characteristics
- secular
- uncertain

Picture or Sentence
The Church sent a missionary overseas to teach people its beliefs.

Now use the word map below to explore the meaning of the word *cartography*. You may use your student text, a dictionary, and/or thesaurus to complete each of the four sections.

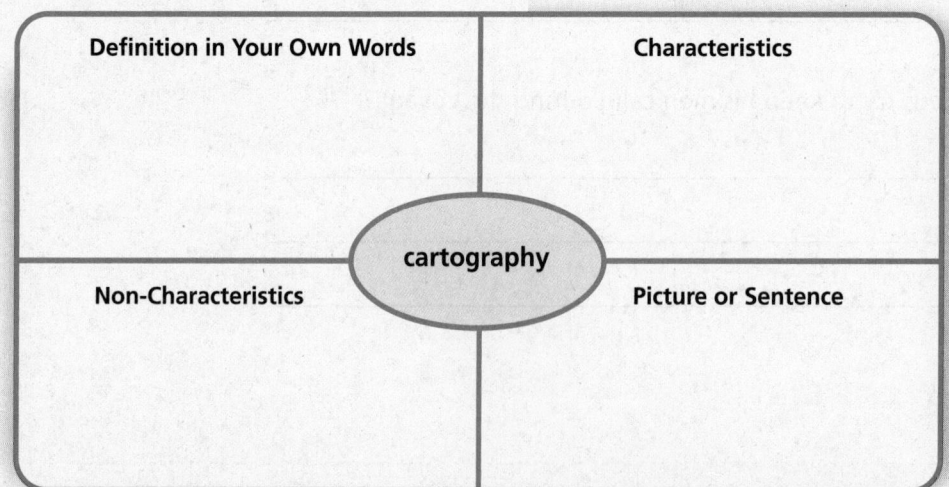

Definition in Your Own Words

Characteristics

cartography

Non-Characteristics

Picture or Sentence

Make word maps of your own on a separate piece of paper for these Key Terms: *caravel, circumnavigate*.

Name _____ Class _____ Date _____

Take Notes

Analyze Cause and Effect Use what you have read about the voyages of discovery to complete the cause-and-effect chart below.

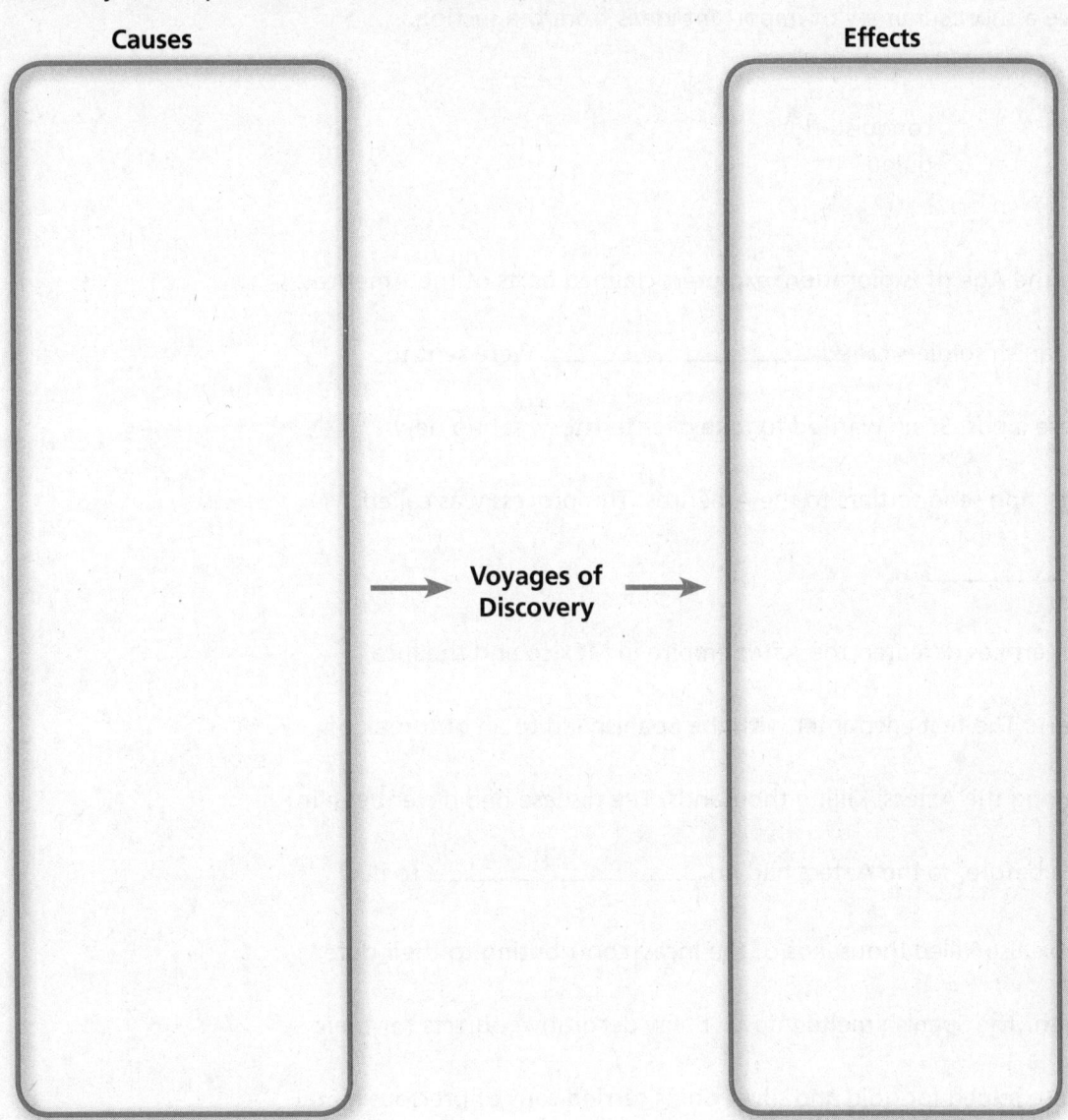

Causes

Effects

Voyages of Discovery

Essential Question

Who gained and who lost because of Italy's control of trade in the Mediterranean? What did Portugal gain by finding an ocean route to India?

_____

_____

_____

Word Wise

Word Bank Choose one word from the word bank to fill in each blank. You might have to change the endings of some words. When you have finished, you will have a short summary of important ideas from the section.

Word Bank
colonization   conquistador
bullion   quipu
immunity

During the Age of Exploration, explorers claimed parts of the Americas

for Spain. Spanish soldiers called _____ were sent to

conquer these lands. Spain wanted to take over territory, set up new

governments, and send settlers to the Americas. This process was called

_____.

Spanish armies defeated the Aztec empire in Mexico and the Inca

empire in Peru. The first encounter with the Spanish led to an outbreak of

smallpox among the Aztecs, killing thousands. The disease had never been in

the Americas before, so the Aztecs had no _____ to it.

Smallpox also killed thousands of the Incas, contributing to their defeat

by the Spanish. The Spanish melted down many decorative objects for their

gold. They also mined for gold and silver. Ships carried tons of precious metal

in bars called _____ back to Spain.

The Spanish believed the Aztec and Incan religions were pagan forms

of worship. The conquerors burned Aztec books and Inca records called

_____. The destruction of artifacts and records resulted in

the loss of much of Aztec and Incan culture.

Name _____   Class _____   Date _____

Take Notes

Sequence Use what you have read about the conquest of the Americas to add important events to the timeline below.

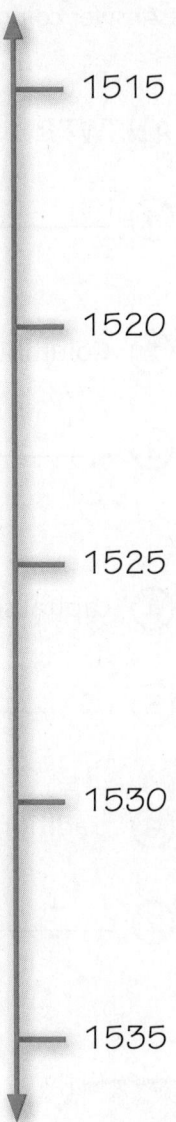

1515

1520

1525

1530

1535

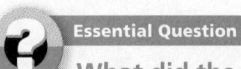

Essential Question

What did the people of the Americas gain or lose from their dealings with the Spanish? Is it possible to have fair trade between a group of conquerors and the people they conquered? Explain.

_____

_____

_____

Word Wise

Vocabulary Quiz Show Some quiz shows ask a question and expect the contestant to give the answer. In other shows, the contestant is given an answer and must supply the question. If the blank is in the Question column, write the question that would result in the answer in the Answer column. If the question is supplied, write the appropriate answer.

QUESTION

(1) In what type of system are the prices of goods and services based on competition?

(2) _____

(3) What is it called when workers manufacture goods at home using their own equipment?

(4) _____

(5) What economic policy promotes the expansion of trade?

(6) _____

(7) What term describes a rise in prices and an increase in available cash?

ANSWER

(1) _____

(2) Columbian Exchange

(3) _____

(4) capitalism

(5) _____

(6) traditional economy

(7) _____

Name _____ Class _____ Date _____

Take Notes

Summarize Use what you have read about the growth of trade to record important consequences of trade on the chart below.

The Growth of Trade	
Columbian Exchange	**Economic Changes**

Essential Question

Who benefited more from mercantilism, European nations or their colonies? Explain. How did the rise in land prices cause benefits for some people and losses for others?

_____

_____

_____

Name _____ Class _____ Date _____

What are the consequences of trade?

Prepare to Write

Throughout this chapter, you have explored the Essential Question in your text, journal, and On Assignment at myworldhistory.com. Use what you have learned to write an essay about the consequences of trade during the Age of Exploration.

Workshop Skill: Write an Introduction and Thesis Statement

Review the four types of essay. Then decide which type of essay you will write. Which type of essay have you chosen?

_____

Develop your thesis, which is your response to the Essential Question. Begin by making a list of the most important results of trade that you have read about in this chapter.

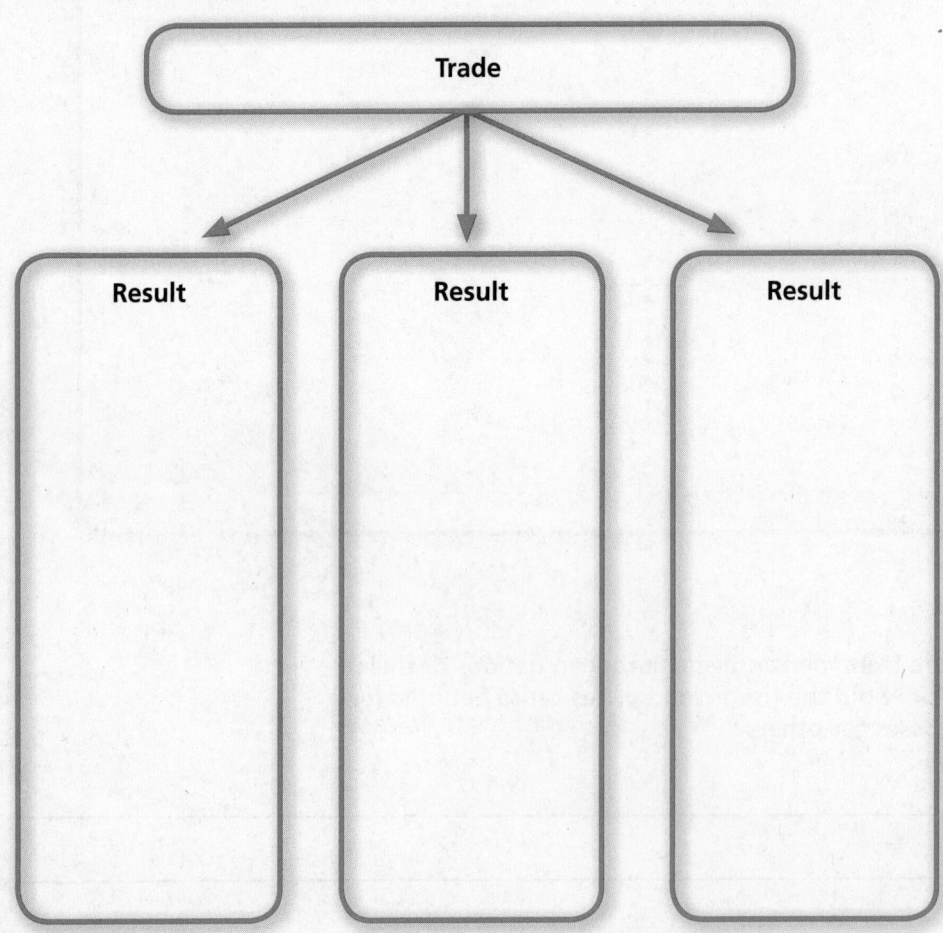

Write Your Thesis Statement

Your thesis statement states your position and three reasons that support it. The thesis statement will be the last sentence(s) in your introductory paragraph. For example: *The major consequences of trade during the Age of Exploration were* _____, _____,

and _____.

If your sentence is too long, break it up into two sentences.

Now write your thesis statement:

_____

Write Your Introduction

The first paragraph of an essay introduces the topic to the reader. An introduction has three parts:

1. A statement indicating what the essay is about

Example *Trade during the Age of Exploration had consequences that*

_____.

2. An indication of why the subject or issue is important

Example *Understanding the consequences of trade is essential to*

understanding _____.

3. A thesis statement

Write your introductory sentence: _____.

State the subject's importance: _____.

Write your thesis statement, including three supporting reasons:

_____

Draft Your Essay

Introduction Rewrite your introductory paragraph on your own paper.
Body Paragraphs Develop each reason to support your position in a separate paragraph. Include details and examples.
Conclusion Summarize your reasons. When you have finished, proofread your essay.

Places to Know!

Map Skills Use the maps in this unit to identify the Places to Know! on the outline map. Before the name of each place below, write the letter that shows its location on the map.

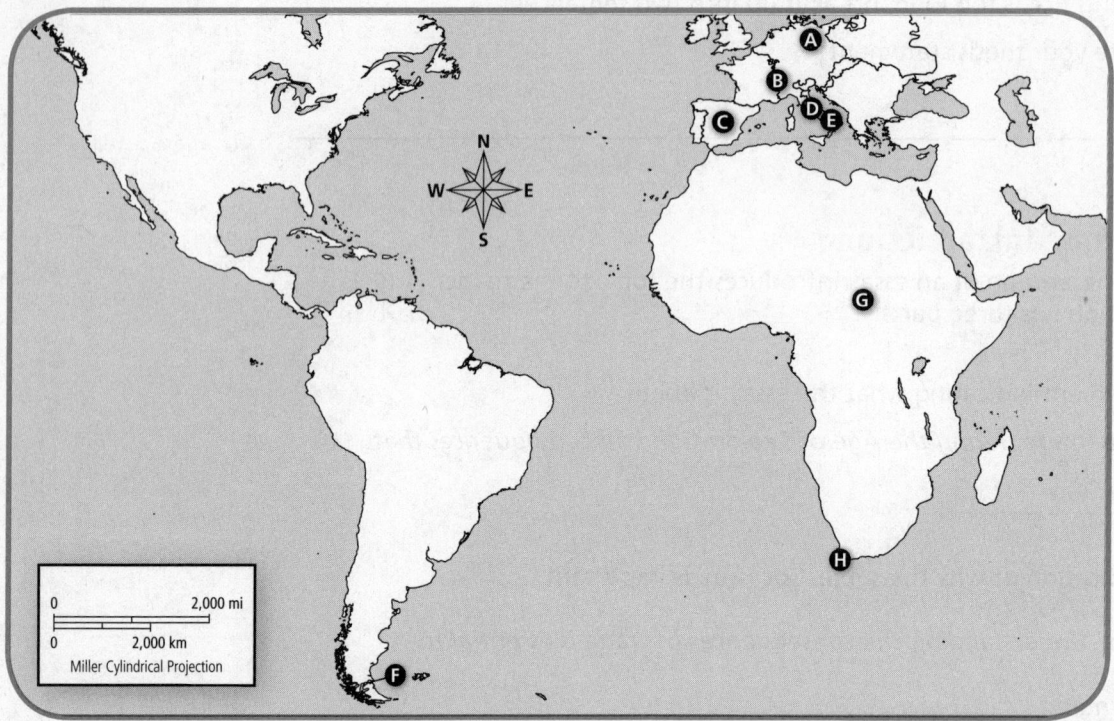

_____ Wittenberg, Germany   _____ Italy

_____ Geneva, Switzerland   _____ Strait of Magellan

_____ Spain   _____ Africa

_____ Rome   _____ Cape of Good Hope

Name _____ Class _____ Date _____

Key Events

Timeline Use what you have read about the rise of Europe to complete the timeline below. Draw a line from each event to its correct position on the timeline. Then write a brief description of each event.

1425

1455 _____
_____

1533 _____
_____

1450

1475

1492 _____
_____

1500

1545 _____
_____

1525

1517 _____
_____

1550

1588 _____
_____

1575

1600

Name _____ Class _____ Date _____

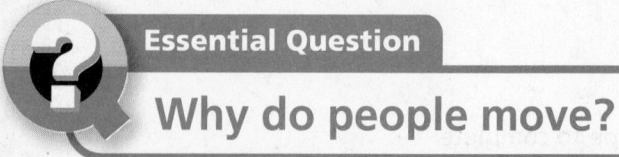

Why do people move?

Preview Before you begin this chapter, think about the Essential Question. Understanding how the Essential Question connects to your life will help you understand the chapter you are about to read.

Connect to Your Life

① Have you or anyone you know ever moved? What was the reason for the move?

_____

_____

② Under each category in the table, list reasons why people move. Include reasons that attract people to move and force people to move.

Reasons Why People Move				
Economic	Geographic	Political	Family	Military

Connect to the Chapter

③ Before you read the chapter, skim the headings, maps, and pictures. How do you think the movement of people affects cultures and nations? Record your predictions in the table below.

Effects of Movement on Communities, Cultures, Nations				
Languages	Culture	Government	Technology	Public Life

④ At the end of the chapter, come back to this page. Circle any predictions you made that were not accurate.

Name _____ Class _____ Date _____

Connect to myStory: Malinche: Mother of Mexico

(1) This story describes how Malinche helped Cortés and his soldiers deal with a new culture. Have you ever known a newcomer to your school? How did the teachers and students help this person deal with new surroundings?

_____

_____

_____

(2) How did Malinche help the Spanish? How did the Spanish change Malinche? Write your answers in the appropriate categories in the table.

	Religion	Language	Politics
How Malinche Helped the Spanish			
How the Spanish Changed Malinche			

(3) How do you think the Spanish changed the geography, language, and politics of Mexico? Write at least three predictions.

_____

_____

_____

Word Wise

Word Bank Choose one word from the word bank to fill in each blank. You may have to change the endings of some of the words.

Word Bank
mestizo   encomienda
creole   viceroy
peninsulare   mulatto
missions

By the 1570s, many Spaniards had settled in the Americas. In order to govern efficiently, the king of Spain appointed a(n) _____, an officer who ruled in the name of the king.

Under the _____ system, colonists demanded labor or tribute from Native Americans in a certain area. This system resulted in the enslavement of Native American laborers.

Jesuit and Franciscan priests came to the Spanish colonies to begin _____, or communities dedicated to spreading the faith or to educating and protecting people. Unfortunately, life in these communities was harsh.

Eventually, a class system developed in Spanish colonial society. At the top were _____, people born in Spain. Next came _____, American-born descendants of Spanish settlers land. The lower class included _____, people of Native American and European descent and _____, people of African and European descent. Native Americans and people of African descent occupied the lowest social classes.

Name _____ Class _____ Date _____

Take Notes

Identify Main Ideas and Details Use what you have read about the Spanish empire in the Americas to complete the concept web below.

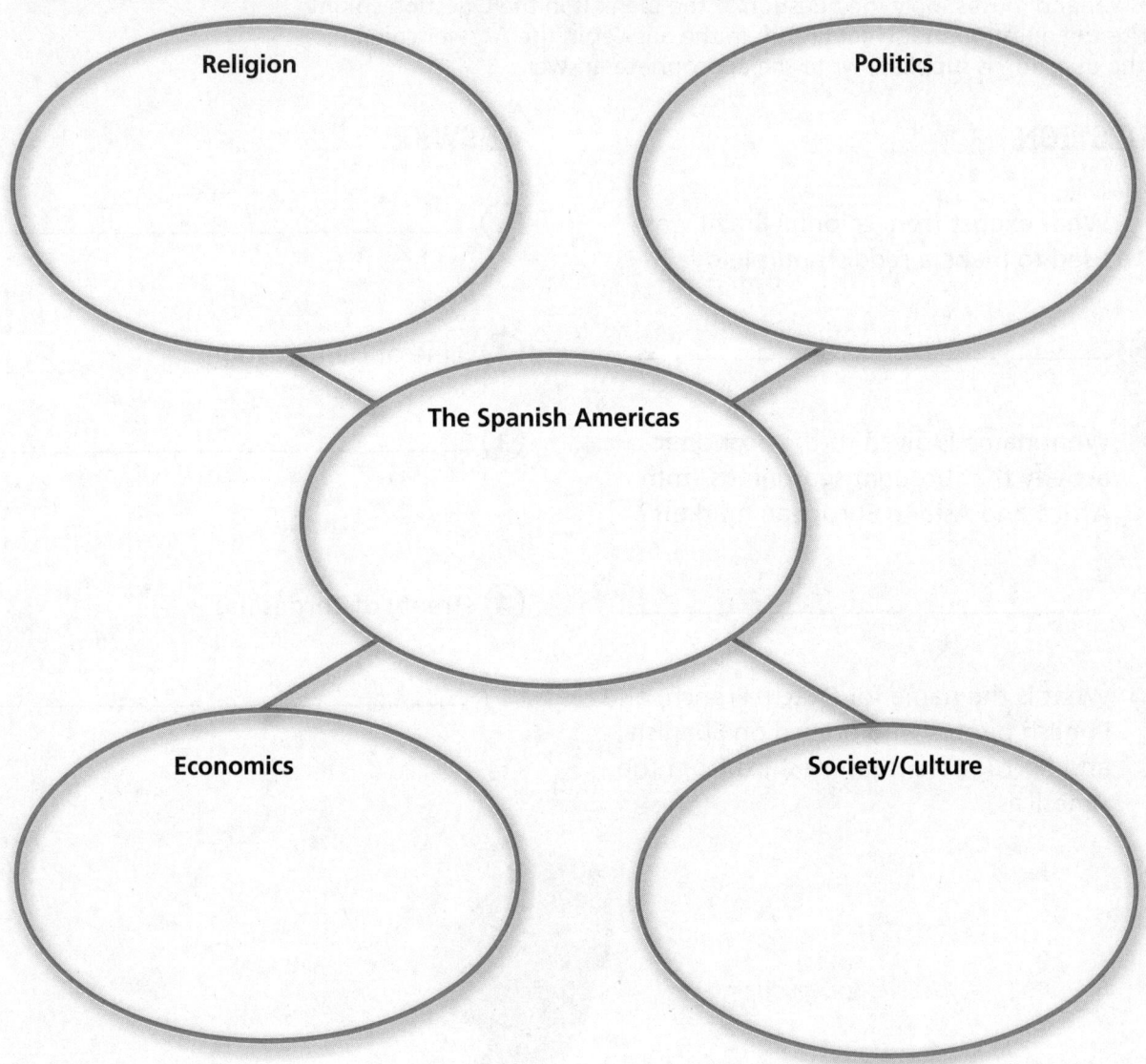

Religion

Politics

The Spanish Americas

Economics

Society/Culture

Essential Question

Why did members of the Jesuit and Franciscan religious orders move to the Americas?

_____

_____

_____

Name _____ Class _____ Date _____

Word Wise

Vocabulary Quiz Show Some quiz shows ask a question and expect the contestant to give the answer. In other shows, the contestant is given an answer and must supply the question. If the blank is in the Question column, write the question that would result in the answer in the Answer column. If the question is supplied, write the appropriate answer.

QUESTION

ANSWER

(1) What export from colonial Brazil was used to make a reddish-purple dye?

(1) _____

(2) _____

(2) Line of Demarcation

(3) What name is given to the economic activity that brought seasonings from Africa and Asia to European markets?

(3) _____

(4) _____

(4) Treaty of Tordesillas

(5) What is the name for Dutch, French, and English pirates who preyed on Spanish and Portuguese treasure ships from the Americas?

(5) _____

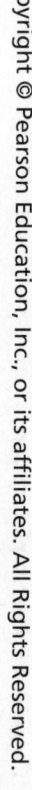

Name _____ Class _____ Date _____

Take Notes

Analyze Cause and Effect Use what you have read about the Portuguese empire to complete the cause-and-effect chart below. In the left column, list at least three ways that the Portuguese strongly influenced life in the Americas. In the right column, fill in the effects of those influences.

Causes

Spain feared that Portugal would compete for the lands and riches in the Americas.

_____
_____

Portuguese settlers need labor to work on the plantations.

_____
_____
_____

Vasco da Gama led voyages to India.

Afonso de Albuquerque conquered Goa, Malacca, and Hormuz.

_____
_____
_____

Effects

_____
_____
_____

Portugal claimed Brazil as part of its empire.

_____
_____
_____

Jesuits came into conflict with colonists.

_____
_____
_____
_____

Portugal's empire dissolves.

Essential Question

Why did Portuguese explorers travel to India?

_____
_____
_____

325

Word Wise

Words in Context For each question below, write an answer that shows your understanding of the boldfaced key term.

(1) Why did the **Pilgrims** come to North America?

_____

_____

_____

(2) What was the **northwest passage**?

_____

_____

_____

(3) What are **push-pull factors**?

_____

_____

_____

(4) How did **indentured servants** gain passage to North America?

_____

_____

_____

(5) How did the **Treaty of Paris** change North America?

_____

_____

_____

Name _____ Class _____ Date _____

Take Notes

Compare and Contrast Use what you have read about the colonization of
North America to record similarities and differences between the French and
English colonies on the Venn diagram below.

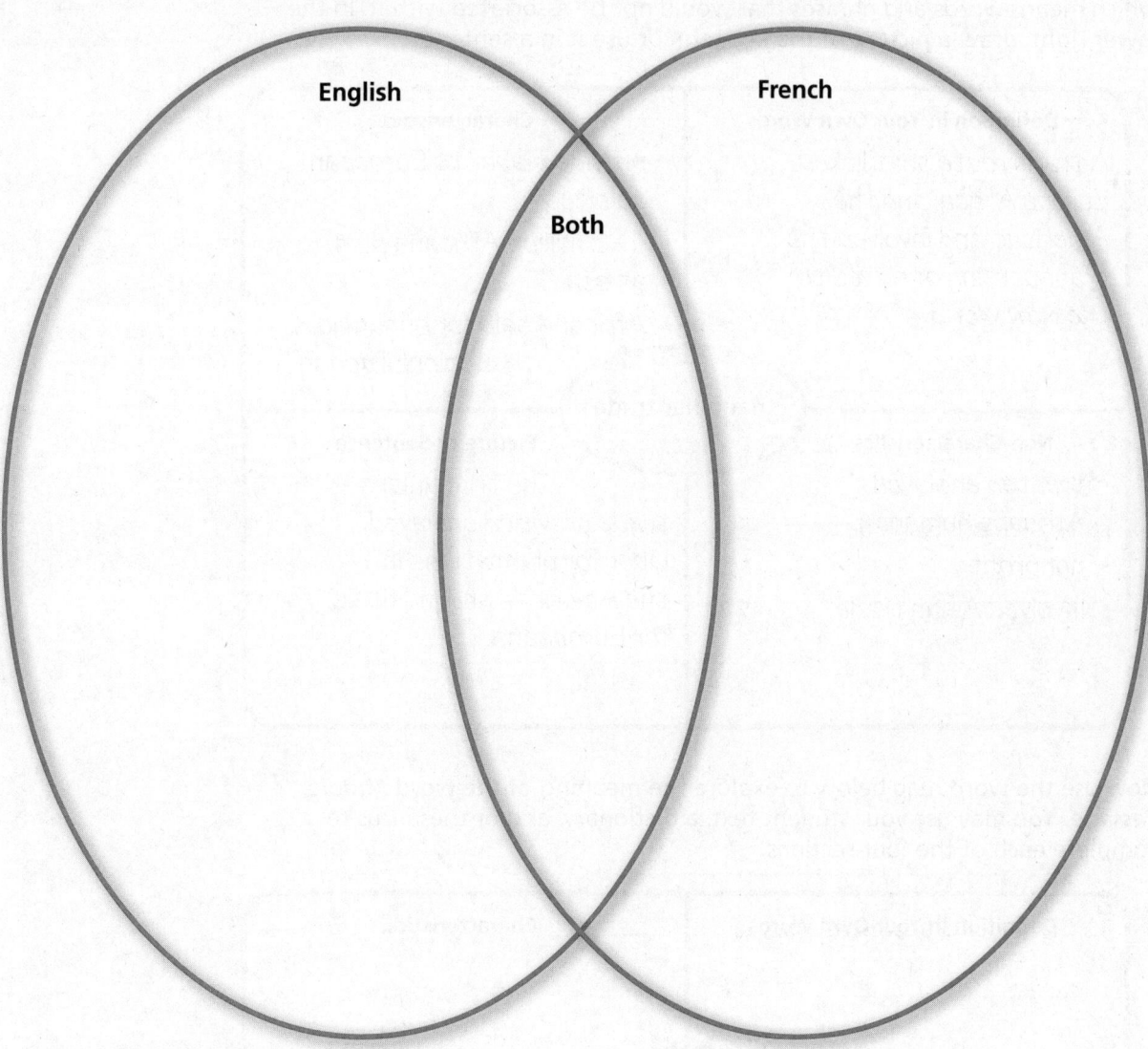

English

French

Both

 Essential Question
**What valuable resource drew many French settlers to North
America?**

_____

_____

Word Wise

Make a Word Map Follow the model below to make a word map. The key term *triangular trade* is in the center oval. Write the definition in your own words at the upper left. In the upper right, list Characteristics, which means words or phrases that relate to the term. At the lower left, list Non-Characteristics, which means words and phrases that would not be associated with it. In the lower right, draw a picture of the key term or use it in a sentence.

Definition in Your Own Words	Characteristics
A trade route that linked Europe Africa, and the Americas and involved the transporting of slaves to the New World	• provided labor to European colonies • 1–2 million Africans died at sea • Africans sold for sugar, gold, other colonial goods

triangular trade

Non-Characteristics	Picture or Sentence
• treated enslaved Africans humanely • nonprofit • involved Asian trade	The triangular trade provided enslaved labor for plantations in the Americas and profits for Europeans.

Now use the word map below to explore the meaning of the word *Middle Passage*. You may use your student text, a dictionary, and/or thesaurus to complete each of the four sections.

Definition in Your Own Words	Characteristics

Middle Passage

Non-Characteristics	Picture or Sentence

Make word maps of your own on a separate piece of paper for these Key Terms: *mutiny, chattel*.

Name _____ Class _____ Date _____

Take Notes

Summarize Use what you have read about the transatlantic slave trade to record the main ideas about this trade on the chart below.

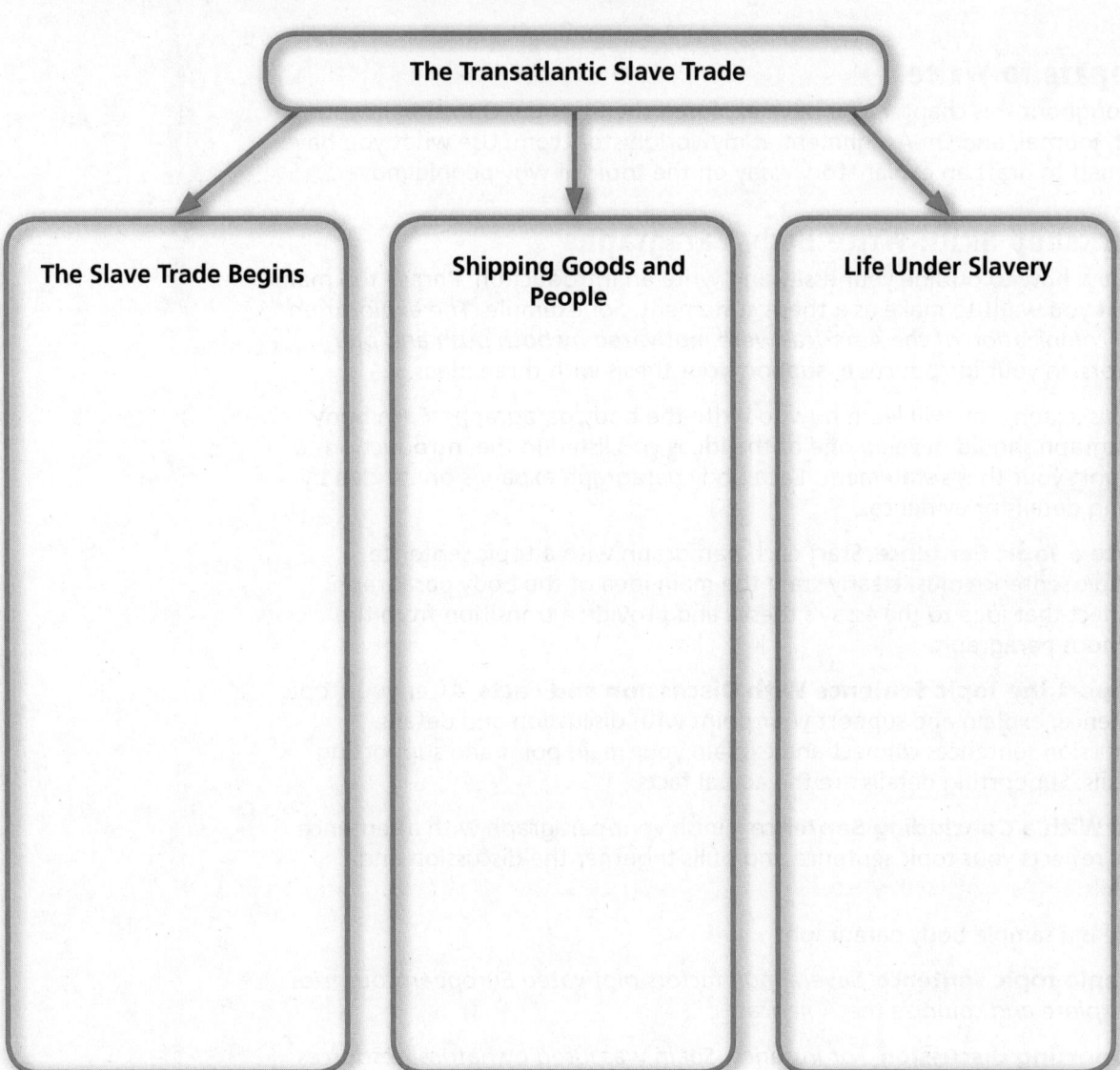

The Transatlantic Slave Trade

The Slave Trade Begins

Shipping Goods and People

Life Under Slavery

Essential Question

How did the Africans' reason for moving to the Americas differ from the Europeans' reasons?

_____

_____

_____

329

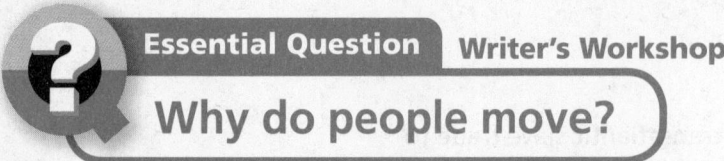

Essential Question   Writer's Workshop

Why do people move?

Prepare to Write

Throughout this chapter, you have explored the Essential Question in your text, journal, and On Assignment at myworldhistory.com. Use what you have learned to draft an explanatory essay on the topic of why people move.

Workshop Skill: Write Body Paragraphs

Review how to outline your essay and write an introduction. Phrase the main point you want to make as a thesis statement. For example, *The exploration and colonization of the Americas were motivated by both push and pull factors*. In your introduction, support your thesis with three ideas.

In this lesson, you will learn how to write the body paragraphs. Each body paragraph should develop one of the ideas you listed in the introduction to support your thesis statement. Each body paragraph expands on its idea by giving details or evidence.

Write a Topic Sentence Start each paragraph with a topic sentence. A topic sentence must clearly state the main idea of the body paragraph, connect that idea to the essay's thesis, and provide a transition from the previous paragraph.

Support the Topic Sentence With Discussion and Facts After your topic sentence, explain and support your point with discussion and details. Discussion sentences connect and explain your main point and supporting details. Supporting details are the actual facts.

End With a Concluding Sentence Finish your paragraph with a sentence that reflects your topic sentence and pulls together the discussion and details.

Here is a sample body paragraph:

Sample topic sentence *Several pull factors motivated European countries to explore and colonize the Americas.*

Supporting discussion *For instance, Spain was lured by natural resources to explore and colonize Mexico and areas of South America.*

Supporting detail *The mining of resources such as gold, silver, and tin in the Americas made Spain a wealthy nation.*

Supporting discussion *Also, English investors were attracted by the possibility of setting up profitable colonies in eastern North America, and the French government wanted to set up a fur trading business in Canada.*

Concluding sentence *So the potential for gaining wealth pulled European nations to the Americas. However, pull factors also involved political competition.*

Write a Body Paragraph

Now write your own body paragraph for your essay.

Topic sentence

_____

_____

Supporting discussion

_____

_____

Supporting detail

_____

_____

Supporting detail

_____

_____

Supporting discussion

_____

_____

Concluding sentence

_____

_____

Draft Your Essay

Use the body paragraph above in your complete essay written on your own
paper. Be sure that each of your body paragraphs has a topic sentence,
supporting details, and a concluding sentence.

Name _____ Class _____ Date _____

What should governments do?

Connect to Your Life

1. The government affects your life every day in large and small ways. In the table below, list a specific example in each category.

Government's Role in My Life			
Taxes	Laws	Environmental Protection	Issuing Licenses

2. Do you agree with the ways government affects your life? Why might some people support a particular government action and others oppose it?

_____

_____

Connect to the Chapter

3. Preview the chapter by skimming the chapter's heads, photographs, and graphics. Then think about ways that monarchies played a role in different European countries. List your ideas in the table below.

Government's Role in Early Modern Europe			
Spain	France	Russia and Central Europe	England

4. Read the chapter. Then update your table, adding new ideas, moving ideas to different columns, or crossing out ideas that no longer make sense to you.

Connect to myStory: The Battle of the Spanish Armada

1 Think about how England's planned attack occurred during a time of conflict between Catholics and Protestants. Have you ever disagreed with someone over your personal beliefs? If so, were you able to resolve your differences? Explain your answer.

_____

_____

2 Think about the power struggle between Queen Elizabeth and Philip II. How did each leader's beliefs differ?

_____

_____

3 The Armada seemed to be unbeatable because of its size. What disadvantages did Spain have as it faced England in battle?

a. _____

b. _____

c. _____

d. _____

e. _____

4 Read the passage from Queen Elizabeth's speech before the battle with Spain. Why do you think it might have inspired her people?

_____

_____

Word Wise

Vocabulary Quiz Show Some quiz shows ask a question and expect the contestant to give the answer. In other shows, the contestant is given an answer and must supply the question. If the blank is in the Question column, write the question that would result in the answer in the Answer column. If the question is supplied, write the answer.

QUESTION

ANSWER

① What is the term for a ruler who has complete power over the government and people's lives?

① _____

② What are the lands of the Habsburg royal family known as?

② _____

③ _____

③ armada

④ _____

④ inflation

Name _____ Class _____ Date _____

Take Notes

Identify Main Ideas and Details Reread the text under each red heading in your textbook. Take notes about information under each heading to complete the concept web below.

Spain, a Global Power

Powerful Monarchs

Main Idea

_____

_____

Details

_____

_____

_____

_____

Spain's Golden Age

Main Idea

_____

_____

Details

_____

_____

_____

_____

Essential Question

How did Charles V and Philip II use their power?

_____

_____

_____

335

Name _____ Class _____ Date _____

Word Wise

Words in Context For each question below, write an answer that shows your understanding of the boldfaced key term.

1 In which ways was the palace of **Versailles** a symbol of King Louis XIV's power?

_____

_____

_____

2 How did an **assassin** affect the history of France in 1610?

_____

_____

_____

3 How did Louis XIV's belief in the **divine right** of kings affect his leadership?

_____

_____

_____

4 Why was the **War of the Spanish Succession** significant for King Louis XIV?

_____

_____

_____

Name _____ Class _____ Date _____

Take Notes

Summarize Reread this section and summarize information about each leader to complete the chart below. Remember that a summary gives an overview of information, not specific details.

```
┌─────────────────────────────────────────────────────────┐
│                France's Absolute Monarchy                 │
└─────────────────────────────────────────────────────────┘
        │                    │                    │
┌───────────────┐    ┌───────────────┐    ┌───────────────┐
│    Henry IV    │    │ Cardinal Richelieu │ │   Louis XIV    │
│                │    │                │    │                │
│                │    │                │    │                │
│                │    │                │    │                │
│                │    │                │    │                │
│                │    │                │    │                │
└───────────────┘    └───────────────┘    └───────────────┘
```

 Essential Question

Describe France under the rule of Henry IV, Cardinal Richelieu, and Louis XIV.

_____

Name _____ Class _____ Date _____

Word Wise

Crossword Puzzle The *Across* clues are definitions of key terms from this section. Fill in the numbered *Across* boxes with the correct key terms. Then do the same with the *Down* clues.

Across	Down
2. divide up	1. landowning Russian noble
4. peasant who is legally bound to live and work on land owned by lords	3. Russian emperor

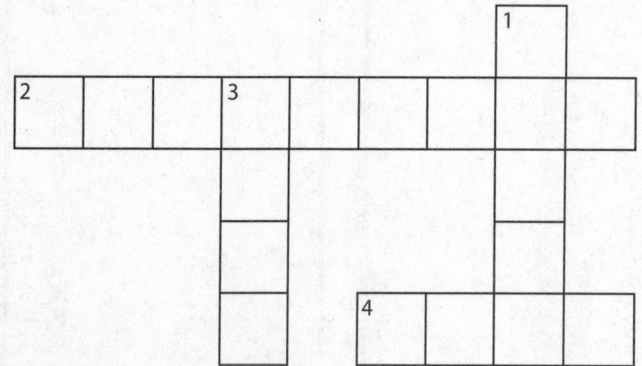

Name _____ Class _____ Date _____

Take Notes

Compare and Contrast Use what you have read about absolute monarchies across Central and Eastern Europe to compare and contrast leaders from this section of the chapter in the table below.

Peter the Great	Catherine the Great	Maria Theresa	Frederick the Great
•	•	•	•
•	•	•	•
•	•	•	•

Essential Question

How did powerful leaders rule Russia and Central Europe?

_____

Word Wise

Use a Word Bank Choose one word from the word bank to fill in each blank. When you have finished, you will have a short summary of important ideas from the section.

Word Bank

republic	English Civil War
Restoration	Glorious Revolution
treason	English Bill of Rights
Puritan	constitutional monarchy

The _____ took place from 1642 to 1651 between

nobles known as Cavaliers and their opponents, who were called

Roundheads. Many Roundheads were _____, Protestants

who wanted to reform the Church of England. The Roundheads were led by

Oliver Cromwell. Cromwell defeated Charles I, who was executed for

_____, which is the betrayal of one's country. England

was declared a _____. Cromwell became England's new

leader, but when he died, his son could not hold on to power. In 1660,

Parliament voted to bring back the monarchy. The new king, Charles II,

treated Parliament with respect. This time period was known as the

_____. Charles II was succeeded by James II, who did not

deal as well with Parliament. James II was forced from power. His bloodless

overthrow became known as the _____. Parliament asked

James II's daughter Mary and her husband, William II of Orange, to become

England's monarchs. Parliament demanded limits on their power and passed

the _____. This list of the constitutional rights of English

citizens established a _____, a monarchy limited by law.

Name _____ Class _____ Date _____

Take Notes

Analyze Cause and Effect The column headings in the table below match the headings in your textbook. Reread the information under each heading in this section. Analyze the causes and effects of the struggle for power between English monarchs and Parliament by filling in the table below.

Limited Monarchy in England

Monarchs Versus Parliament	Civil War and Commonwealth	Restoration and Revolution
Cause _____	Cause _____	Cause _____
Effect _____	Effect _____	Effect _____
Cause _____	Cause _____	Cause _____
Effect _____	Effect _____	Effect _____
Cause _____	Cause _____	Cause _____
Effect _____	Effect _____	Effect _____

 **Essential Question**

How did disagreements between the monarchy and Parliament shape England's history?

_____

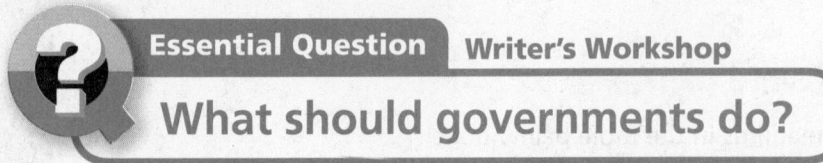

Essential Question Writer's Workshop

What should governments do?

Prepare to Write

Throughout this chapter, you have explored the Essential Question in your text, journal, and On Assignment at myworldhistory.com. Use your notes and what you have learned to write an essay describing the role of government during the rise of European monarchies.

Workshop Skill: Write a Conclusion

An essay requires writing a thesis statement, an introduction, three body paragraphs, and a conclusion. The conclusion wraps up your essay and summarizes your main points. In this lesson, you will learn how to write the conclusion.

Preparing to Write Your Conclusion Before you write your conclusion, reread your essay. Think about your thesis and the main ideas and details that support it. Do any questions come to mind as you reread your work? Is there another topic you want to explore that relates to points you made about what governments should do? After you reread, brainstorm responses to your new questions. This will help you come up with an interesting and unique conclusion.

Summarize Your Main Points Review each of the main points you made in your essay. Write one or two sentences that summarize the main points of your body paragraphs. Remember, your summary should avoid going into too much detail, but should clearly restate your main points.

Use a Checklist Sometimes making a checklist can help you organize your thoughts and ideas. You may wish to follow a checklist like the one below. As you complete each task, check it off your list.

_____ Restate your thesis to remind the reader of the main point of your essay.

_____ Summarize the most important ideas that support your thesis.

_____ Include a few sentences that introduce a new idea or raise questions about your topic.

_____ Explain the importance of your topic and suggest its deeper meaning.

What Makes a Strong Conclusion? A strong conclusion should tie together the different strands of your essay. It should give the reader the feeling that everything adds up and makes sense. At the same time, your conclusion should be interesting and thought-provoking.

Sample Conclusion Here are some sample sentences that could be used to form a cohesive conclusion:

- **Restatement of the Thesis:** *The role of government during the rise of European monarchies involved power struggles and religious conflict.*

- **Summary of an Important Idea:** *Parliament placed strict limits on England's monarchs, causing monarchs to work with Parliament to carry out their own policies.*

- **A New Idea:** *If Parliament had not demanded limitations on England's monarchy, its government would likely be quite different today.*

- **Why This Topic Is Important:** *Studying the governments of the past can help us better understand how and why our own government was formed.*

Write Your Conclusion

Now write your own concluding paragraph for your essay.

Restatement of the Thesis _____

_____

Summary of Important Idea #1 _____

_____

Summary of Important Idea #2 _____

_____

Summary of Important Idea #3 _____

_____

A New Idea or Question _____

_____

Why the Topic is Important _____

_____

Draft Your Essay

Use the concluding paragraph above in your completed essay. Then write your essay on a separate piece of paper and proofread it with a writing partner.

Name _____ Class _____ Date _____

What is power? Who should have it?

Preview Before you begin this chapter, think about the Essential Question. Understanding how the Essential Question connects to your life will help you understand the chapter you are about to read.

Connect to Your Life

① Define the following government terms:

a. legislator _____

b. dictator _____

c. president _____

d. judge _____

e. constitutional monarch _____

② Place the letter of the term above onto the line below to show where each falls on the power scale, from little power to great power.

Little Power   **Great Power**
0   10

Connect to the Chapter

③ Now preview the chapter to find out who held power in America and France. Then, fill in the blank rows of the table.

Who Held Power in America?				
When	Before the American Revolution	After the American Revolution	Under the Articles of Confederation	Under the U.S. Constitution
Who held power?				
Who Held Power in France?				
When	Before the Enlightenment	After the Fall of the Bastille	During the Reign of Terror	In 1799
Who held power?				

④ After reading the chapter, return to this page. Change any answers that were incorrect.

344

Connect to myStory: Thomas Jefferson: Tense Summer Days in Philadelphia

① Have you ever been asked to write something important that would be read aloud to other people? How did it make you feel?

_____
_____

② In the myStory, why was Thomas Jefferson tense?

_____
_____

③ Identify three events that occurred in Massachusetts that motivated the colonists to declare independence from Britain.

_____
_____
_____

④ At what meeting did Jefferson write the Declaration of Independence?

_____

⑤ What problems plagued Jefferson as he wrote?

_____
_____

⑥ What main ideas about the role of government did Jefferson include in the Declaration of Independence?

_____
_____

Word Wise

Vocabulary Quiz Show Some quiz shows ask a question and expect the contestant to give the answer. In other shows, the contestant is given an answer and must supply the question. If the blank is in the Question column, write the question that would result in the answer in the Answer column. If the question is supplied, write the answer.

QUESTION	ANSWER
① _____	① rationalism
② _____	② heliocentric theory
③ What is a belief that goes against the teaching of the Church called?	③ _____
④ _____	④ inductive reasoning
⑤ What process is followed by using observation, experiments, and careful reasoning to gain new knowledge?	⑤ _____

Name _____ Class _____ Date _____

Take Notes

Identify Main Ideas and Details Use what you read about the Scientific Revolution to complete the diagrams below. For each main idea, write details that support it.

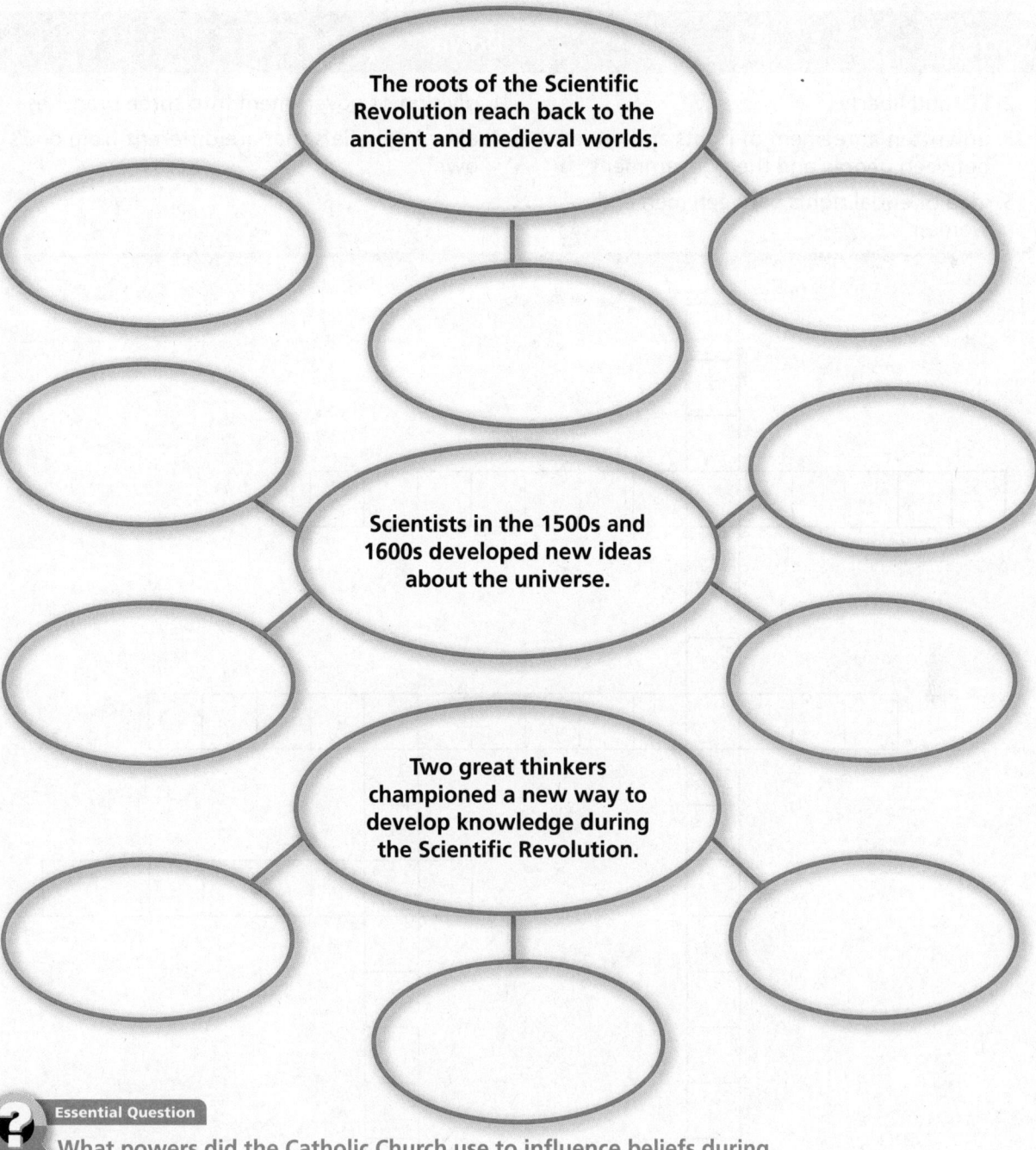

Essential Question

What powers did the Catholic Church use to influence beliefs during this time?

_____

_____

Word Wise

Crossword Puzzle The *Across* and *Down* clues are definitions of key terms from this section. Fill in the numbered *Across* boxes with the correct key terms. Then do the same with the *Down* clues.

Across	Down
2. life and liberty	1. division of government into three branches
3. unwritten agreement of rights and duties between people and their government	4. allowing beliefs that are different from one's own
5. idea of equal rights between men and women	

Name _____ Class _____ Date _____

Take Notes

Summarize Use what you have read in Section 2 to fill in key ideas about the topics in the table below. Then use the key ideas to write a summary statement about the Enlightenment.

Different Ways of Thinking	Political Thought	Social and Economic Thought
The Enlightenment's Roots _____ _____ _____	**Natural Rights** _____ _____ _____ _____	**Religious Tolerance** _____ _____ _____ _____
Thinking About the World _____ _____ _____ _____ _____ _____ _____	**Separation of Powers** _____ _____ _____ _____ **The Social Contract** _____ _____ _____ _____	**The Rights of Women** _____ _____ _____ **Free Trade and Free Markets** _____ _____ _____ _____

Summary Statement: _____
_____

Essential Question

How did Baron de Montesquieu think power should be divided? Why did he think this division was necessary?

_____

Word Wise

Sentence Builder Finish the sentences below with a key term from this section. You may have to change the form of the words to complete the sentences.

Word Bank

alliance   boycott
constitution   massacre
militia

① Early battles of the American Revolution were fought by armies of

citizen volunteers who trained to fight during emergencies, or

_____.

② Delegates from the states met in Philadelphia in 1787 to write a

document that lists the basic principles and structure of a government,

or _____.

③ The killing of a large number of helpless people is called a

_____.

④ France and the American colonies made a formal agreement to help

one another, or a(n) _____.

⑤ To show disapproval by refusing to buy certain goods is a

_____.

Name _____ Class _____ Date _____

Take Notes

Analyze Cause and Effect Use what you read about the American Revolution to complete the information below. For each cause given, write the effect. For each effect given, write the cause.

Causes

1. _____

   _____

2. A group of colonists stage a protest known as the Boston Tea Party.

3. Thomas Paine writes *Common Sense,* arguing that, among other things, the colonies should not be ruled by a government located across the ocean.

4. _____

   _____

5. Under the Articles of Confederation, individual states are given more power than the central government.

6. At the Constitutional Convention, large states and small states argue over representation in the legislature.

7. _____

   _____

Effects

1. Colonists try to persuade Parliament to change its policies, and some colonists take part in violent protests.

2. _____

   _____

3. _____

   _____

4. The French government is convinced that the colonists can defeat Britain, and it forms an alliance with the Americans.

5. _____

   _____

6. _____

   _____

7. Framers of the Constitution divide power among the national government and state and local governments.

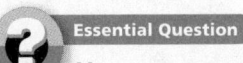 **Essential Question**

How was government power distributed first under the Articles of Confederation, and then under the U.S. Constitution?

_____

_____

Name _____ Class _____ Date _____

Word Wise

Words In Context For each question below, write an answer that shows your understanding of the boldfaced key term.

(1) Into what three **estates** was French society divided before the French Revolution?

_____

_____

(2) How did **radicals** cause the Reign of Terror during the French Revolution?

_____

_____

(3) Why do many scholars believe that Napoleon's most important achievement was the **Napoleonic Code**?

_____

_____

(4) Why did Napoleon **abdicate** in 1814?

_____

_____

Name _____ Class _____ Date _____

Take Notes

Sequence Use what you have read in this section to add details to the timeline below.

The French Revolution	
May 1789	1. _____ _____
	• Parisians storm the Bastille on July 14.
August 1789	2. _____ _____
	• The National Assembly ends the monarchy's absolute power in the Constitution of 1791.
	• France declares war on Austria and Prussia.
1793	3. _____ _____
1794	4. _____ _____
	• France's government is weak and disorganized.
1799	5. _____ _____
1804	6. _____ _____
	• Napoleon creates a strong central government, writes the Napoleonic Code, and invades almost all of Europe.
1812	7. _____ _____
1814–1815	8. _____ _____

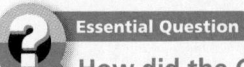

Essential Question

How did the Constitution of 1791 change the power of the French monarchy?

_____

_____

_____

Name _____ Class _____ Date _____

What is power? Who should have it?

Prepare to Write

Throughout this chapter, you have explored the Essential Question in your text, journal, and On Assignment at myworldhistory.com. Use what you have learned in this chapter to write an essay about power and who held it before and after the Scientific Revolution, the Enlightenment, the American Revolution, and the French Revolution.

Workshop Skill: Revise Your Work

Review the outline of your essay, and then write and develop an introduction, body paragraphs, and a conclusion. Consider the main point you want to make in your essay and phrase it as a thesis statement. For example: *The American colonists were very aware of power and who should hold it.* In your introduction, list three reasons why the American colonists were aware of government power. In each body paragraph, develop one of these reasons using details and evidence to support it.

You will learn more about how to revise your essay in this lesson. Revision has several important goals: First, you should clarify main ideas and connect them to both your audience and your writing purpose. Second, you should evaluate each piece of evidence to ensure that it fits your thesis. Third, you should review sentences to make sure that they make sense and contain no grammar, punctuation, or spelling errors.

Identify Your Main Points

_____ Check that each paragraph has a main point.

_____ This point should be clearly stated and is usually the first or last sentence.

_____ Circle all your main points, including your thesis statement.

Think About Your Readers and Purpose

_____ Keep in mind who your reader will be—your teacher.

_____ Be sure that your language is formal. Rewrite slang terms, and do not use personal pronouns.

_____ Review your purpose in writing. Is it to persuade? To explain? To describe? To tell a story? Use the writing prompt to guide your purpose.

_____ Look back at your essay to make sure you have connected the causes and effects.

Evaluate Your Evidence

_____ Reread each circled main point. Carefully read the rest of the paragraph.

_____ Does the evidence support the main point?

_____ Is the evidence organized in a logical or chronological manner?

_____ Make sure the evidence supports your thesis.

_____ Reword your thesis slightly if necessary to fit the points you have made. Sentences that do not support the thesis and main ideas should be eliminated.

Be Clear and Correct

_____ Read your essay aloud. Never skip this step! Hearing your sentences will help you notice when they do not flow or if they do not make sense.

_____ Ask yourself what you meant to say and use that restatement to rewrite confusing sentences.

_____ Reread silently or use a computer grammar and spelling checker to find and correct any errors.

Revise Your Essay

Now look critically at one paragraph from your essay and make revisions to improve it. Write your corrected paragraph below.

_____

_____

_____

_____

_____

_____

_____

_____

_____

Draft Your Essay

Copy the revised paragraph into your essay. Use it as a guide in revising the remaining paragraphs. Be sure to check each paragraph for a main idea, supporting evidence, and appropriate spelling, grammar, and punctuation.

Name _____ Class _____ Date _____

Places to Know!

Map Skills Use the maps in this unit to identify the Places to Know! on the outline map. Before the name of each place below, write the letter that shows its location on the map. Write a brief sentence or phrase that explains an interesting historical fact about each location.

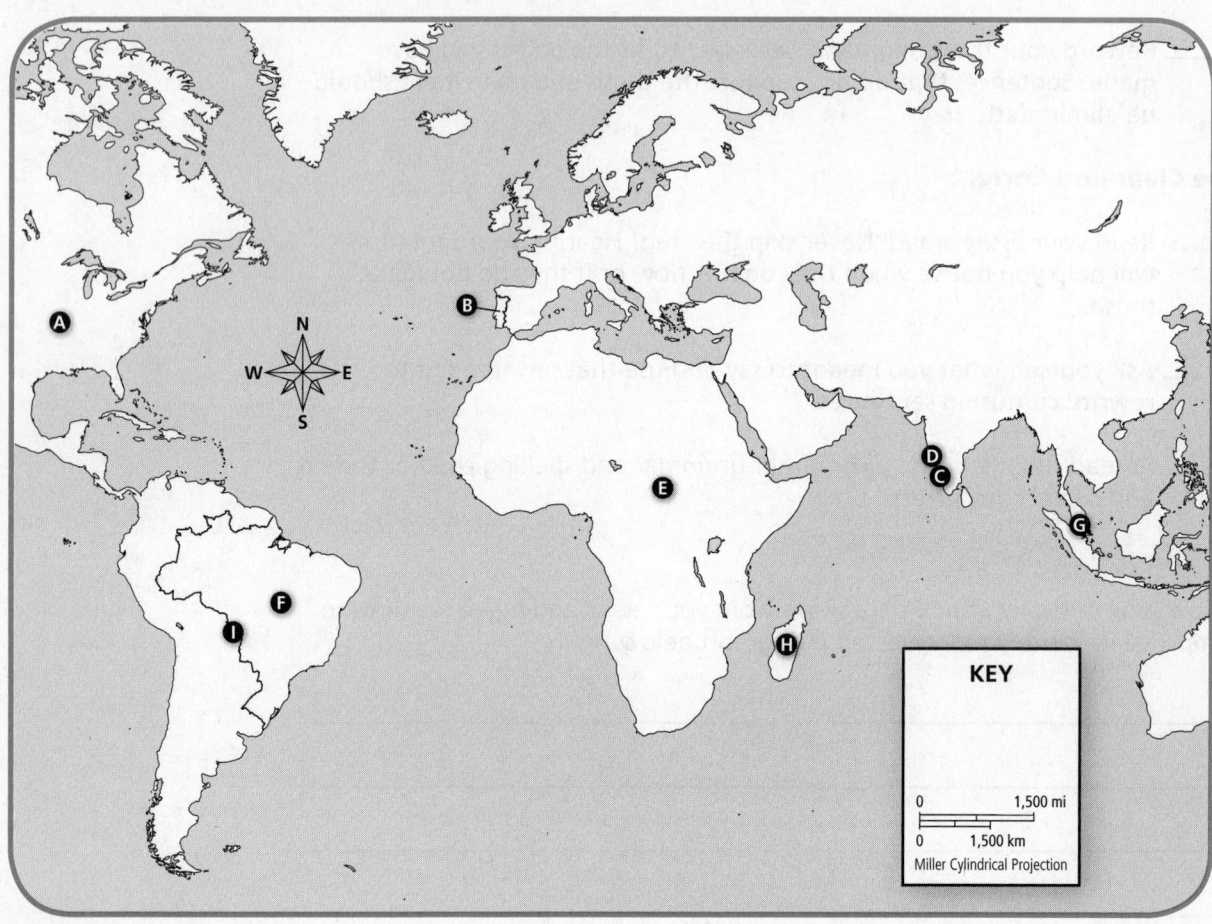

_____ Brazil

_____ Portugal

_____ North America

_____ South America

_____ Africa

_____ Mozambique

_____ Malacca

_____ Calicut

_____ Goa

Key Events

Timeline Use what you have read about the early modern world to complete the timeline below. Draw a line from each event to its correct position on the timeline. Then write a brief description of each event.

1497 _____
_____

1518 _____
_____

1616 _____
_____

1620 _____
_____

1643 _____
_____

1450

1500

1550

1600

1650

1700

1750

1800

1689 _____
_____

1690 _____
_____

1776 _____
_____

1789 _____
_____

? **Essential Question**

What are the consequences of technology?

Preview Before you begin this chapter, think about the Essential Question. Understanding how the Essential Question connects to your life will help you understand the chapter you are about to read.

Connect to Your Life

(1) Think about chores or jobs that you do to help around the house or earn some extra money. In the table below, list the types of technology you use, along with the effect of each. Then write whether the effect is positive or negative.

Ways Technology Affects My Life

Technology	Its Effect	Positive or Negative?

(2) Now think about one type of technology that you don't have but would like to use to do your chores. Why do you want that technology?

_____

_____

Connect to the Chapter

(3) Preview the chapter by skimming the heads, photographs, and graphics. In the table below, name a technological advance for each category. Then predict how that technology changed life in Europe and the United States.

	Technology	Prediction
Food Production		
Manufacturing		
Energy		
Transportation		

(4) Read the chapter. Then review the predictions you listed in the table. Circle the predictions that were correct.

Name _____ Class _____ Date _____

Connect to myStory: Harriet Hanson Robinson's Lost Eden

① How was Harriet's life different from your life? How was it similar?

_____

_____

_____

② If you had been Harriet, how would you have felt about changing your way of life and going to work in a mill?

_____

_____

_____

③ Now think about what the story shows about the ways that technology changed the lives of people in the 1800s. Record the changes on the table below.

Before 1800s	Change
Most workers were men.	
Workers lived and worked at home or nearby.	
Goods were made by hand.	
Workers set their own hours.	

④ What was the proudest moment of Harriet's life? Explain why it meant so much to her.

_____

_____

_____

359

Word Wise

Vocabulary Quiz Show Some quiz shows ask a question and expect the
contestant to give the answer. In other shows, the contestant is given an
answer and must supply the question. If the blank is in the Question column,
write the question that would result in the answer in the Answer column.
If the question is supplied, write the appropriate answer.

QUESTION	ANSWER
(1) What is the feeling of unity that people within a nation share?	(1) _____
(2) _____	(2) Carbonari
(3) What term is used for a state in which citizens are united by shared interests such as religion, language, or culture?	(3) _____

Name _____ Class _____ Date _____

Take Notes

Sequence Use what you have read about nationalism in Europe to add important events to the timeline below.

1780

1800

1820

1840

1860

1880

Essential Question

Why did Bismarck introduce welfare programs as Germans moved to work in factories?

_____

_____

_____

Word Wise

Word Map Follow the model below to make a word map. The key term *Industrial Revolution* is in the center oval. Write the definition in your own words at the upper left. In the upper right, list Characteristics, which means words or phrases that relate to the term. At the lower left, list Non-Characteristics, which means words and phrases that would *not* be associated with it. In the lower right, draw a picture of the key term *or* use it in a sentence.

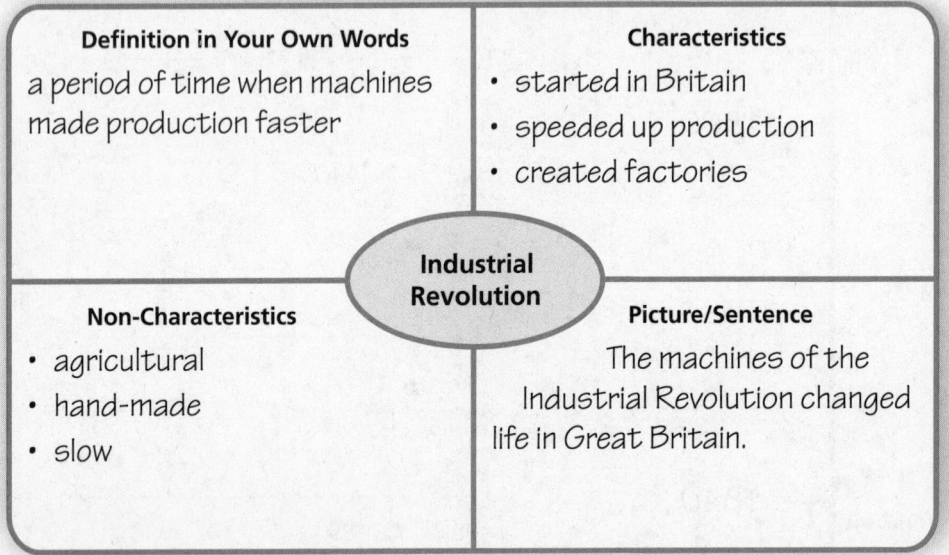

Definition in Your Own Words
a period of time when machines made production faster

Characteristics
• started in Britain
• speeded up production
• created factories

Industrial Revolution

Non-Characteristics
• agricultural
• hand-made
• slow

Picture/Sentence
The machines of the Industrial Revolution changed life in Great Britain.

Now use the word map below to explore the meaning of the word *enclosure.* You may use your student text, a dictionary, and/or a thesaurus to complete each of the four sections.

Definition in Your Own Words

Characteristics

enclosure

Non-Characteristics

Picture/Sentence

Make word maps of your own on a separate piece of paper for these Key Terms: *socialism* and *communism.*

Take Notes

Analyze Cause and Effect Use what you have read about the Industrial Revolution to list the effect of each change listed in the table.

Change	Effect
1. Advances in farming made food production more efficient.	1. _____ _____
2. Inventors made machines to spin thread and weave cloth more quickly.	2. _____ _____
3. James Watt invented the steam engine.	3. _____ _____
4. Business owners built factories in which to manufacture goods.	4. _____ _____
5. Landowners enclosed lands to create large commercial farms.	5. _____ _____
6. Cities grew rapidly as people moved there for industrial jobs.	6. _____ _____

Essential Question

How did the Industrial Revolution change people's lives?

_____

_____

_____

Word Wise

Word Bank Choose one word from the word bank to fill in each blank. When you have finished, you will have a short summary of important ideas from the section.

Word Bank

concessions   gunboat diplomacy
imperialism

European empires controlled most of the world by the 1800s. Ships

carried raw materials from distant lands back to the powerful European

states. This control of foreign lands by stronger states is called

_____. There were many reasons for European domination

of the world. One was industrialism. Europe needed raw materials for its

factories. Another reason was nationalism. The British, in particular, were

eager to expand their empire.

The European empires carved up the world among them. In China,

different European nations had separate "spheres of influence." When the

Chinese tried to stop Great Britain's opium trade to China, the two countries

went to war. Britain won, and the Chinese were forced to offer

_____, or trading rights, to Europeans.

Japan, alarmed by events in China, restricted contacts with the West.

However, in 1853, the United States sent Matthew Perry to Japan to demand

diplomatic relations and trading rights. Fearful of bombardment by the

guns on Perry's ship, the Japanese agreed. This _____,

threatening to use firepower to gain concessions, was often used by Western

powers.

Name _____ Class _____ Date _____

Take Notes

Identify Main Ideas and Details In the table below, record details that support each of these main ideas from the section.

1. Causes of Imperialism	2. Carving Up the World	3. Southeast and East Asia	4. Nationalism Spreads
Many factors helped European nations and the United States gain colonies around the world.	European powers took control of most of Africa and India to gain trade and raw materials.	Western powers used advanced weapons to force Asian states to trade with the West.	Nationalistic ideas spread and helped non-Europeans throw off colonial rule.

Essential Question

How did Western powers use technology to build empires?

_____

_____

_____

Name _____ Class _____ Date _____

Word Wise

Words In Context For each question below, write an answer that shows your understanding of the boldfaced Key Term.

(1) What benefit did a business gain from practicing **vertical integration**?

_____

_____

(2) How does an **assembly line** work?

_____

_____

(3) What happens when employees go on **strike**?

_____

_____

(4) What were women asking for when they demanded **suffrage**?

_____

_____

(5) What were **tenements,** and where were they located?

_____

_____

(6) What is the purpose of a **union**?

_____

_____

Name _____ Class _____ Date _____

Take Notes

Summarize On the chart below, write a one-or-two-sentence summary of each of the major topics related to the second Industrial Revolution.

```
                    ┌─────────────────────────────────────────┐
                    │     The Second Industrial Revolution      │
                    └─────────────────────────────────────────┘
```

Industry and Business

• **Power and Productivity**

  _____
  _____
  _____

• **New Inventions**

  _____
  _____
  _____
  _____
  _____

• **Big Business**

  _____
  _____
  _____

Industrial Society

• **Higher Standard of Living**

  _____
  _____
  _____

• **People on the Move**

  _____
  _____
  _____

The Push to Reform

• **Workers in the Age of Industry**

  _____
  _____
  _____

• **Workers Form Unions**

  _____
  _____
  _____

• **Child Labor Laws**

  _____
  _____
  _____

• **Education and Health**

  _____
  _____
  _____

• **Women's Rights**

  _____
  _____
  _____

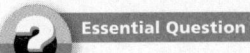
Essential Question

How did technology change life in the late 1800s?

_____

_____

_____

Essential Question Writer's Workshop

What are the consequences of technology?

Prepare to Write

Throughout this chapter, you have explored the Essential Question in your text, journal, and On Assignment at myworldhistory.com. Use what you have learned to write a letter about how technology changes people's lives.

Workshop Skill: Write a Letter

Review what you have already learned about writing letters, including appropriate greetings and conclusions and what the body of a letter includes. Remember that letters can be formal or informal. Use formal letters to write to newspapers, businesses, governments, and other institutions. Use informal letters to write to friends and family.

In this assignment, you will write a formal letter to answer the question, *What are the consequences of technology?* First, decide who will receive your letter. You might write to a government official, the president of a business, or a newspaper editor. Your purpose will be to explain how technological change affects people's lives.

Who will receive your letter? _____

The Parts of a Letter Your letter will include the following parts: date, heading, inside address, greeting, body, conclusion, closing, and signature.

Date, Heading, and Inside Address In a formal letter, the heading includes your return address and the date in the upper right corner. Skip a line and put the inside address, the address of the person who will receive the letter, at the left. It is a good idea to address the letter to a specific person, even if you are writing to a company. Include the person's title, such as *Mr., Mrs., Ms., Dr.* or *Senator*, followed by the person's full name.

Greeting After the inside address, skip another line and add the greeting. Most formal letters use "Dear," followed by a title and the person's full name. In a formal letter, use a colon after the greeting instead of a comma.

Body Use the body to explain your purpose. Why did you choose to write to this person? What ideas about technology do you want to express? For example, you might want to mention the ways that technology helps you communicate or keep up with the news. Discuss both positive and negative ways that technology has affected your life.

Conclusion, Closing, and Signature Conclude by briefly restating your main point. You might want the person to reply with his or her thoughts on the matter. Be sure to mention this in your conclusion. Below the conclusion, skip a line and write a closing such as "Sincerely yours," or "Yours truly," followed by a comma. Sign your full name below it.

Draft Your Letter

Use the format below to write the first draft of your letter.

(Your address and
the date; do not
include your name) _____

_____

_____

_____ (Inside address: full
name and address
of the person you
are writing to)

_____

_____

Dear _____:

Body _____

_____

_____

_____

_____

_____

_____

_____

Conclusion _____

_____

_____

Closing _____

Your Signature _____

Finalize Your Letter

Remember to follow the steps of the writing process to revise and edit your letter. Then neatly copy it onto a clean sheet of paper.

Name _____ Class _____ Date _____

Essential Question

How should we handle conflict?

Preview Before you begin this chapter, think about the Essential Question. Understanding how the Essential Question connects to your life will help you understand the chapter you are about to read.

Connect to Your Life

① Think about conflicts between friends. Now consider conflicts between nations. What might such conflicts have in common?

_____

_____

_____

② Record examples of conflict that you have either observed or experienced and a conflict in the news in the following table.

	Type of Conflict	Effect of Conflict
Conflict Observed or Experienced		
Conflict in News		

Connect to the Chapter

③ Skim this chapter's text, subheads, and visuals to find information about World War I, postwar revolution and depression, and World War II. In the table below, make predictions about the effects of these conflicts or challenges.

Chapter Sections	Who Was Involved?	Effect of Conflict(s)
World War I		
Revolution and Depression		
World War II		

④ After reading the chapter, return to this page. Circle any predictions that were incorrect.

370

Name _____ Class _____ Date _____

Connect to myStory: Anne Frank: Living in Hiding

1 Compare your typical day with that of Anne Frank when she was in hiding. Using information from the story, write what Anne Frank did at each time of the day listed below. Then write what you do at the same time of day.

Time	What Anne Frank Did	What You Do
6:45 A.M.		
8:30 A.M.		
9:00 A.M.		
1:00 P.M.		
1:15 P.M.		
5:30 P.M.		
10:00 P.M.		

2 How would you have spent your day if you had been in hiding like Anne? What would you have done each day if you had lived in the Secret Annex?

_____

_____

3 Think about what happened to Anne Frank and her family. Could something similar happen in the United States? Why or why not?

_____

_____

_____

4 Think about the hardship caused by Hitler and the Nazis during World War II. What lessons can we learn from what was done to Anne Frank and her family?

_____

_____

Word Wise

Sentence Builder Complete the sentences using the information you learned in this section. You might have to change the form of some words to complete the sentences.

① Sometimes called the Great War, _____ was the first

truly global conflict.

② A policy of aggressive military buildup is known as

_____.

③ Germany and Austria-Hungary were known as the _____

during World War I.

④ _____, or fighting from deep holes dug in the

ground, had never happened on such a large scale before World War I.

⑤ To win the support for the war effort, both sides used _____,

which is the spreading of ideas to promote or to harm a cause.

⑥ Germany was forced to pay _____, or payment for war

damages, following World War I.

Name _____ Class _____ Date _____

Take Notes

Identify Main Ideas and Details Reread the text under each red heading in your textbook. Take notes about information under each heading in the table below.

Causes of World War I	War Breaks Out	War Ends
Main Idea: _____ _____	Main Idea: _____ _____	Main Idea: _____ _____
Imperialism and Nationalism _____ _____ _____	Assassination Leads to War _____ _____ _____	U.S Entry into the War _____ _____ _____
Militarism and Alliances _____ _____ _____	A Stalemate Develops _____ _____ _____	Postwar Treaties _____ _____ _____
	A New Kind of Warfare _____ _____ _____	
	Other Fronts _____ _____ _____	
	Life on the Home Front _____ _____ _____	

Essential Question

Describe the causes, course, and effects of World War I.

_____

_____

_____

373

Word Wise

Crossword Puzzle The *Across* and *Down* clues are definitions of key terms from this section. Fill in the numbered *Across* boxes with the correct key terms. Then do the same with the *Down* clues.

Across	Down
1. idea that a government should have total control over its people	2. massive collection of economic and social government programs
5. a deep worldwide economic slump that lasted through the 1930s	3. radical group under Vladimir Lenin
6. territory administered by the Allied powers	4. political system that stresses national strength, military might, and the belief that the state is more important than individuals

Name _____ Class _____ Date _____

Take Notes

Summarize The column headings in the table below match the red headings in your textbook. Reread each section. Summarize information under each column's subheadings to complete the chart below. Remember that a summary is one or two sentences that give an overview of information, not specific details.

Revolution and Depression			
The Russian Revolution	**Widespread Discontent**	**Prosperity to Depression**	**Rise of Totalitarianism**
•	•	•	•
•	•	•	•
•	•	•	•
	•		•

Essential Question

How did conflict and change affect people around the world between 1910 and 1940?

_____

_____

_____

Name _____ Class _____ Date _____

Word Wise

Word Map Follow the model below to make a word map. The key term *World War II* is in the center oval. Write the definition in your own words at the upper left. In the upper right, list Characteristics, which means words or phrases that relate to the term. At the lower left, list Non-Characteristics, which means words and phrases that would *not* be associated with it. In the lower right, draw a picture of the key term *or* use it in a sentence.

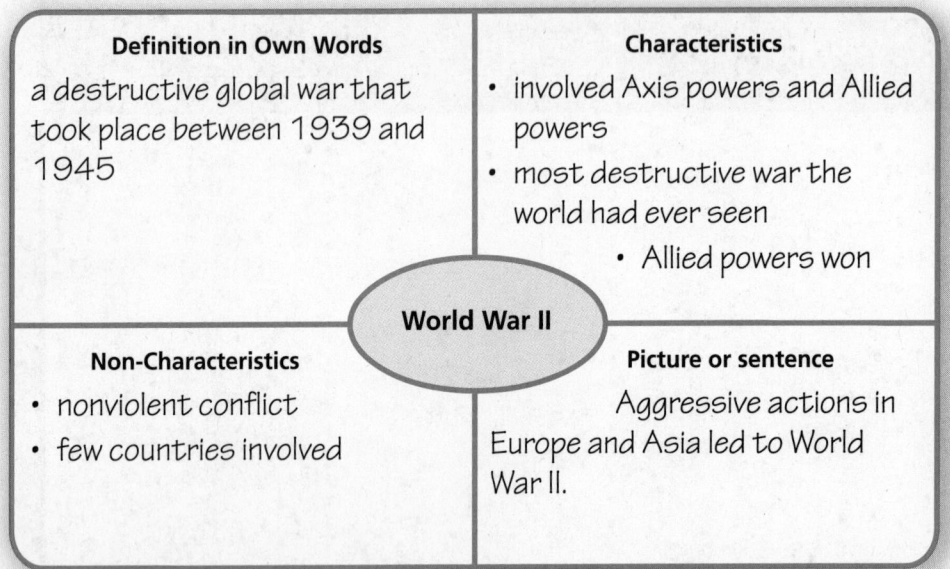

Definition in Own Words

a destructive global war that took place between 1939 and 1945

Characteristics

• involved Axis powers and Allied powers
• most destructive war the world had ever seen
  • Allied powers won

World War II

Non-Characteristics

• nonviolent conflict
• few countries involved

Picture or sentence

Aggressive actions in Europe and Asia led to World War II.

Now use the model above to explore the meaning of the word *blitzkrieg*. Use your student text and a dictionary or thesaurus to complete each of the four sections to understand the meaning of this word.

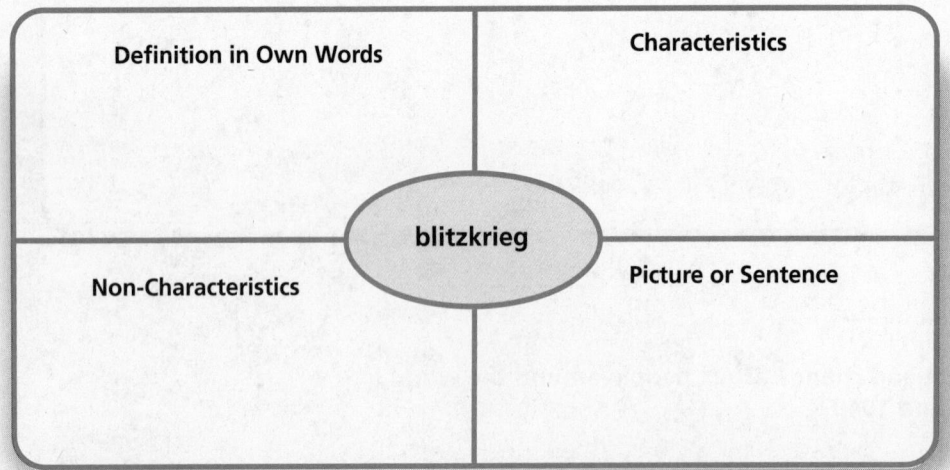

Definition in Own Words

Characteristics

blitzkrieg

Non-Characteristics

Picture or Sentence

Make word maps of your own on a separate piece of paper for the Key Terms: *Axis powers, nonaggression pact, appeasement, Holocaust,* and *genocide*.

Name _____ Class _____ Date _____

Take Notes

Sequence Label each date on the timeline with the event that happened at that time. Fill in a fact about the event on the space provided. Then, identify how the dates in the top row are similar by filling in the box at top left. Identify how the dates in the bottom row are similar by filling in the box at bottom left.

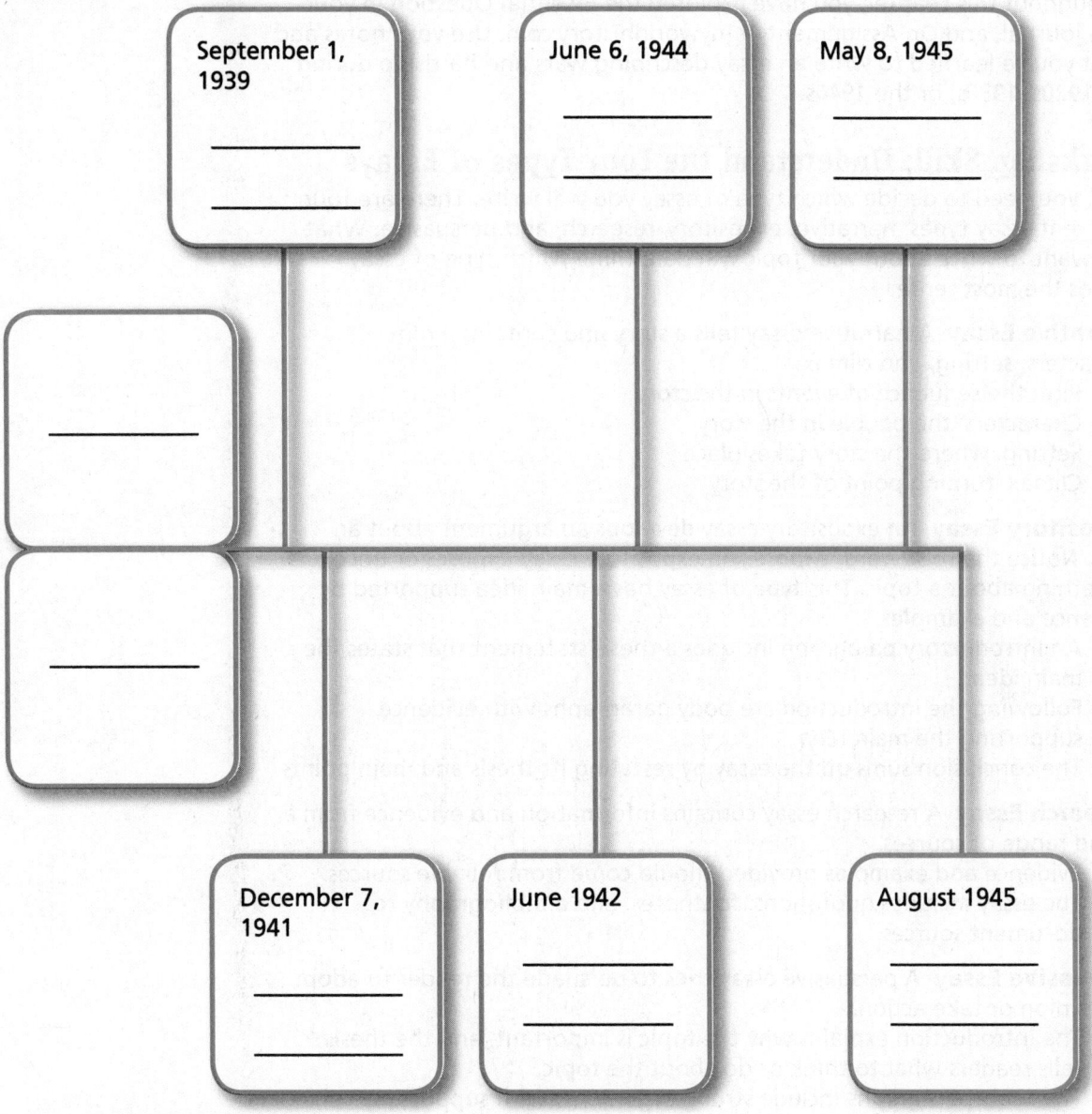

September 1, 1939

_____

_____

June 6, 1944

_____

_____

May 8, 1945

_____

_____

_____

_____

December 7, 1941

_____

_____

June 1942

_____

_____

August 1945

_____

_____

Essential Question

What were the major events of World War II, including the events that led to the war?

Essential Question | Writer's Workshop

How should we handle conflict?

Prepare to Write

Throughout this chapter, you have explored the Essential Question in your text, journal, and On Assignment at myworldhistory.com. Use your notes and what you've learned to write an essay describing wars and hardship during the 1920s, 1930s, or the 1940s.

Workshop Skill: Understand the Four Types of Essays

First, you need to decide which type of essay you will write. There are four different essay types: narrative, expository, research, and persuasive. What you want to write about your topic will determine which type of essay makes the most sense.

Narrative Essay A narrative essay tells a story and contains a plot, characters, setting, and climax.
- Plot: the sequence of events in the story
- Characters: the people in the story
- Setting: where the story takes place
- Climax: turning point of the story

Expository Essay An expository essay develops an argument about an idea. Notice the root word, *expose*. An expository essay exposes or uncovers something about a topic. This type of essay has a main idea supported by evidence and examples.
- An introductory paragraph includes a thesis statement that states the main idea.
- Following the introduction are body paragraphs with evidence supporting the main idea.
- The conclusion sums up the essay by restating its thesis and main points.

Research Essay A research essay contains information and evidence from a broad range of sources.
- Evidence and examples provided should come from reliable sources.
- The essay includes quotations, footnotes, and a bibliography to document sources.

Persuasive Essay A persuasive essay tries to persuade the reader to adopt an opinion or take action.
- The introduction explains why the topic is important, and the thesis tells readers what to think or do about the topic.
- The body paragraphs include strong arguments with supporting evidence to prove each point.
- The conclusion reviews the main points and urges the reader to adopt an opinion or take action.

Identify Essay Types

Now that you have learned about the different essay types, test your knowledge by reading the four descriptions in the following table. In the column on the right, write which type of essay the sentence describes.

Essay Description	Type
1. The essay discusses how the Allied powers defeated the Axis powers in World War II. The essay uses maps, charts, statistics, and quotations with sources in a bibliography.	_____
2. The essay urges readers to support Holocaust awareness in order to prevent future genocide by fanatical leaders.	_____
3. The essay tells a story about a successful banker and his family during the Great Depression. After the stock market crash, the family works together to survive.	
4. The essay discusses how totalitarian regimes can cause political unrest and tensions among nations. The essay explains problems that occur when totalitarian governments suppress their citizens, often leading to revolution.	_____

Plan Your Essay

Use the following questions to help you make some decisions about your essay.

(1) What do I want to say about wars and hardship during the time period I have chosen?

_____

_____

_____

(2) Do I want to tell a story, explain an idea, present evidence, or persuade others?

_____

_____

_____

(3) Which essay type will best help me to accomplish my goal? _____

Draft Your Essay

Write an outline for your essay. Remember, you will need an introductory paragraph, three body paragraphs, and a conclusion. Use notes from the outline to write your essay. Then, read your essay, making corrections as needed. Proofread your essay carefully.

Name _____ Class _____ Date _____

What is power? Who should have it?

Preview Before you begin this chapter, think about the Essential Question. Understanding how the Essential Question connects to your life will help you understand the chapter you are about to read.

Connect to Your Life

(1) Think about positions in local, state, or federal government and list some of the positions below. What do these people have the power to do or change? Write ideas next to each position.

a. _____

b. _____

c. _____

d. _____

e. _____

(2) Place the letter next to each position you identified on the line below to show where each falls on the power scale, from little power to great power.

Little
Power
0

Great
Power
10

Connect to the Chapter

(3) Preview the chapter. Skim the chapter headings, images, and captions. Use this table to list your predictions about who gained or lost power at different times in the modern world.

Place, Time	Who Gained Power?	Who Lost Power?
India, 1947		
China, 1949		
Ghana, 1957		
Algeria, 1962		
East Germany, 1989		

(4) Read the chapter, and then circle the predictions that were not correct.

Connect to myStory: The Two Worlds of Jomo Kenyatta

1 Think of people you know who are influenced by more than one culture. How are these influences different from those that affected Jomo Kenyatta?

_____

_____

2 In the diagram below, list important events in Kenyatta's journey toward leadership of Kenya. Next to each event, write *K* if the event reflects influence of *Kenyan* culture and *B* if it reflects influence of *British* culture. Write both letters to show influence of both cultures.

	Important Events	Cultural Influence(s)
Boyhood		
Studies		
Activism		
Leadership		

3 Think about Kenyatta's story and life experiences. What struggles for power occur? How might these struggles be repeated in other nations? Write your predictions on the lines below.

_____

_____

_____

_____

_____

_____

_____

_____

_____

_____

Word Wise

Crossword Puzzle The *Across* and *Down* clues are definitions of key terms from this section. Fill in the numbered *Across* boxes with the correct key terms. Then do the same with the *Down* clues.

Across	Down
1. economic system in which government makes most decisions	1. long conflict between the United States and Soviet Union
4. relaxation of tensions between the United States and Soviet Union	2. U.S. policy to keep Soviet Union from expanding its post-war influence
5. Soviet policy of openness about discussing the political system	3. country with the power to influence world events
6. economic system based on private ownership of property	

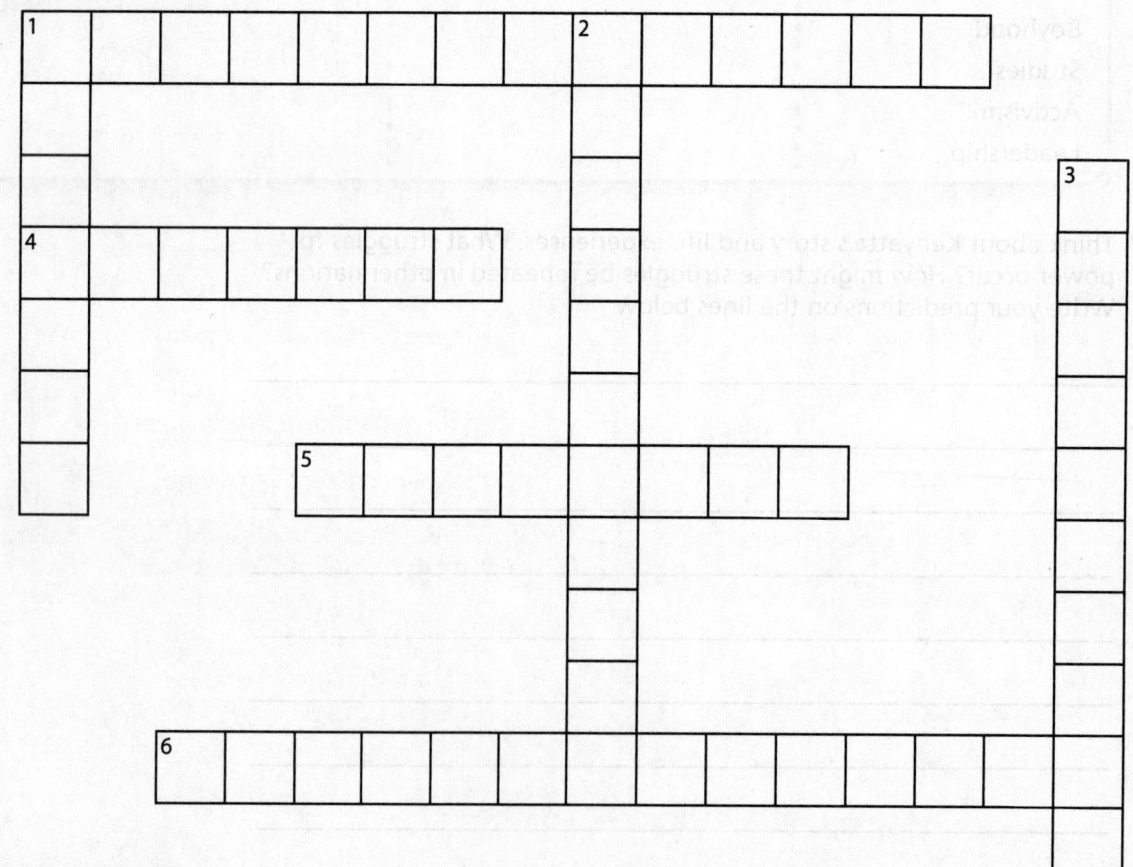

Name _____ Class _____ Date _____

Take Notes

Sequence Study the events listed below. Identify the year in which each event occurred and then place the events in order in the boxes below, from earliest to latest.

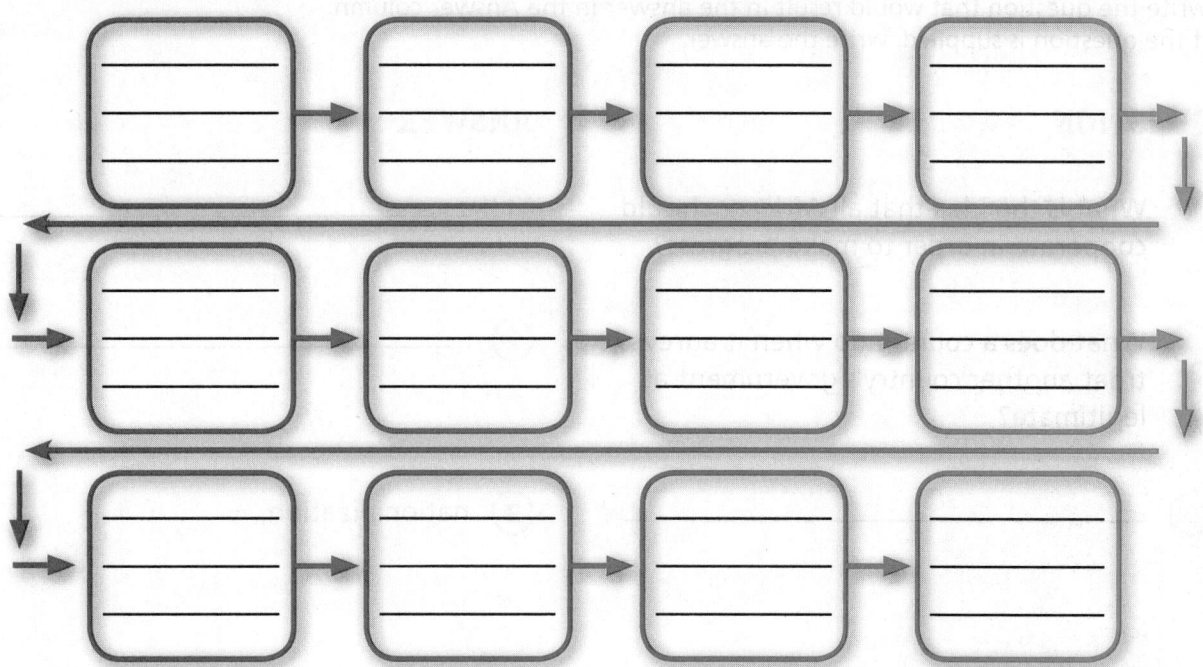

<table>
<tr><td>

United States and Allies

United States and allies form NATO.

United States develops hydrogen bomb.

Vietnamese communists take control of a united Vietnam as the war ends.

U.S.-Soviet relations improve under détente.

Cuban Missile Crisis raises U.S.-Soviet tension.

United States puts men on the moon.

</td><td>

Soviet Union and Allies

Soviets occupy Eastern Europe after World War II.

Soviets and allies form Warsaw Pact.

Soviets develop hydrogen bomb.

Gorbachev introduces glasnost, which leads to end of Soviet Union.

East Germany builds Berlin Wall.

Soviets put a satellite into space.

</td></tr>
</table>

 Essential Question

During the Cold War, who held political and economic power under the Soviet system? How did this differ from the American system?

_____

_____

Word Wise

Vocabulary Quiz Show Some quiz shows ask a question and expect the
contestant to give the answer. In other shows, the contestant is given an
answer and must supply the question. If the blank is in the Question column,
write the question that would result in the answer in the Answer column.
If the question is supplied, write the answer.

QUESTION

1. What is the idea that all Africans should
cooperate in order to make progress?

2. What does a country do when it agrees to
treat another country's government as
legitimate?

3. _____

ANSWER

1. _____

2. _____

3. nationalization

Name _____ Class _____ Date _____

Take Notes

Analyze Cause and Effect In the web below, trace the end of imperialism and the rise of nationalism. For each region, list the names of newly independent countries with the approximate dates of their independence. Next to each, list its former colonial ruler.

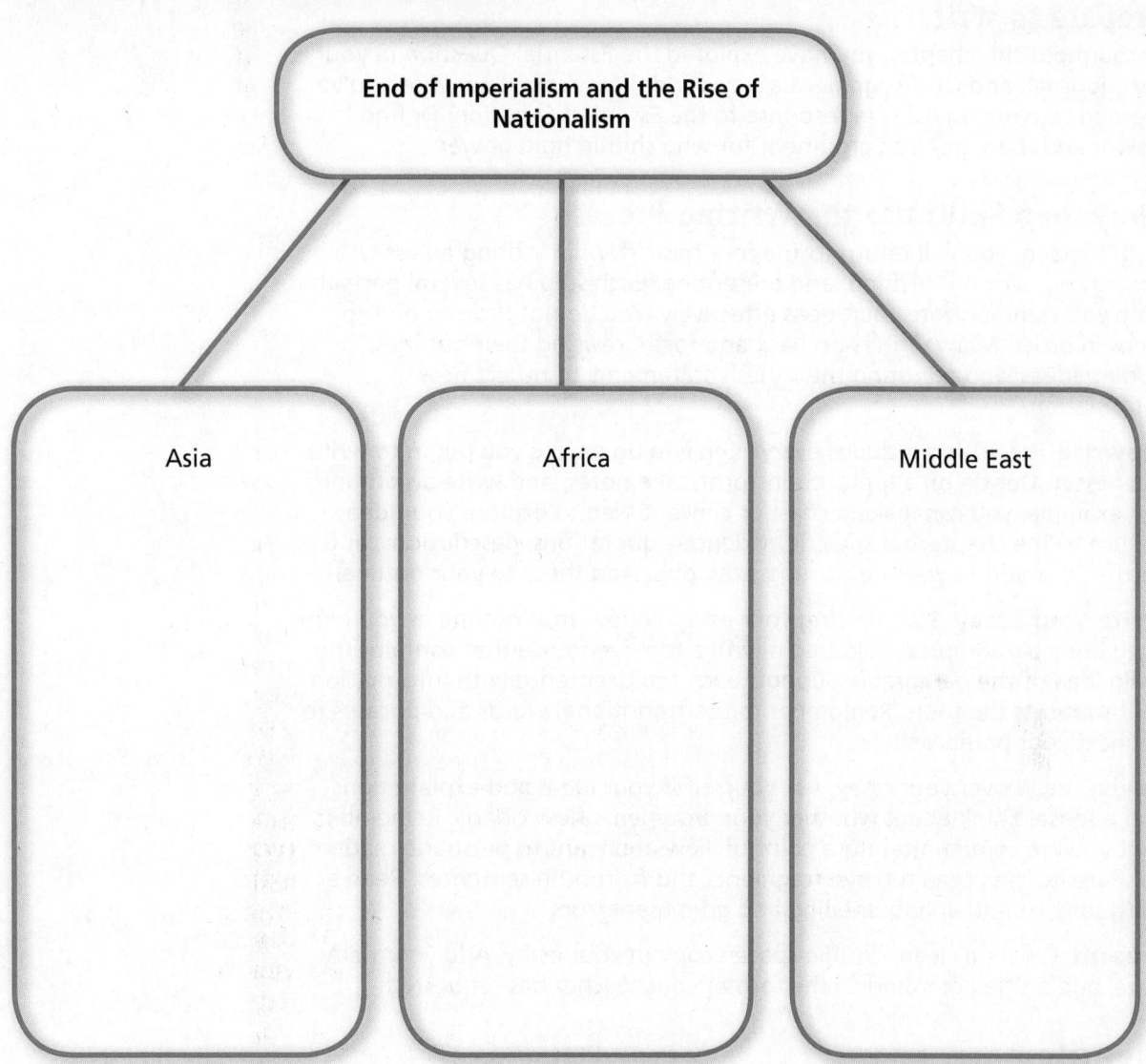

End of Imperialism and the Rise of Nationalism

Asia

Africa

Middle East

Essential Question

How are struggles for power over a region often linked to natural resources? Give two examples from this section.

_____

_____

_____

385

Name _____ Class _____ Date _____

Essential Question **Writer's Workshop**

What is power? Who should have it?

Prepare to Write

Throughout this chapter, you have explored the Essential Question in your text, journal, and On Assignment at myworldhistory.com. Use what you've learned to write an essay in response to the Essential Question. Define power and then make an argument for who should hold power.

Workshop Skill: Use the Writing Process

In this lesson, you will return to the four basic steps in writing an essay: prewriting, writing, revising, and presenting. Each step has several parts that help you communicate your ideas effectively. You do not have to do the steps in order. Many writers go back and forth, revising their outlines, adding ideas, and adjusting their thesis statements to reflect new information.

Prewrite Prewriting includes everything you do before you begin to write your essay. Decide on a topic, brainstorm, take notes, and write an outline. For example, you can make a chart or concept web to explore your ideas. Return to the chapter for specific evidence—quotations, descriptions, and so forth—that add to your supporting examples. Add these to your outline.

Write Your Essay Start writing your essay. Follow your outline as you write. Each body paragraph should begin with a topic sentence that contains the main idea of the paragraph. Support each topic sentence with information that supports the topic. Remember to use transitional words and phrases to connect your paragraphs.

Revise Read over your essay. Ask yourself if your ideas and explanations make sense. Think about whether your arguments flow clearly. Remember that you are communicating a point of view and want to persuade readers to share it. Then read remove fragments and fix run-on sentences. Read a third time to find and fix spelling and grammar errors.

Present Create a clean, double-spaced copy of your essay. Add your name, date, and a title according to the format your teacher has requested.

Prewrite

Here is a sample graphic organizer to help you brainstorm a definition of power. Think about the ideas you identified when you reviewed the chapter.

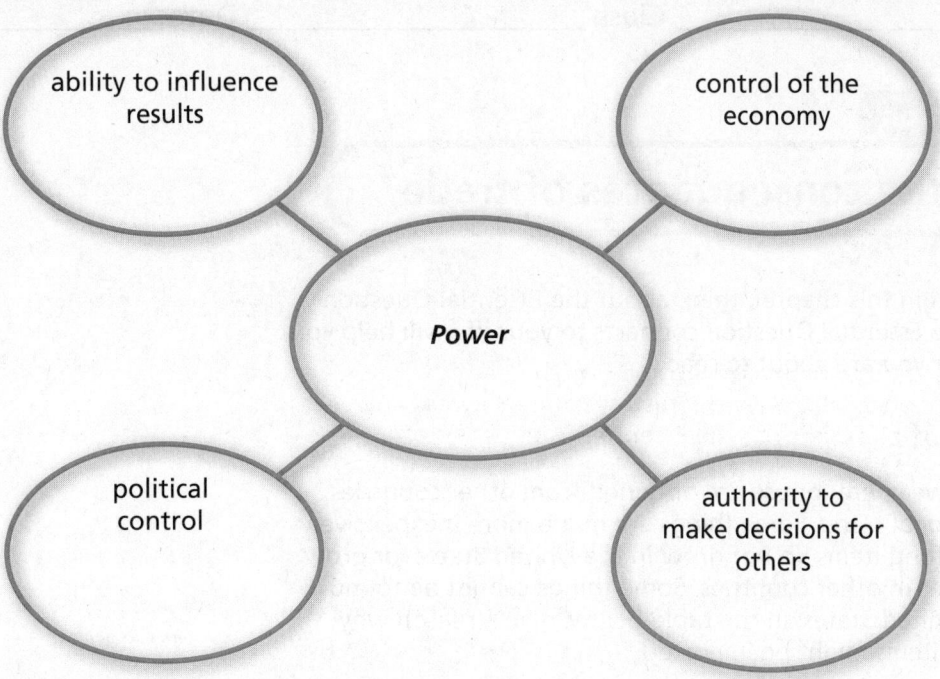

Use a Graphic Organizer Now create and complete your own graphic organizer to organize ideas to support your argument. Try a three-column table with one column for each supporting example.

Thesis Statement _____		
Topic sentence 1 _____ _____	Topic sentence 2 _____ _____	Topic sentence 3 _____ _____
Supporting Arguments 1. _____ _____ _____ 2. _____ _____ _____ 3. _____ _____ _____	Supporting Arguments 1. _____ _____ _____ 2. _____ _____ _____ 3. _____ _____ _____	Supporting Arguments 1. _____ _____ _____ 2. _____ _____ _____ 3. _____ _____ _____

Draft Your Essay

Use the graphic organizers you created to collect ideas for your essay. Then follow the steps in this workshop to draft and revise your paper on separate paper. Be sure that you complete all four steps in the writing process.

Name _____ Class _____ Date _____

Copyright © Pearson Education, Inc., or its affiliates. All Rights Reserved.

❓ Essential Question

What are the consequences of trade?

Preview Before you begin this chapter, think about the Essential Question. Understanding how the Essential Question connects to your life will help you understand the chapter you are about to read.

Connect to Your Life

(1) Many things you wear, eat, or use are obtained from other countries through international trade. Some things are made more inexpensively elsewhere. Some food items do not grow in the United States, or grow at different seasons in other countries. Some things cannot be found naturally in the United States. In the table below, give a reason why each of the trade items might be imported.

Trade Item	Possible Reason It Is Imported
bananas	
chromium	
shoes	
manganese	
mangoes	

(2) How does trade affect you personally? Explain.

_____

Connect to the Chapter

(3) Before you read the chapter, flip through it. Look at the headings and images. Predict ways in which trade in the modern world affects developed nations and developing nations.

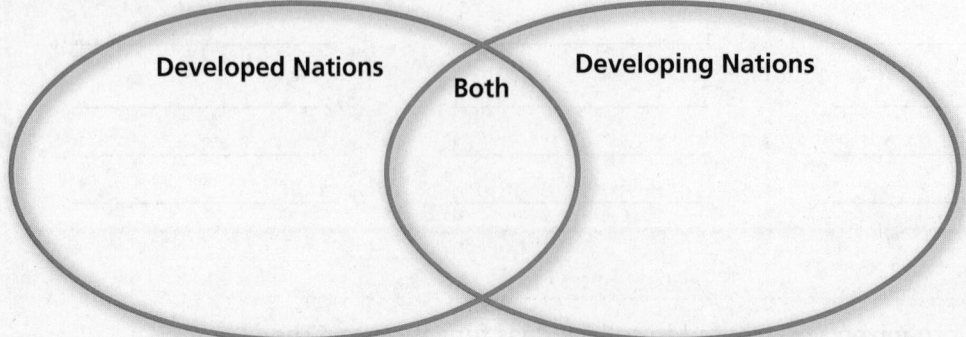

(4) After you finish reading the chapter, look at this chart again. Circle the predictions that were correct.

Connect to myStory: Sonia Gandhi: A Family Legacy

① What challenges did Sonia face when she married Rajiv?

_____

_____

② How did she react after he was killed?

_____

_____

③ Name a woman you know or know about who is in a position of power, such as an elected official or the head of a business or humanitarian organization. What challenges do you think she faces? Explain.

_____

_____

_____

④ Complete the table below to compare the political lives of Indira and Sonia Gandhi.

	Indira Gandhi	Sonia Gandhi
Position held		
Ties to former political leaders of India		
Means of obtaining position		
Events leading to leadership role		

⑤ How do leaders in the modern world rise to positions of power? Write at least two predictions.

_____

_____

_____

Word Wise

Sentence Builder Complete the sentences using the information you learned in this section.

conflict   refugee
segregation   integrate
fundamentalism apartheid
terrorism

(1) Someone who is displaced by war is a _____.

(2) The African National Congress fought against the unjust

system of _____.

(3) _____ is sometimes related to terrorist acts.

(4) Ending _____ was a goal of the civil rights

movement.

(5) The 2001 attack on the World Trade Center was an

act of _____.

(6) A ruling by the U.S. Supreme Court forced schools

to _____.

(7) Disagreements and wars are both forms of _____.

Name _____ Class _____ Date _____

Take Notes

Summarize In the table below, briefly describe the two types of conflict and give all the examples of each that you have read about in this section.

Conflict	
Fights for Human Rights	**Terrorism**

Essential Question

How did other nations use trade to encourage South Africa to end apartheid?

_____

_____

_____

Word Wise

Word Map Follow the model below to make a word map. The key term *import* is in the center oval. Write the definition in your own words at the upper left. In the upper right, list Characteristics, which means words or phrases that relate to the term. At the lower left, list Non-Characteristics, which means words and phrases that would *not* be associated with it. In the lower right, draw a picture of the key term *or* use it in a sentence.

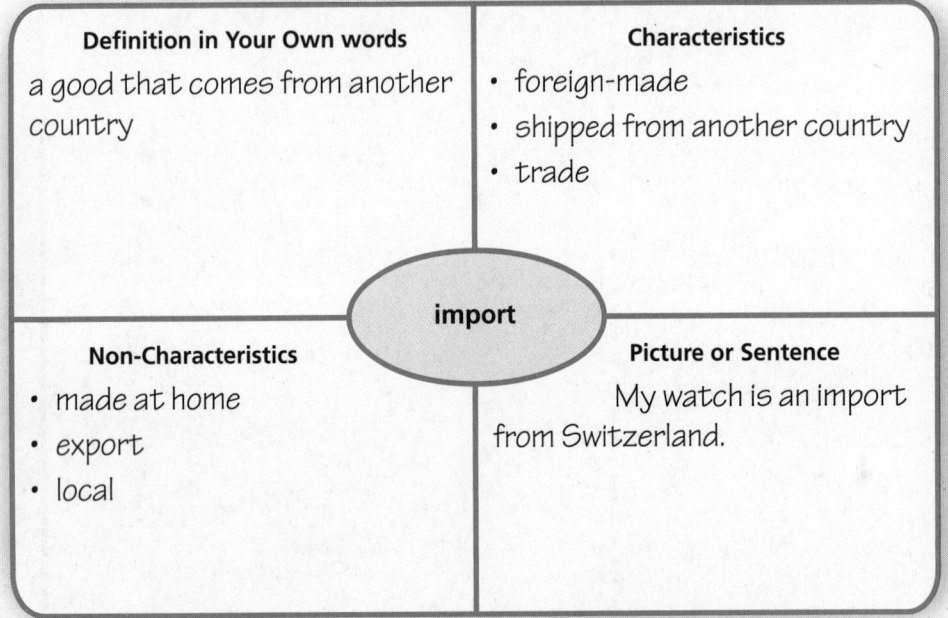

Definition in Your Own words

a good that comes from another country

Characteristics

- foreign-made
- shipped from another country
- trade

import

Non-Characteristics

- made at home
- export
- local

Picture or Sentence

My watch is an import from Switzerland.

Now use the word map below to explore the meaning of the term *free trade*. Use your student text and a dictionary or thesaurus to complete each of the four sections to understand the meaning of this word.

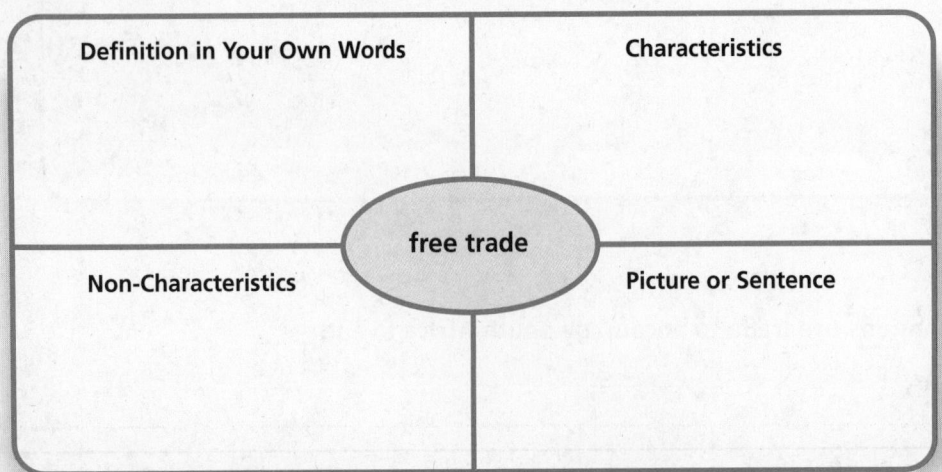

Definition in Your Own Words

Characteristics

free trade

Non-Characteristics

Picture or Sentence

Make a word map of your own on a separate piece of paper for the Key Term *inflation*.

Name _____ Class _____ Date _____

Take Notes

Identify Main Ideas and Details In this section you read about cooperation and trade. Use the top half of the concept web below to record main ideas and details about three international organizations. Use the lower half to record main ideas and details about the global economy.

International Organizations

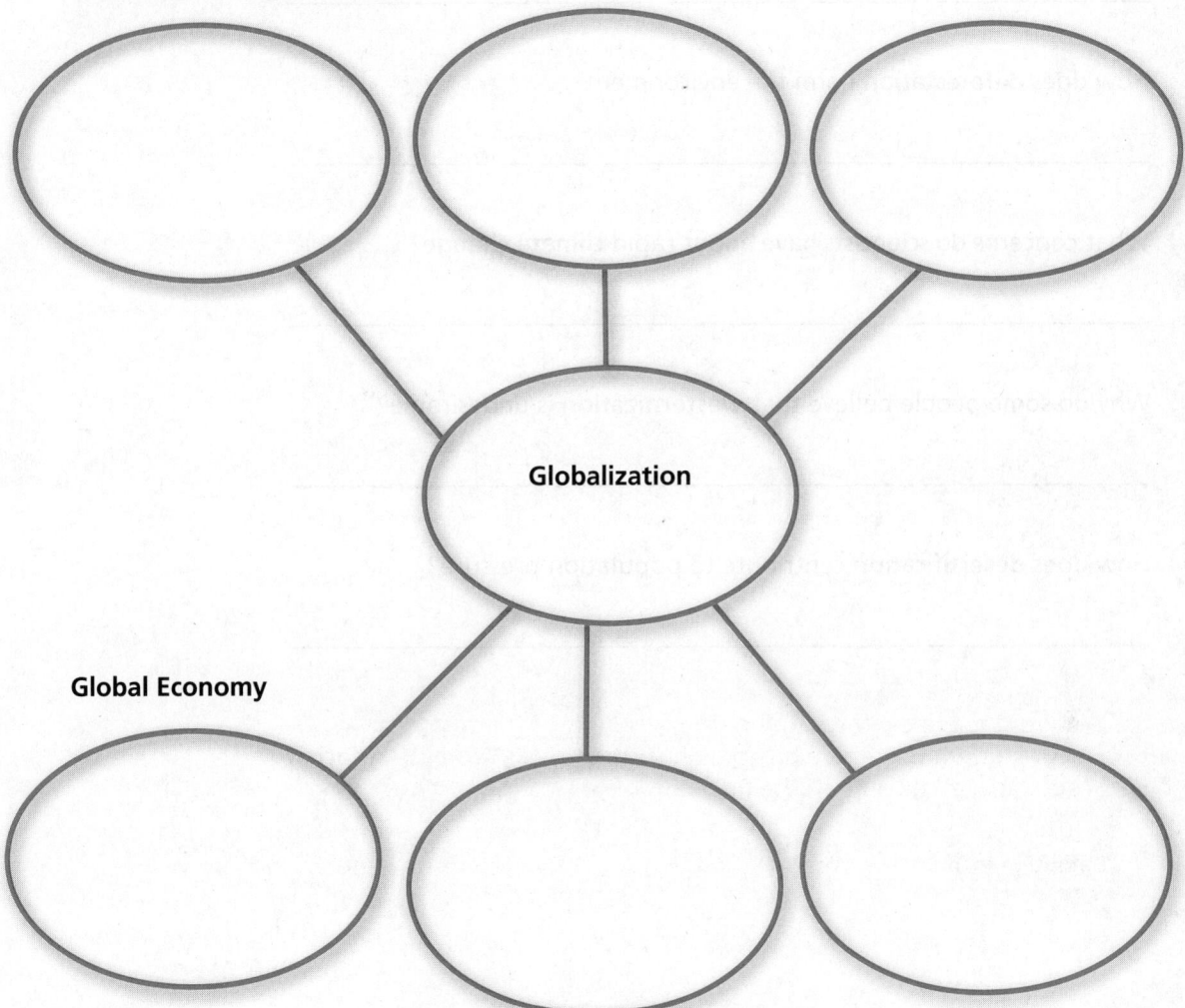

Globalization

Global Economy

Essential Question

How has free trade affected developing nations?

_____

_____

_____

Word Wise

Words In Context For each question below, write an answer that shows your understanding of the boldfaced key term.

(1) What does **genetic engineering** involve?

_____

(2) How does **deforestation** harm the environment?

_____

(3) What concerns do scientists have about rapid **climate change**?

_____

(4) Why do some people believe that **westernization** is undesirable?

_____

(5) How does **desertification** contribute to population pressure?

_____

Name _____ Class _____ Date _____

Take Notes

Analyze Cause and Effect In the box on the left, write three modern developments that are having widespread effects. In the box on the right, write at least one effect of each.

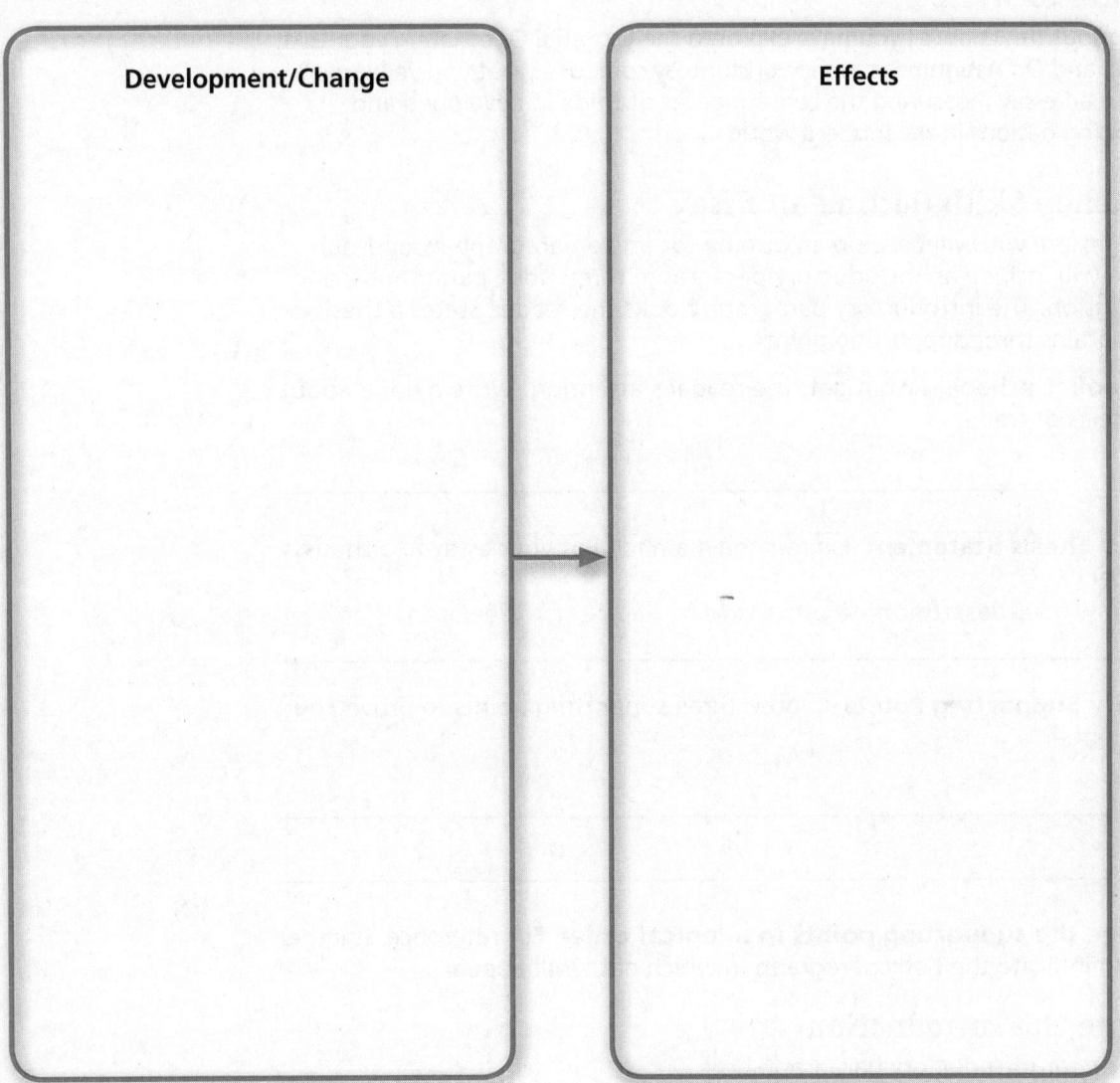

Development/Change

Effects

Essential Question

How is trade related to westernization?

_____

_____

_____

Name _____ Class _____ Date _____

What are the consequences of trade?

Prepare to Write

Throughout this chapter, you have explored the Essential Question in your text, journal, and On Assignment at myworldhistory.com. Use what you've learned to write an essay measuring the consequences of trade in developed and developing nations in the modern world.

Workshop Skill: Outline an Essay

In this lesson, you will develop an outline for a five-paragraph essay. Your outline will include an introductory paragraph, three body paragraphs, and a conclusion. The introductory paragraph hooks the reader, states a thesis, and contains three supporting points.

The Hook The hook is what gets the reader's attention. Write a hook about the effects of trade.

Hook _____

Write a Thesis Statement Express the main idea of your essay in a thesis statement.

_____

_____

Identify Supporting Points Choose three supporting points to prove your statement.

_____

_____

Arrange the supporting points in a logical order For reference, number them to indicate the body paragraph in which each will appear.

Outline the Introduction

Outline your introductory paragraph here.

Hook _____

Thesis Statement _____

_____

Sentence Summarizing Supporting Points _____

_____

End with a Concluding Sentence Finish your paragraph with a sentence that reflects your topic sentence and draws the discussion and details together.

Outline Body Paragraphs

For each paragraph, write a topic sentence. The topic sentence states the main idea of the paragraph and expresses one of your three supporting points. Add two or three key examples or important details to support the main idea of the paragraph. Sum up the information in the paragraph with a concluding sentence. Repeat this process for each body paragraph.

First Body Paragraph

Topic sentence

_____

Supporting detail

_____

Supporting detail

_____

Concluding sentence

_____

Follow this format to write two more body paragraphs.

Outline Your Conclusion

In this final paragraph, review your thesis. Summarize your supporting points and explain how they proved your thesis. Then tell the reader why the topic matters.

_____

_____

Conclusion

Restate the Thesis _____

Summary of Supporting Points _____

What the Supporting Points Prove _____

Why the Topic Matters _____

Draft Your Essay

Write your essay on your own paper. Use the outline as a guide. When you have finished, proofread your essay with a partner.

Places to Know!

Map Skills Use the maps in this unit to identify the Places to Know! on the outline map. Before the name of each place below, write the letter that shows its location on the map.

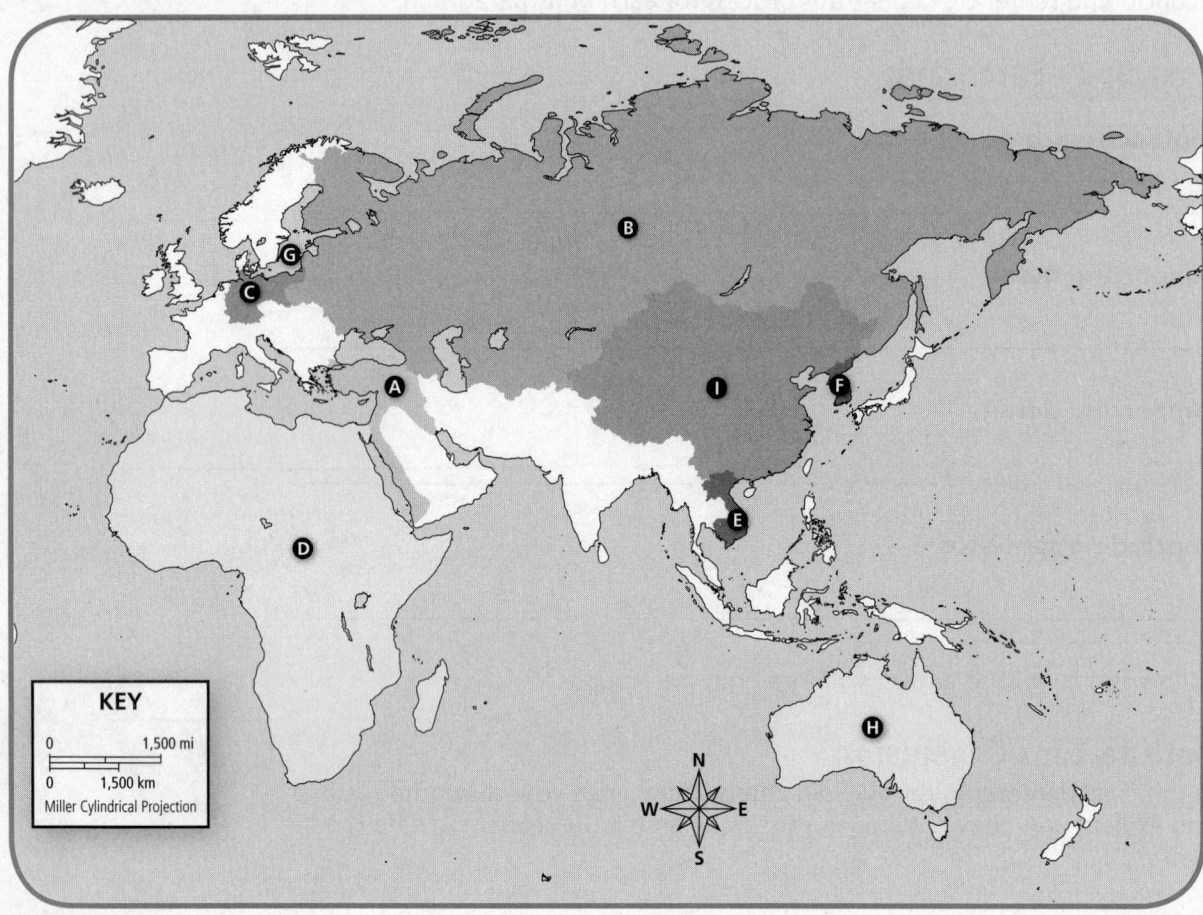

KEY

0   1,500 mi

0   1,500 km

Miller Cylindrical Projection

_____ Vietnam

_____ Ottoman empire

_____ China

_____ Russia

_____ Korea

_____ Australia

_____ Baltic Sea

_____ Africa

_____ Germany

Key Events

Timeline Use what you have read about the modern world to complete the timeline below. Draw a line from each event to its correct position on the timeline. Then write a brief description of each event.

1858 _____
_____

1871 _____
_____

1914 _____
_____

1929 _____
_____

1939 _____
_____

1945 _____
_____

1850

1875

1900

1925

1950

1975

2000

2025

1948 _____
_____

1949 _____
_____

1962 _____
_____

1993 _____
_____

2001 _____
_____

Acknowledgments

Maps

XNR Productions, Inc.

Photography

2, Andy Crawford/Dorling Kindersley; 4, O. Louis Mazzatenta/National Geographic; 5, SAUL LOEB/AFP/Getty Images; 9, Todd Gipstein/Corbis; 12, Jeff Greenberg/PhotoEdit; 15, Stone/Getty Images; 16, SuperStock/age fotostock; 19, Pearson; 21, Stephane De Sakutin/AFP/Getty Images; 22, Matthew Ward/Dorling Kindersley; 28, John Reader/ Photo Researchers, Inc.; 30, Richard Hook/Dorling Kindersley; 36, R Juniors Bildarchiv/ Alamy; L Imagebroker/Alamy; M Juniors Bildarchiv/Alamy; 46, The Art Archive/Musée du Louvre, Paris/Gianni Dagli Orti; 48, Mesopotamian/Louvre, Paris, France/Giraudon/ The Bridgeman Art Library International; 60, Shutterstock, Inc.; 62, SSPL/Science Museum/Art Resource, NY; 68, Private Collection/Look and Learn/The Bridgeman Art Library International; 70, Victoria & Albert Museum, London, UK/The Bridgeman Art Library International; 72, SuperStock; 80, Commoner28th/Getty Images; 81, Robert Harding Picture Library/SuperStock; 84, dbimages/Alamy; 86, Friedrich Stark/ Alamy; 92, Indian School/National Museum of India, New Delhi, India/Giraudon/The Bridgeman Art Library; 94, Danita Delimont; 100, De Agostini/Superstock; 102, The Art Archive/National Palace Museum Taiwan; 104, Karl Johaentges/Age Fotostock; 110, Tomb of Qin shi Huang Di, Xianyang, China/The Bridgeman Art Library International; 112, Panorama/The Image Works; 122, Private Collection/Look and Learn/Bridgeman Art Library; 128, John Hios/akg-images; HIP/Art Resource, NY; 130, De Agostini/Getty Images; 134, ANCIENT ART & ARCHITECTURE/DanitaDelimont.com; 136, Sandro Vannini/Corbis; 138, Araldo de Luca/Corbis; 140, Matthias Kulka/Corbis; 152, Pearson; 160, Shutterstock, Inc.; 162, De Agostini/Getty Images; 168, Shutterstock, Inc.; 171, Shutterstock, Inc.; 176, Erich Lessing/Art Resource, NY; 178, The Metropolitan Museum of Art/Art Resource, NY; 186, Tim E. White/Alamy; 190, Private Collection/Archives Charmet/The Bridgeman Art Library International; 192, Photo Researchers/Alamy Stock Photo; 200, M. Jon Arnold Images Ltd./Alamy; L. Michael Dwyer/Alamy; T. Michael Nichols/National Geographic Society; 202, Christoph Henning/Das Fotoarchiv/Black Star/Alamy; 204, De Agostini/Superstock; 212, Bridgeman-Giraudon/Art Resource, NY; 214, Ms Pers.; 113, f; 29, Genghis Khan (c.1162–1227) Fighting the Tartars, from a book by Rashid-al-Din (1247–1318) (gouache), Persian School, (14th century)/Bibliothéque Nationale, Paris, France/The Bridgeman Art Library International; 224, AP Photo/Shizuo Kambayashi; 231, Pacific Press Service/Alamy; 238, Gianni Dagli Orti/Corbis; 244, The Trustees of the British Museum/Art Resource, NY; 254, World History Archive/Alamy Stock Photo; 256, Sonia Halliday Photo Library/Alamy; 264, Akg-images/British Library/ Newscom; 266, Bettmann/Corbis; 270, Topham/The Image Works; 276, R union des Mus es Nationaux/Art Resource; 278, Bildarchiv Preussischer Kulturbesitz/Art Resource; 280, G. Nimatallah/akg Images; 290, Erich Lessing/Art Resource, NY; 294, Dorling Kindersley; 300, The Bridgeman Art Library International; 314, World History Archive/Alamy Stock Photo; 324, Axiom Photographic/Masterfile; 326, Collection of The NewYork Historical Society, 1885.5; 334, Everett-art/Shutterstock; 338, State Russian Museum, St. Petersburg, Russia/Giraudon/The Bridgeman Art Library International; 346, British Library, London, UK/Bridgeman Art Library; 350, Nikreates/Alamy; 352, The Granger Collection, New York; 360, Massimo Listri/Corbis; 362, North Wind Picture Archives/ Alamy; 372, Bettmann/Corbis; 374, Photos12/Alamy; 384, Shutterstock, Inc.; 390, David Turnley/Corbis.